MODERN
SCHOLARSHIP ON
EUROPEAN
HISTORY

HENRY A.
TURNER, JR.

General Editor

THE AX WITHIN

THE AX WITHIN
ITALIAN FASCISM IN ACTION

Edited with an Introduction by

ROLAND SARTI

NEW VIEWPOINTS
A Division of Franklin Watts, Inc.
New York   1974

56681

Library of Congress Cataloging in Publication Data

Sarti, Roland, 1937–   comp.
The ax within: Italian fascism in action.

(Modern scholarship on European history)
Bibliography: p. 223-254
1. Fascism—Italy.   2. Italy—Politics and
government—1922–1945.   I. Title.
DG571.S276   320.9′45′091   73-9559
ISBN 0-531-06367-4
ISBN 0-531-06498-0 (pbk.)

Text design by Rafael Hernandez
Cover design by Nicholas Krenitsky

Manufactured in the United States of America.

ACKNOWLEDGMENTS

Giuseppe Rossini, "Fascism Between Legality and Revolution, 1922–1924," from Giuseppe Rossini, ed., *Il delitto Matteotti tra il Viminale e l'Aventino* (1966). By permission of Società Editrice Il Mulino, Bologna.

Francesco Margiotta Broglio, "Fascism and the Church, 1922–1925," from Francesco Margiotta Broglio, *Italia e Santa Sede dalla Grande Guerra alla Conciliazione* (1966). By permission of Editore Laterza, Bari.

Giorgio Rochat, "The Fascist Militia and the Army, 1922–1924," from Giorgio Rochat, *L'esercito italiano da Vittorio Veneto a Mussolini (1919–1925)* (1967). By permission of Editore Laterza, Bari.

Adrian Lyttelton, "Fascism in Italy: The Second Wave," from *Journal of Contemporary History* I (1966). By permission.

Renzo De Felice, "From the Liberal State to the Fascist Regime: The First Steps." Translated by permission of Harcourt Brace Jovanovich, Inc., from *Mussolini il fascista* by Renzo De Felice. Copyright © 1968 by Giulio Einaudi editore s.p.a., Torino.

Alberto Aquarone, "The Rise of the Fascist State, 1926–1928," from Alberto Aquarone, *L'organizzazione dello Stato totalitario* (1965). Copyright © 1965 by Giulio Einaudi editore s.p.a., Torino.

Roland Sarti, "Fascist Reforms and the Industrial Leadership in Italy 1919–1940," from Roland Sarti, *Fascism and the Industrial Leadership in Italy 1919–1940* (1971). Originally published by the University of California Press; reprinted by permission of the Regents of the University of California.

Cesare Vannutelli, "The Living Standard of Italian Workers, 1929–1939," from *Rassegna di Statistiche del Lavoro* X, 3 (1958). By permission.

Enzo Santarelli, "The Economic and Political Background of Fascist Imperialism," from Enzo Santarelli, *Storia del movimento e del regime fascista* (1967). By permission of Editori Riuniti, Roma.

Luigi Preti, "Fascist Imperialism and Racism," from Luigi Preti, *Impero fascista, africani ed ebrei* (1968). Copyright © 1968 by U. Mursia & C., Milano. By permission.

Alberto Aquarone, "Public Opinion in Italy Before the Outbreak of World War II." By permission of Edzioni Scientifiche Italiane, Società per Azioni, Napoli.

viii

To our parents, Joseph and Jennie Alia

NOTE ON THE SELECTIONS

Nine of the eleven selections that make up this anthology appear in English for the first time. Since translations occupy such a prominent place in this work, a word about them is perhaps in order. The translations convey the meaning of the original as accurately as possible, but translators are often called upon to exercise their personal judgment in trying to convey nuances of meaning. Precisely because translations inevitably reflect the translator's judgment in subtle but important ways, the reader should be aware that no translation can be an adequate substitute for the original. No truly rigorous study is possible without the language skills necessary to consult primary and secondary sources in their original language.

A comparison with the original texts will reveal that a number of changes have been made in the translations. While the editor has avoided making any changes that might alter the meaning of the original, he has not hesitated to make several minor changes in the text for the sake of brevity, clarity, or stylistic uniformity. Such changes include the insertion of a few introductory words, first names, or titles when a figure appears in the text for the first time, shortening a few excessively long passages, paraphrasing an occasional sentence in order to avoid awkward expressions, breaking up long paragraphs, and substituting approximate equivalents for a few official titles with which few nonspecialized readers are likely to be familiar. In order to avoid cluttering the text with an exceedingly large number of brackets or parentheses, such minor changes are not indicated in the final version. However, lengthy editorial summations, background explanations running to more than a few words, and omissions of certain passages are clearly indicated in the text. With very few exceptions, the original footnote apparatus has been retained intact.

The editor wishes to express his appreciation to Dr. Thelma Canale-Parola of North Amherst, Massachusetts, for her invaluable help in preparing preliminary drafts of five translations. The editor takes complete responsibility for all translations as they appear in their final form.

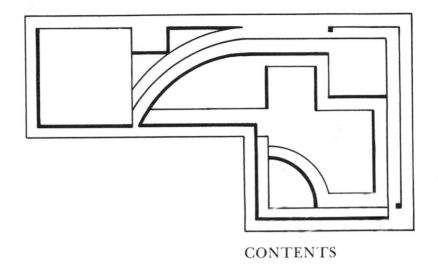

CONTENTS

THE AX WITHIN

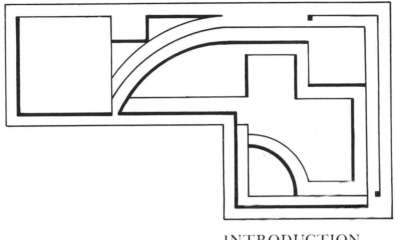

INTRODUCTION

Fascism is more of a puzzle today than in the days when Hitler and Mussolini dominated newspaper headlines. Our uncertainty over the nature of fascism is probably compounded by the current indiscriminate use of the word as a political epithet. The term is bandied about with an imprecision that would have been inconceivable when people could see real fascism in action. Another source of confusion, however, is our increasing awareness of how the Fascist regimes functioned behind their monolithic façades. The more we learn about how power was distributed and how decisions were made in Fascist regimes, the more we have to rethink our definitions of fascism. Ideological labels that unequivocally associate fascism with revolution or reaction are the least satisfactory. Unlike other "isms," fascism lacked compact ideological sources and social bases to help make it intelligible. Communism, for instance, found in the writings of Karl Marx and in its appeal to the proletariat a visible ideological and social identity. Fascism, on the other hand, drew its doctrines and support from an exceptionally broad array of thinkers and social groups. This mixed ideological and social basis poses special problems for the student of fascism.[1]

When fascism appeared in Italy immediately after World War I, the only obvious trait of the new movement was its vehement nationalism. It was only later that it also became what today would be called a law-and-order movement. The political activists who found a precarious unity under the sign of the fasces had little in common beyond their nationalism and their rebellious mood. Fascism developed in Italy as a loose coalition of competing and often incompatible groups, ranging all the way from ultraconservative landowners to anarcho-syndicalists. The internal diversity was appropriately reflected in the fasces, the bundle of sticks with an ax blade protruding that became the political emblem of the movement, and historians ever since have wondered whether to attach greater significance to the diversity of the components or to the bond that held them together. Although the Fascists insisted and outsiders often assumed that the components formed an indissoluble whole, new evidence clearly indicates that the so-called totalitarian state was in reality something quite different from what it was popularly believed to be.

The generation that experienced the tragic events of the 1930's and the holocaust of World War II was understandably ready to accept the validity of Mussolini's boast that fascism and totalitarianism were synonymous and turn that boast into a moral condemnation of fascism.[2] A younger generation of scholars is equally sensitive to the moral issues raised by fascism but is trying to draw its own lessons by looking at fascism in its historical context. The scholarly literature of the last ten years in particular has often attempted "on the one hand, to avoid separating fascism from the context of Italian reality . . . and on the other, to go beyond the external image of fascism, seeking rather to reveal its complex nature by emphasizing the interaction of its component elements." [3]

The components were indeed varied: they included laissez-faire liberals whose only concern was to liberate business from public controls, revolutionary syndicalists hostile to capitalism, idealist youths disillusioned with the materialism of their elders, self-seeking opportunists, intransigent disciplinarians, and democratic revisionists. Many of the selections presented here explore the relationship between these groups, dealing both with their rivalries and with the bonds that kept them together in a show of formal discipline. They provide historical explanations to help reconcile appearances and realities.

The nature of the Fascist bond is indeed worth examining. We may recognize in it the historical novelty that its large and enduring political constituency was based more on shared resentments than on affinities. Its members were attracted mostly by what fascism rejected: liberalism, democracy, and communism. The generation that was under thirty when World War I ended professed complete disillusionment with the safe but unexciting values of the old liberal order as personified in Italy by Premier Giovanni Giolitti, the aging conjurer of parliamentary majorities. Young Fascists and many older conservatives agreed that he was largely responsible for the ills of the country, particularly the alleged lack of nationalistic fervor among the masses and the drift into socialism. The "positive" postulates of fascism, such as nationalism and the glorification of war, derived their political justification and potency from the polemics against Giolitti's system of government and its alleged catering to Socialist demands. The Fascists were nationalists because the Socialists were internationalists; they glorified war because the Socialists and Giolittians had been neutralists; they preached love of danger and adventure because they argued that Giolittians and Socialists were part of the same conservative establishment that was insensitive to the higher aspirations of idealistic elites.

The rejection of the liberal order was fascism's political trump card even when Mussolini's method of government held

3

out the possibility of a reconciliation between liberalism and fascism. It was difficult for fascism to develop a more positive program because to do so it would have had to make unequivocal choices that, in turn, would have alienated important segments of its constituency. That constituency can be divided into two broad groups: the Fascist activists who fought in the action squads and who expected that once in power fascism would change things in unspecified but fundamental ways, and the vast coalition of supporters, sympathizers, and fellow travelers who expected fascism to correct what they considered to be the aberrations of liberalism but not to abolish such pivotal liberal institutions as parliament and the monarchy.[4]

In order to keep this constituency united, fascism had to have a leader astute enough to pose credibly as a traditionalist, reformer, and revolutionary all in one. Ambiguity had to be the essence of Fascist politics and the Fascists had only one leader who was sufficiently versatile to play that kind of game. Benito Mussolini became the pivotal figure of the Fascist regime largely because of his ability to be all things to all men.

When King Victor Emmanuel III appointed Mussolini prime minister in October 1922 and the Fascist columns marching on Rome were shipped back home after having been allowed to parade through the city, there were probably not many Italians who thought they had just witnessed a revolution. There were few indications that the march on Rome was the first political victory of an international movement that was destined to dominate the world scene for the next quarter of a century. Conservatives who accepted fascism on pragmatic grounds felt reassured by the fact that the march on Rome had been a bloodless affair and that the crisis had been resolved in a civilized manner by negotiations between responsible leaders. There were few convinced Fascists outside the squads and the *squadristi* were probably under one hundred thousand (approximately twenty-six thousand took part in the march on Rome). Prominent military figures, business leaders, and members of the king's entourage supported Mussolini's bid for power (with varying degrees of enthusiasm) because they expected that the responsibilities of government would transform fascism into a pillar of the state. Their expectations were clearly at variance with those of many Fascists who believed in the revolutionary mission of fascism.

The victory of fascism was thus based on a misunderstanding of Fascist goals which Mussolini did nothing to dispel. As long as the nature of fascism remained vague and fluctuating, he could move according to the needs of the moment and the prompting of his keen political instinct. There was no need for him to stimulate dissension among his followers; they were already so divided that all he had to do was exploit their inevitable quarrels. Although Mussolini did take full advantage of their rivalries to consolidate his position in the government and in the party, he was also compelled to play the role of mediator. Once in power he needed a pliable party ready to second his political game. Divisions among party members could not be allowed to develop into open warfare without endangering the survival of his government. He did not want a party united and powerful enough to challenge his leadership, but neither did he want a party perpetually at war within itself. He began to favor collaborators who either had no ideas of their own or who could accommodate themselves to his politics regardless of what they believed.

Within these limits, Mussolini welcomed the collaboration of revolutionary syndicalists and capitalists, libertarians and martinets, intellectuals and men of action, revisionists and intransigents. The greater the internal diversity, the greater his freedom of action. For the sake of political expediency, he was perfectly willing to work with individuals who were personally repellent to him. A good example was Roberto Farinacci, an intransigent Fascist who liked to pose as the conscience of the regime, criticized laxity and corruption in high places, and harbored ill-concealed ambitions to become Mussolini's successor. Although Mussolini eventually tried to destroy Farinacci's political power, he admitted once that "if he had not existed I would have invented him." [5]

The Fascist regime could be described as a prolonged exercise in political equivocation. Mussolini's manipulation of contending factions in the party, his choice of collaborators, concessions to powerful interest groups, alternate posturing as a man of law and order and as a revolutionary, the slow evolution of the corporative state, were all aspects of his strategy to delay making important decisions and to eventually make them in such a way that few people would feel immediately threatened. It was a situation that called for a special kind of leadership. Anyone who approached the problem of government with a doctrinaire mentality did not survive politically for very long. The 1920's witnessed a steady exodus of disillusioned Fascists from the centers of power. A prominent casualty in the early years of the regime was Mussolini's first minister of finance, Alberto de Stefani, a determined laissez-faire man whose persistent efforts to reduce government spending, lower protective tariffs, and generally keep government and business in separate compartments pleased neither the business leadership who wanted greater access to government nor the revolutionary Fascists who wanted government to actively curb the power of big business.

Political success required either resilience in the face of repeated frustrations and partial victories or an indifference to programs and ideas. People with firm ideas survived only if they could trim their sails according to the prevailing political winds. The best example of the intellectual in politics was Giuseppe Bottai who fought in every political battle of the regime, scoring minor victories and suffering impressive defeats. His name is associated with the hopeless fight to make the party more democratic in the early 1920's and with an inconclusive reform of the school system in the late 1930's. At the other extreme we find Achille Starace who became party secretary in the 1930's mostly because of his mindless disciplinarianism and blind loyalty to Mussolini.[6]

Mussolini is still the most enigmatic figure. To his contemporaries he was either the political opportunist who sacrificed every principle in order to reach and retain power or the "new

6

man" of politics who could be rigid or pliable, depending on the political realities of the moment.[7] Interpretations of Mussolini range too far and wide to be discussed here.[8] However, recent studies based on new archival sources do shed some light both on the man and the politician. Stimulating insights abound, for instance, in Renzo De Felice's ongoing monumental biography of Mussolini.[9] Some of De Felice's arguments have already aroused bitter controversy, particularly his contention that up to the end of 1920 Mussolini remained a genuine revolutionary. His argument that there was coherence and continuity in Mussolini's political career has been rejected in no uncertain terms by those who see Mussolini as a demagogic agitator rather than as a revolutionary.[10] Regardless of how one views De Felice's work, he has made it abundantly clear that Mussolini aimed at strengthening his own and the state's authority at the expense of the party and at making himself the indispensable mediator between fascism and the nation. By following Mussolini's career we have rediscovered that fascism emerged as a combination of discordant elements.[11]

The realization that Mussolini was more often a mediator than an initiator poses a new problem for historians. We must ask ourselves why we are so familiar with the figure of the domineering Duce and so unfamiliar with that of the adroit politician. Part of the answer certainly lies in the effectiveness of his own propaganda. His balcony oratory, stiff bearing, and peremptory public statements were obviously calculated to convey the image of a "leader who leads." There is also, however, the fact that Mussolini and fascism changed noticeably in the course of time. To mention one minor but revealing detail, in the 1920's Mussolini often appeared in public in civilian dress. In the following decade he and his close collaborators were rarely seen out of military uniform. More significantly, Mussolini's reputation in the 1920's was based on such alleged accomplishments as making the trains run on time (an echo and a vulgarization of certain modernizing aspirations of fascism), stepping up the production of wheat, strengthening the currency, and turning the political

7

tide against bolshevism. What was missing from the public image of the 1920's is precisely that which is most deeply etched in our memory: Mussolini in his role of warlord and international troublemaker.

It would be foolish to argue that the fascism of the 1930's bears no relationship to that of the 1920's. It would be more accurate to say that what was implicit in fascism from the very beginning became explicit only in the 1930's. We can go on from there to discuss the points of transition and the forces that impelled fascism along its historical course. The purpose of this anthology is not to acquaint the reader with the classic interpretations of Italian fascism. The views of seminal figures like Benedetto Croce, Piero Gobetti, and Antonio Gramsci can be consulted in other works.[12] Our main purpose is to present the internal history of the Fascist regime as accurately as the current state of research will allow.

Some turning points in the history of the Fascist regime are fairly obvious: from the appearance of Mussolini's first *fasci di combattimento* in March 1919 through most of 1920 Mussolini apparently thought that social revolution might be imminent in Italy and hesitated to cut his ties with the radical tradition (the Fascist program consequently stressed social justice); as the prospect of revolution faded in 1921–1922 fascism became more conservative and courted the support of specific vested interests (business, landowners, army, monarchy, etc.); from the march on Rome through most of 1924 fascism went through a "liberal" phase in which Mussolini solicited the support of non-Fascists and governed through parliament in spite of the fact that the political opposition was still strong there; from 1925 to 1934 fascism suppressed the political opposition, Mussolini consolidated his personal dictatorship, and the corporative state evolved on a piecemeal basis; after 1934 the regime pursued an expansionist policy by military means and international considerations took precedence over domestic concerns.

In the sphere of domestic concerns, the most significant change occurred from June 1924 to January 1925 in the course of the crisis that followed the assassination of the Socialist leader Giacomo Matteotti by Fascist thugs. The first four selections deal with developments up through the Matteotti crisis. They draw attention to such questions as Mussolini's efforts to gain mastery over his Fascist followers, his careful dealings with two powerful vested interests, the church and the army, and how the Matteotti crisis affected the struggle for power within the party. Mussolini's system of government during this period was certainly anti-democratic but not necessarily illiberal, particularly if we keep in mind the fact that Italian liberals had always had an ambivalent attitude toward the idea of democratic government. They believed that government should reflect a multiplicity of interests, but not that it should necessarily respond to popular pressures. The electoral law, which the Fascists pushed through parliament in November 1923, assured the Fascists and their conservative supporters a dominant position in parliament but stopped far short of creating a one-party system of government. Revolutionary Fascists actually feared that this and other "transformist" reforms might eventually reconcile fascism to the status quo.

That the thrust of Fascist ideology was totalitarian from the very beginning seems clear enough. It is equally clear, however, that Mussolini's method of government was anything but ideological. Whether fascism would indeed have been transformed into a straightforward authoritarian dictatorship, like that of Francisco Franco in Spain, had Mussolini been allowed to pursue his initial political goals is a matter of pure speculation. That possibility was effectively precluded by the outcome of the Matteotti crisis and Mussolini's speech of January 3, 1925.

The speech of January 3 is usually seen as marking the beginning of the totalitarian phase of Italian fascism. It certainly led to a more systematic regimentation of Italian society. The process whereby the government set up the machinery for suppressing the opposition, muzzling the press, and giving Fascists a monopoly over the representation of all groups is thoroughly described by Alberto Aquarone. But these innovations do not in themselves tell the whole story. Long after the speech of Janu-

9

ary 3 Mussolini continued his fight against the intransigents in general and Farinacci (who was then secretary of the party) in particular. It has been suggested that Mussolini was much more receptive to the views of authoritarian Nationalists, like Minister of Justice Alfredo Rocco and Minister of the Interior Luigi Federzoni who simply wanted to strengthen the state, than to the urgings of those Fascists who wanted to concentrate power in the hands of the party.[13]

As Aquarone himself states, with the speech of January 3 it was not so much that fascism triumphed, but that Mussolini triumphed—"and not Mussolini as head of the party but as head of the government." [14] The intransigents demonstrated that they lacked the leadership and the vision to rise above primitive political resentments and the use of violence as a cure-all. The result of the so-called *leggi fascistissime* (most Fascist laws) was to greatly expand the power of the police and the prefects rather than the power of the party. And Mussolini made discreet use of these new powers. Only minimal pressure was applied against organized business, whose leaders, for the most part, indicated their willingness to accept constitutional changes as long as they remained influential in the new institutions of the Fascist state. Outright repression was reserved mostly for the labor unions that were still under Catholic, Communist, or Socialist control. The performance of the Fascist labor unions that took over is a good indication of the limits of the Fascist revolution.

The party itself was profoundly transformed in the course of time. Although it was always a formidable organization on paper, its role after 1928 became mostly choreographic. Its membership grew spectacularly but many new members joined only for reasons of opportunity. A stifling bureaucracy settled upon old and new members alike. Mussolini thus achieved his goal of "making the party pay decreasing attention to political problems and give him as little trouble as possible." [15]

It would be wrong, however, to dismiss the party's choreographic role as insignificant. Its main function in the 1930's was to keep nationalist feelings at a high pitch. Party secretary Starace became an object of resentment and ridicule because of his mania for rallies, parades, uniforms, and salutes, but it was Mussolini who was ultimately responsible for these developments. All the evidence indicates that it was Mussolini who decided that the time had arrived to start fulfilling the old promises of national glory. The making of foreign policy was his exclusive prerogative and he guarded it jealously. It is also true, however, that he found many willing collaborators. When the party ceased to be the forum in which political alternatives could be discussed, there was nothing to do except become the cheerleader of the nation. In that role it was acceptable to everyone who rallied behind the regime because nationalism was the only thing they all shared. The party actually became the symbol of national unity as soon as the regime turned to aggression. It was due largely to the efforts of its organizers that the crowds filled the nation's squares to roar their approval of the Duce's fulminations against the League of Nations and the Western democracies. The goal of expansion abroad, which had been pursued by peaceful diplomacy in the 1920's, was to be pursued by military means in the 1930's.[16]

The last three selections deal with the latter phase of Fascist expansionism and attempt to establish connections between domestic developments and foreign policy. Although it is not always possible to document clear cause and effect relationships between the two, there are certain juxtapositions that cannot be ignored. We may note, for instance, that fascism turned to military aggression after the myth of the continuing revolution had been exhausted at home with the enactment of the corporative reform of 1934 and when the regime had to confront the great depression without being able to promise major social innovations. The reader can decide for himself whether the aggressive foreign policy of fascism after 1934 was perhaps an attempt to prolong the revolutionary image of fascism by military means. This is an area in which much work remains to be done; it is interesting to note, however, that Farinacci and the so-called revolutionary intransigents reemerged from political obscurity as

11

champions of the alliance with Nazi Germany and as advocates of an Italian policy of racism.

Fascism ended logically enough by acting out its basic premise that success in war is the ultimate test of a people's will and right to prevail. The successful war against Ethiopia probably confirmed that belief and encouraged Mussolini to continue on the same course. But, while there is every indication that the war against Ethiopia was popular, the same cannot be said for the subsequent involvements in the Spanish Civil War and World War II. It is always difficult to sustain nationalist enthusiasm for long periods of time and in the face of mounting deprivations. Popular support for the regime dwindled as the economic and social burdens of war increased. Disaffection with the regime was widespread on the eve of Italy's entrance in World War II. Mussolini's decision to enter the war was almost certainly based on his erroneous estimate that a German victory was imminent, but that does not answer the larger question of why Mussolini felt that he had to make the decision to go to war. One possible answer is that Mussolini realized his regime could not survive an additional proof of its spiritual bankruptcy. To avoid the test of war would have revealed that the warlike ethic of fascism was as false as its promises of social renewal. And the man who wanted to be recognized as the founder of a new world order would have been revealed as merely a clever politician.

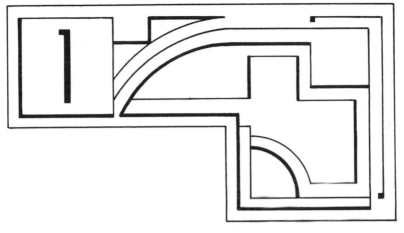

FASCISM BETWEEN LEGALITY AND REVOLUTION, 1922–1924 *

Fascism came to power in a semilegal way that left many questions about its nature and goals unanswered. The Fascist armed squads that marched on Rome at the end of October 1922 certainly gave the impression that the government was being taken over by force. Force, however, was only one element of the Fascist effort to seize power. Although the march on Rome was the most visible part of that effort, the decisions that won Mussolini the king's invitation to form the government were made in Mussolini's headquarters in Milan where the future

* From Giuseppe Rossini, ed., *Il delitto Matteotti tra il Viminale e l'Aventino* (Bologna: Il Mulino, 1966), pp. 59–83. Reprinted by permission of the publisher.

15

Duce negotiated with the country's business and political notables. Coercion and compromise were thus from the very beginning inseparable traits of Fascist government in Italy. The history of Italian fascism could easily be written by describing how the "mix" changed over the years.

For approximately two years after the march on Rome, moderation and restraint prevailed in spite of the fact that violence could and did break out at almost any moment. The violence, however, was sporadic and Mussolini's government made definite efforts to contain it. There were no constitutional changes during this period and the various proposals of the Fascist government were enacted through regular legislative channels. Mussolini seemed to be primarily concerned with restoring public confidence in the government, maintaining the unity of the party, and convincing public opinion that he was the only leader strong enough to restrain those restless Fascists who wanted to continue the revolution.

The politics of compromise gave way to that of violence when Fascist thugs assassinated the Socialist leader Giacomo Matteotti on June 10, 1924. Although the degree of Mussolini's personal responsibility in the crime has never been ascertained, the assassination provoked a major political crisis that seriously impaired the effectiveness of his government. Sensing that the general consensus behind his government was weakening, Mussolini felt that he had no choice but to rely more heavily on the support of those Fascists who insisted on the need for greater intransigence in dealing with the opposition.

Giuseppe Rossini, a well-known scholar born in 1923 and a graduate of the University of Rome who has written extensively on fascism and on the Catholic movement in Italy, takes the Matteotti crisis as his starting point. In studying the behavior of the Fascist leaders during the crisis, he explores its political background and antecedents. His study therefore sheds considerable light on Mussolini's political motivations and tactics after the march on Rome. We get a picture of fascism that should correct the widespread but simplistic impression of a regimented, monochromatic movement. The Mussolini who emerges from these pages is also strikingly different from the Duce of Fascist propaganda. We meet here the adroit backstairs politician who was bent on consolidating his own power by undercutting his collaborators, playing one faction against another, and posing as national reconciler. A knowledge of these hidden aspects of fascism is necessary to understand how fascism took root in Italy. By implication, it can perhaps also help us to understand how fascism can emerge anywhere out of something initially quite different. It is indeed paradoxical that a stifling Fascist regime should have been imposed upon a country by a movement in which ultra-individualists played such a large role. This selection will be particularly useful if the reader tries to identify the various ideological currents noticeable within fascism during these early years, the rival factions that fought for power, and Mussolini's efforts to strike a convincing balance between impartial statesman and revolutionary leader.

■

From the march on Rome to the elections of April and the assassination of the Socialist deputy Giacomo Matteotti in June 1924, Mussolini believed that the basic political problem of fascism was to develop ways of achieving national reconciliation in order to broaden the consensus behind the regime. We will not attempt to judge the sincerity of the various efforts to restore legality, particularly because these efforts were accompanied during 1923 and the first half of 1924 by contradictory developments such as the so-called "minor aggressions" against several political opponents and dissident Fascists and by the establishment of the *Ceka (Fascist secret police—Ed.)*. These episodes of Fascist violence are legally and politically significant because they culminate in the most serious of all social crimes, political assassination. But, after expressing our moral revulsion, we are still left with the problem of ascertaining whether Mussolini and fascism faced the crisis of June 1924 with the intention of breaking with the opposition, or whether Matteotti's murder prevented an understanding with parliament and violently interrupted progress

17

toward a settlement that would have been welcomed by some Fascist groups and opposed by others.

Matteotti's murder certainly made it difficult, if not impossible, for Mussolini to carry out his plan of posing as a moderate by indicating that he stood apart from those Fascists who had a reputation for violence. General Emilio De Bono's behavior as chief of police throws light on this problem, particularly if considered in relation to the debates that developed within fascism during 1923 and 1924. To appreciate the significance of his activities, however, we must momentarily set aside the simplistic notion that members of the *Ceka* carried out the tragic mission on direct orders from their chief.

De Bono's official attitude as chief of police in the period preceding Matteotti's murder is amply documented. . . . Telegrams, circulars, and notes make it sufficiently clear that the government wished to convince the prefects (*government officials responsible for law enforcement in the provinces—Ed.*) that it would not "unconditionally protect the Fascists" regardless of what they did.[1] In case of provocation, the police were to prevent Fascist reprisals, but "if the Fascists, or people claiming to be such, are intemperate, provocative, or arrogant, the guilty or responsible parties must be punished without hesitation. The punishment must be especially swift when those involved use fascism as an excuse to settle personal or factional resentments." Extremists were to be told that the Fascist Militia should be called into action only rarely and cautiously, not only because "we must not give hostile observers the opportunity to say that the Royal Guards (*riot police organized in 1919—Ed.*) have been abolished and the *Carabinieri* diminished in number only to set up a new police unit," but also because the Militia should be mobilized only for political reasons and not to deal with common crimes.[2]

As late as February 1923 there were still orders that the Militia must not be equipped with arms.[3] Army corps commanders were responsible for preventing the distribution of weapons in order to reduce the number of "more or less politically motivated" incidents, which occurred mostly on weekends. . . .[4] Following the establishment of the Militia, "no other military group or association was to be allowed, either armed or unarmed," nor were any other demonstrations, gatherings, or parades featuring "shirts or blouses of any other color than black" to be permitted.[5] Individuals were to surrender all weapons, with some allowance to be made only for Blackshirts, at least until their squads had been fully incorporated into the Militia.[6]

Both Mussolini and De Bono requested that special consideration be shown for religious organizations, which were not to be disturbed in any way.[7] Mussolini personally addressed this request to De Bono in May, complaining to him that he had just received a strong protest from the president of Catholic Action, Luigi Colombo, deploring acts of violence against youthful members of his organization and the wrecking of their premises. Finally, there is an energetic telegram from Mussolini to the prefects with the usual request that all weapons be confiscated but also urging surveillance of all subversive elements, including "self-proclaimed nationalist movements operating at the edges of fascism under such labels as *rinnovamento* and *rinascita*." The document is particularly useful because it shows that, less than a year after the march on Rome, Mussolini expected the prefects not only to safeguard public order, but also to provide him with information on the alignments within fascism and on the infiltration, for instance, of Mafia elements into the party.[8] Mussolini intended to use government agencies against such groups of dissident Fascists as those headed by Ottavio Corgini in Reggio Emilia and Raimondo Sala in Alessandria:[9]

> The prefect, and no one but the prefect, represents the authority of the government in the provinces. I have repeated this many times, the last time before the Senate. All party representatives are subordinate to the prefect. Since fascism is the dominant party, it is understood that the prefect must maintain close contacts with the local *fascio* to avoid dissension and public disturbances.[10]

19

The recognition that the preservation of public order was the primary responsibility of the prefects can only be explained by referring to the situation within the Fascist party before the assassination of Matteotti, and particularly during 1923. The party was plagued by an overexpanded membership, by a split between a moderate current unhappy over the government's failure to resolve administrative problems, by a left wing exasperated by the way the "revolution" had dissolved into mere politics, and particularly by the presence in the government of Catholics and Liberals and the division of the country into spheres of influence each dominated by a *ras,* or local party boss. The centrifugal thrust of peripheral forces was not restrained within the party by a correspondingly strong central power. The centralization of power thus had to be achieved by relying upon the traditional agencies of government because no others were available, and even when they were available, were controlled by people who did not agree with Mussolini. . . .

Strange as it may seem, even the establishment of the Militia, decided by the Grand Council in December 1922 and introduced by royal decree on January 14, 1923, was a step in Mussolini's drive to achieve normalcy. Although the anti-Fascist opposition considered the Militia unconstitutional, in relation to what was going on within fascism its establishment made it possible, at least in principle, to effectively contain the centrifugal impetus of *rassismo (the phenomenon whereby many local party bosses tended to behave like independent potentates—Ed.),* which was always a threat to public order and to the normal development of the political process.

Condemnations of excesses and violence were heard from within fascism. Mussolini and Cesare Rossi, a close personal collaborator who was Mussolini's liaison with the press from November 1922 to June 1924, had requested at the time of the treaty of pacification *(an understanding between Fascist and Socialist representatives negotiated at Mussolini's initiative in early August 1921 and designed to end street fighting between the two groups —Ed.)* stricter discipline and careful selection of recruits. They were particularly critical of the Fascists of Emilia and Romagna who, they claimed, were guilty of engaging in "violence for its own sake" to the point that "the name of fascism has become synonymous of terror among those populations, including those who are not Socialists."

These charges stemmed from Mussolini's political calculation that the more zealous Fascists were the "white guards" of the privileged classes ready to protect the interests of the employers. The old argument that fascism represented class interests had already been challenged by Cesare Rossi when, writing in Mussolini's review *Gerarchìa* in August 1922, he had stated that the landowners who understood the renovating thrust of fascism considered it "more immediately and profoundly dangerous than the Socialist party whose turbulence was inevitably illusory and accidental." [11] Not even Roberto Farinacci, the outspoken Fascist boss of Cremona, who had a well-deserved reputation for violence, was willing to endorse the notion that the party "was the avant garde of conservative reaction," pointing out that there were more than one million workers enrolled in the Fascist corporations. [12] When, after the march on Rome, Mussolini's newspaper *Il Popolo d'Italia* began to search for the more or less distant precursors of fascism, it gave first priority to Mussolini's socialism, which it traced back to "the attitude of the former editor of *Avanti* (*Mussolini was editor of the Socialist newspaper* Avanti *from December 1912 to October 1914—Ed.*) and of the amazing editor of *Il Popolo d'Italia* from 1915 to 1918." This tracing of antecedents was an obvious effort to prevent the polemics against socialism, then in full sway, from degenerating into a crude campaign against labor. [13]

It is understandable that, given these pronouncements, some observers should begin to think that socialism had survived into fascism as if to take revenge from beyond the grave, thus creating the risk that the demagogic policies of socialism might reappear in Fascist syndicalism. And so it happened, at least until Fascist labor leaders realized (and they realized it quickly) that their aims and those of Mussolini's government were far apart. Their

21

revolutionary expectations faded in a matter of months, mostly because of the confusion and contradictions in the party. An example of this confusion around the middle of December 1922 was the uncertain relationship between Gabriele d'Annunzio and Mussolini and between the Fascist squads and the Fiume legionnaires (*nationalist followers of d'Annunzio who had followed the poet in his seizure of Fiume in September 1919 in protest against the failure of allied peace negotiators at Versailles to award that disputed city to Italy—Ed.*), who were often being arrested and harassed by the police. Farinacci had already called for a clarification with explicitly controversial language: "The country must now know what the poet d'Annunzio really thinks." By alternating flattery with threats, he aimed basically at preventing d'Annunzio from joining the opposition and, specifically, at thwarting an understanding between the poet and Gino Baldesi and Tito Zaniboni, two moderate Socialists who tried to use d'Annunzio's influence in bringing about an understanding between the Socialist and Fascist labor unions. The vague possibility that d'Annunzio might turn to the left made many Fascist leaders uneasy:

> Here are the very same people, namely Baldesi, Zaniboni, and their followers, who only yesterday were using the masses brutalized by class hatred to insult you and the cause for which you have shed your blood (*reference to d'Annunzio's wartime exploits in the course of which he suffered the loss of one eye— Ed.*), once again misleading the crowd with new words but with the same vile intent of yesterday and they are now saying: the Soldier-Poet is on our side.[14]

In contrast to the open-ended political aims and tactics of Mussolini, the police staged a resolute campaign against real or presumed Fiume legionnaires by placing the headquarters of the *Arditi* (*shock troops demobilized soon after the war, many of whom had rallied to d'Annunzio during the seizure of Fiume— Ed.*) under surveillance and confiscating their records: "it seems that their unlawful activity is to expand from Milan to other major centers, and gradually throughout the kingdom; the fusion of undesirable elements mentioned above has reportedly already begun with great circumspection in various cities, including Bologna, Florence, Rome, Turin. . . . Please take note of the fact that action must be taken even against genuine Fiume legionnaires whenever justified by their sectarianism or criminal precedents." [15] And these steps were being authorized by the Ministry of the Interior, where one of the undersecretaries was Aldo Finzi, himself a former Fiume legionnaire.

The party was clearly intent on eliminating all actual or potential rival organizations. Not even the appearance of the Militia was unanimously welcomed within the party . . . precisely because it was suspected that it would isolate Mussolini from the party and would protect Mussolini against the restless provincial *ras* who had no intention . . . of settling down.[16] "As far as they were concerned," commented Massimo Rocca, "local Fascist chiefs had no intention of disbanding the squads that were often their only source of support against enemies within or outside the party, or against local government authorities whom they were in the habit of disobeying." [17] Hence the efforts to prevent the members of the squads from joining the Militia, particularly because it was to be commanded by former army officers in an effort to smooth relations between the Militia and the regular army. . . .

The opposing factions . . . clashed bitterly during a session of the Grand Council, which began to meet on January 12, 1923.[18] Turning to Farinacci and to the "gentlemen in the second row," Mussolini warned them that "the country can perhaps put up with one Mussolini, but not with several dozen." [19] He called upon the squads to demobilize and join the Militia. Rossi and Rocca supported his request, while Achille Starace, Attilio Teruzzi, Farinacci, and Francesco Giunta sided with the opposition in defense of the "revolutionary spirit" that would have been compromised by the union of the squads and the Militia. . . . The debate lasted for several sessions but proved inconclusive because "Mussolini needed the party Militia to consolidate his power, while the local chieftains needed the protection of the squads against government authorities and possibly even against Mussolini, who had tried in vain to use the central oligarchy to control the oligarchs in the provinces." The only thing that emerged clearly from this complicated system of checks and balances was the persistence of the old "camorrist, demagogic, utilitarian" mentality that was reinforced by the influx of new recruits after the march on Rome. . . . (*Efforts by the party directorate to halt recruitment, transform the original Fascists into an elite, and sever ties with the Masons failed to reform the party—Ed.*) [20]

The internal predicament of fascism a few months after the allegedly revolutionary march on Rome is illustrated in a report presented by party vice-secretary Giuseppe Bastianini. (*The author quotes at length from the report, which points to an "uneasiness within the party" that resulted from various developments: a widespread feeling that the leadership was indecisive, conflicts between pro-labor and anti-labor factions, conflicts between the "Fascists of the first hour" and subsequent arrivals, conflicts between Fascists and Nationalists, the presence of discontents who felt that they had not been properly rewarded, the persistence of "democratic attitudes" among rank and file members, poor organization, and a lack of discipline among party leaders—Ed.*) [21]

Mussolini thus had to bear the burden of a party that was only minimally united and composed of socially heterogeneous groups that made it seem both anti-capital and anti-labor. He faced a particularly difficult situation because the march on Rome was only a few months behind and the slightly heretical influence of socialism was still ideologically significant within fascism where it had not yet been co-opted by power politics.[22]

Fascism unquestionably failed politically in the course of 1923 because it could not master these problems, a failure that in turn caused confusion in the ranks and conflicting decisions. Mussolini, who was constant only in his tendency to vacillate, telegraphed the following message to the secretary of the party on March 26: "Our great victory cannot be questioned. It is ques-

24

tioned only by those Fascists who do not accept our stern discipline and persevere in their idiotic and unheroic, illegal ways, which I am determined to suppress because they sully the purity of fascism and endanger the future of the nation." Mussolini could thus easily pretend for the sake of public opinion that he stood apart from the movement that he had guided until then but which now seemed unable to adjust to what *Il Popolo d'Italia* described as "the new condition" of fascism. He was exploiting the contrast . . . between the Fascist government and fascism in the provinces in order to win the support of special interest groups, who were still reluctant or fearful, by trying to solve the problem of the squads . . . with the creation of a theoretically apolitical organization, the Militia, that would be capable of absorbing all those illegal tendencies originating in a mentality scornful of traditional authorities, particularly of the judges and prefects who still represented the Giolittian system. . . .[23]

Mussolini could not avoid taking into account the demands of all those interest groups who faced him and with whom he had to deal laboriously. Near the end of his political career, shortly before July 25, 1943, when he was overthrown by Fascist conspirators and by the king, he made a revealing comment to his old friend, the revolutionary syndicalist Ottavio Dinale:

> If you could only imagine what an enormous effort it was to reach an arrangement that would not create conflicts between mutually jealous and suspicious rival powers: the government, the party, the monarchy, the Vatican, the army, the Militia, the prefects, party officials, heads of various national associations, powerful trusts, etc.; you understand; these are the indigestions of totalitarianism which was unable to absorb the hereditary institution, the monarchy, forced upon me in 1922. It was an effort to overcome the traditional and specific shortcomings of the Italian people, who are both great and petty, who have changed only externally after twenty years of steady therapy.[24]

The Militia inserted itself in the established balance of power with a function of its own. Without it, "the party would have constituted a reserve force to be mobilized in the improbable event that the agencies of the state refused to obey the Fascist government, in other words, in case fascism should have to resort to force once again." [25] In spite of many arguments, including the fact that Militia officers were barred from political posts, no one came forward with a better solution than Mussolini's for harnessing the disorderly and chaotic energies of the Fascist party. The clear-cut separation between fascism and the Militia eventually put the latter under government control, to be utilized in case of need even against the party.[26] As for the party, if it was not relegated to a subordinate role, which it could play through its *gruppi di competenza (advisory groups, also known as "technical councils," made up of technocrats who were expected to advise the government on a wide variety of economic and political problems—Ed.)* . . . , it would interfere violently with the orderly operations of government agencies, using violence haphazardly to assert its own independence and prestige. There was thus a second form of lawlessness, within the party, which tore the party apart and favored the rise of fanatical types at the local level.

Confusion prevailed in the provinces where dissent was spreading because it was rooted . . . in disillusionment over the rejection of the old squads, disregard of seniority, resentment against opportunistic late joiners, and loyalty to the "fascism of the first hour." [27] (*The author discusses two groups of dissidents, the* banda dello sgombero *of Florence and the* vecchia guardia *of Genoa, who wanted to purge the party* [sgomberare] *of all politically unreliable elements that had joined after the march on Rome—Ed.*) The men who wanted to purge the party . . . were intransigent and violent, but they are not to be confused with the many speculators who used the arguments of the intransigents to weaken moral restraints and get their hands on the public till. It is for this reason that, when fascism faced its first crisis, the *banda dello sgombero* sided with the *revisionists*, with Rocca, in spite of the fact that Rocca did not want a narrow, sectarian party run by those whom Bottai called the "senior sharpies."

(The author points out that party discontents developed the habit of professing complete faith in Mussolini in order to safely disregard party policy. This ruse was condemned by Bottai— Ed.):

> It is most reprehensible when people who are discontented, deluded, inept, and unworthy, who make common cause by joining splinter groups, or get together in tight, hostile enclaves within the party, turn to Mussolini. When they cry "Long Live the Duce," or send a telegram pledging loyalty to the Duce when at the same time they break party discipline, they resort to a shabby device which cannot be tolerated. We must shut out these counterfeit Fascists.[28]

(The author discusses several cases of dissident Fascists who either left or were expelled from the party and their motivations. These incidents were interpreted by observers in various ways, but they nevertheless reinforced the impression that Mussolini's policies did not coincide with those of fascism—Ed.)

The revisionist controversy became a major issue in the party during the second half of 1923, . . . Rocca argued that fascism had given the country "only one man, although an immensely great one," and that the party *lived like a parasite* on the shoulders of its leading spokesman in a country "that was all for Mussolini and very little for the Fascists." [29] Whatever positive contributions the party had made were the result of external, even of opposing influences. Its most coherent decisions, such as having promoted the *gruppi di competenza,* having favored corporativism, and having facilitated the appointment of regular army officers to posts in the Militia, had not been welcomed in party circles, which were becoming increasingly more narrow and hostile. Government policy was understood and followed only when it touched on local matters. The *Corriere Italiano,* a newspaper that actively supported Mussolini, commented that it was a case of intellectual laziness to be overcome, according to Giovanni Marinelli, by reorganizing the party whose executive committee and subordinate agencies were out of touch and ignored

27

by local groups. . . .[30] The notion of concentrating leadership in the hands of the original recruits of 1919, or of those who had joined in 1920–1921, was absurd because the party . . . should strive to overcome the crisis of centralization by cautiously returning "to a restricted and informed version of universal suffrage." [31] In August 1923, Augusto De Marsanich argued in *Critica Fascista* that it was absurd to consider "as a human and political subspecies all those citizens who have not felt an impelling need to join our party or all those other people who do not believe that to betray their convictions is more admirable than to remain true to them."

Mussolini escalated his criticism of the more extreme forms of *rassismo* from the end of July to the beginning of September 1923; the revisionist campaign proper began in September with the publication of the already cited article by Rocca, "Fascism and the Country," which raised various previously mentioned possibilities, including that of dissolving the party.[32] Although this last possibility could never be realized, it is nevertheless indicative of a state of mind . . . that favored a reconciliation between fascism and the nation and a more open-minded attitude within the party. The agreement with war veterans (*urged by Mussolini, the Fascist Grand Council on January 13, 1923, had conferred legal status on the Association of War Veterans—Ed.*) and the dialogue with the Confederation of Labor had been a two-pronged effort to reach influential sectors of public opinion and put an end to the party's state of isolation, which was attributable to its failure to understand the need for change. Rocca pointed out how "There are signs that the party understands less and less the need for change and the goals of Mussolini's policies. We humbly and sadly ask the party to make peace with Mussolini's Italy, and in order to achieve this reconciliation, that it abandon its wordy parody of revolution and discipline, its excessive boasting about the victory of violence now that violence is no longer needed." [33]

Replying to Farinacci, who had accused him of favoring the abolition of the party "for the benefit of our enemies," Rocca replied . . . that he was willing to accept only one dictatorship, that of Mussolini, and that he had no intention of yielding to those who proposed to preserve the party in its existing form to bring about the *second wave* of the Fascist revolution. . . . He saw no need, however, to go as far as De Marsanich, who believed that the party ought to be demobilized and eventually reconciled "with many, if not all, our enemies of yesterday." [34]

(*The revisionist campaign in favor of national reconciliation earned Rocca the enmity of the party ras, particularly Farinacci, who engineered Rocca's expulsion from the party. Mussolini, however, prevailed upon the Grand Council to reinstate Rocca on October 12, 1923, thus temporarily strengthening the moderates who wanted to restore the rule of law. The policy of favoring a return to political normalcy prevailed until after the national elections of April 1924 in which the Fascists and their Liberal supporters ran on a common ticket. The struggle between revisionists and intransigents, however, had exposed the lack of unity among the Fascists, thereby endangering the entire party and making it imperative for Mussolini to heal the schism —Ed.*)

Although the revisionists did not really have a doctrine of their own, they made the intransigents more vulnerable to attack by revealing their real motivations. When the executive committee of the party resigned to be replaced on September 30 by a directorate, it seemed as if power had been further concentrated in the hands of an oligarchy.[35] The revisionists had gone too far and could not reap the political rewards that they expected, but in the long run their efforts enabled Mussolini to continue balancing himself between the two opposing sides. . . .

The events of June 1924 interrupted a process of adjustment which . . . should have been accompanied by a constitutional reform to make parliament more representative, while, at the same time, freeing the country from the harmful aberrations of parliamentarianism. Dissident Fascists who agitated restlessly inside and outside the movement made an issue of the failure of the drive to restore legality. Amerigo Dumini, one of the abductors

29

of Matteotti who was eventually found guilty of unpremeditated murder, called them the *dropouts* of fascism when, under questioning by the investigating commission, he justified his resentment of De Bono on the ground that the chief of police was in the habit of protecting all political dissidents. (*The author quotes from Dumini's testimony which revealed the names of several dissident Fascists who were allegedly protected by De Bono —Ed.*)

Mussolini was undoubtedly concerned that the dissidents might gain a foothold in northern Italy were they were led by men of considerable stature . . . such as Cesare Forni and Raimondo Sala, the latter a former mayor of Alessandria, who were beaten up during the electoral campaign of 1924. Giunta, who was then the secretary of the party, issued a circular on March 11, 1924, in which he proposed the use of violence to restrain the movement led by Forni and Sala.[36]

Dumini made the following comments in an undated note that was probably written in the early part of 1924:

> Should the secessionist movement expand, the Forni-Sala group could exert real influence on a considerable part of the Fascist movement in the province of Milan, particularly on the squads. . . . From Cremona Farinacci has sown dissension among virtually all Fascists in the Sorinese area and among the high bourgeoisie of his province. . . . In Milan and throughout that province there are many borderline Fascists who are ready to join whoever wins. . . . Three-fourths of the dissidents in the province are Masons, which means that, since Forni is also a Mason, the party must remain alert to a threat from that quarter. . . . The only group that is still trustworthy are the *arditi* led by Albino Volpi. They are a well-disciplined group who obey the leaders without question, but they find themselves without means of support; they are likely to be disbanded before the election and will probably join the ranks of the dissidents.[37]

(*The author argues that Dumini's statements reveal how the Fascists "of the first hour" resented the influence of the Masonic lodges whose leaders were still active in the party at the end of 1925. The repression that followed the unsuccessful attempt made on Mussolini's life by the Socialist deputy and Mason Tito Zaniboni on November 4, 1925, was aimed primarily at destroying the political power of the Masons—Ed.*)

Without attempting to follow step by step the events leading to the assassination of Matteotti in June 1924 or to describe all the currents within fascism . . . , the fact remains that the prolonged revisionist campaign, the dissidents who managed to even the score with the opposition after Matteotti's murder, those who favored legality and the extremists who looked forward to the *second wave,* the Liberals who advocated a policy of tight spending, the business speculators, the newspapers . . . , all these groups played a partisan role in the Matteotti crisis. Their interpretations of that tragic event reflected their estimate of the nature of fascism and of the goals they wished it to reach.

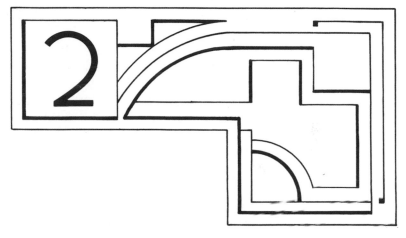

FASCISM AND
THE CHURCH
1922–1925 *

The Fascist claim that the march on Rome was a genuine revolution was hardly supported by the way in which the Fascist government went out of its way to gain the backing of powerful vested interests. Relations with the Church are a good case in point. Mussolini's desire to have the Church on his side was evident from his early days in power. As prime minister, he shed the crude atheism and materialism of his youth in favor of a more spiritual meditative stance. On a more tangible level, he dealt with the Church in the same way he dealt with

---

* From Francesco Margiotta Broglio, *Italia e Santa Sede dalla Grande Guerra alla Conciliazione* (Bari: Laterza, 1966), pp. 250–257. By permission of the publisher.

any powerful organization whose support he coveted. He simply traded specific favors in return for a general endorsement that was calculated to increase the authority of the regime. These tactics worked up to a point. They certainly won him the benevolence of many special interest groups, but that benevolence did not always or necessarily extend to fascism as a political movement or as an ideology. Thus, while fascism remained suspect in many quarters, Mussolini became an indispensable mediator. The basis of Mussolini's dictatorship was established during these early years of the regime when he was acting as healer to the old order and midwife to the new.

Mussolini's effort to initiate a political dialogue with the Church began in January 1923 with a private and for many years secret meeting with the Vatican's secretary of state, Cardinal Pietro Gasparri. Shortly thereafter, the government intervened to save the Vatican-controlled Bank of Rome from bankruptcy. The intervention certainly demonstrated Mussolini's goodwill toward the Church and made it easier to raise and discuss the fundamental issue that kept church and state divided in Italy. The Roman Question, as the conflict between church and state was sometimes called, dated from 1870 when the Italian army had forcibly occupied the papal city of Rome and restricted the pope's temporal authority to the tiny enclave of the Vatican on the right bank of the Tiber. Although in practice the conflict had abated long before Mussolini's rise to power, there were still many unsettled issues and questions of principle that prevented a complete reconciliation.

In the following selection, Francesco Margiotta Broglio, who combines a recognized expertise in Church law with a strong interest in historical research, discusses Mussolini's first and unsuccessful efforts to negotiate a settlement with the Church. Although these initial contacts had no visible results, they did, in fact, establish a framework for the later negotiations that led to the well-known Lateran Pacts of February 1929. The strong desire of the Fascist government to resolve the historical controversy with the Church is evident from many provisions of the

Lateran Pacts. The papacy won a generous financial settlement, its territorial sovereignty over the Vatican was officially recognized by the Italian government, and Catholicism became "the sole religion of the state." Some of the most sensitive issues were treated in the part of the pacts known as the Concordat which, among other things, gave the force of law to religious marriages and introduced compulsory religious instruction in the public schools. This last point, however, did not resolve the fundamental question of whether religious or secular influences were to dominate education. That troublesome question was never resolved in principle because it touched a fundamental aspiration that neither fascism nor the Church could renounce. In most respects, however, the Fascist state made important concessions to the Church that left some radical Fascists rather unhappy. As Margiotta Broglio points out, the signing of the Lateran Pacts was a victory for the conservative elements in fascism. The deference that was customarily shown by the Fascist government toward the Church should alert the reader to the fact that the day-to-day practices of fascism were often at variance with its revolutionary, totalitarian ideology.

■

Under Mussolini, government policy toward the Church followed the same direction and alternatives pursued by the pre-Fascist governments that had come to power in Italy after the outbreak of World War I. To understand why fascism could not develop different policies, we must keep in mind that it was "internally divided" and that "as the Marxist theoretician Antonio Gramsci had clearly perceived, the basic conflicts of Italian society were bound to reemerge within it because they were denied any other outlet." [1]

The ecclesiastical measures taken in 1922–1923 not only followed the political lines established by the governments of Vittorio Emanuele Orlando and Francesco Saverio Nitti, prime ministers from October 1917 to June 1920, but also aimed at eliminating the Popularists from Italian political life. (*The Italian Popular party was formed in December 1918 with the tacit approval of the Vatican. It emerged as a major political force with the elections of November 1919 when it received more than 1,175,000 votes and 100 seats in the Chamber, making it the third largest political bloc after the Liberals with 252 seats and the Socialists with 156 seats. The Church remained officially aloof, but the party was nevertheless recognized as the political arm of Catholicism.—Ed.*) The steps taken in 1922–1923 achieved some of the objectives of the earlier programs. In the final analysis, they even corrected some of their shortcomings as already deplored by the Holy See, such as the lack of specific references to "the pope's full liberty, sovereignty, and independence in his high office." [2]

There is clear evidence to support all these points in the correspondence . . . between Amedeo Giannini, a government official who acted as intermediary between Mussolini and Vatican officials, Mussolini, and Oviglio in the last months of 1923 pertaining to the planned reforms of ecclesiastical laws. It contains explicit statements to the effect that the purpose of the reform and other ecclesiastical measures was to demonstrate that fascism had not only already incorporated the program of the Popularists but had "improved and surpassed it on many points," to hasten the inevitable separation of the "centrists from the leftists" in order to destroy the Popular party, and enable Mussolini to decide whether and how to utilize the Catholic forces that would be left leaderless. [3]

Looking at it from another angle, it is clear that the rather unstable ideological composition of fascism, which resulted from the presence within it of the two incompatible philosophies of revolutionary syndicalism and conservative nationalism, [4] made it impossible for fascism to deal with the Church on the basis of political and juridical formulas deliberately different from those adopted by preceding governments in their efforts to regulate ecclesiastical matters. [5]

If there was any break in the government's religious policy and legislation before the Lateran Pacts, it occurred as a result of the reorientation of the regime that followed Mussolini's speech of January 3, 1925. With that speech, fascism in its true form began to decline because it had to yield to the conservative demands of the Nationalists and the right-wingers in the Popular party. The Vatican had understood as early as May 1923 that the rising influence of conservatives would bring Catholics closer to fascism.[6] As for relations with the Holy See, the speech of January 3 opened the way for the solution of the Roman Question in February 1929 along lines that had been sketched by Alfredo Rocco as early as April 1922: The state must reject the old Liberal program based on the lay nature of the state, on the separation between church and state, and on the state that is indifferent to religion. The Church must renounce its design to strengthen itself domestically and must of necessity expand externally. As a prerequisite, the state must therefore assume "a religious content" and "positively defend Catholicism, which is the faith of the majority of the Italian people," while the Church must give the state its "loyal help in maintaining civil order and the sense of nationality."[7]

It is worth pointing out that the attitudes of Oviglio and Rocco toward the anticipated reform of ecclesiastical laws differed greatly. . . . (*Aldo Oviglio, Mussolini's first minister of justice, wished to resolve the dispute between church and state but believed that negotiations should be delayed until the government had first formulated its own political views on such questions as how to deal with Church properties that were being administered by lay organizations, the desirability of retaining government control over the appointment of religious officials, and the right to discipline religious organizations by sequestering their assets. His successor, Alfredo Rocco, was willing to open negotiations at once and quickly set up a committee of experts to explore the issues.—Ed.*) It was only after the "crisis" of January 3, which was followed by the resignation of Oviglio who . . . throughout 1924 had refused to bring the problem to the attention of the council of ministers in spite of Mussolini's urgings, and Alfredo Rocco's entrance into the cabinet as minister of justice that it became possible to take up the problem and form a special committee. On January 6, 1925, Rocco was already assuring the council of ministers that a reform affecting ecclesiastical holdings was about to be prepared.[8]

It is also worth noting that neither the Fascist government nor its chief ever had clear notions of how to deal with the Catholic Church or developed a Church policy of their own that was truly worthy of the name. Once again, Mussolini's politics did not follow a particular, conscious design, but consisted instead of repeated adjustments and accommodations with events as they developed.[9]

All contacts with the Holy See before the Conciliation, including the direct talks between Mussolini and Father Pietro Tacchi-Venturi, a prelate who enjoyed the confidence of both Mussolini and Cardinal Pietro Gasparri, the papal secretary of state, and perhaps even the negotiations between Domenico Barone (who was eventually replaced by Mussolini) and Francesco Pacelli, brother of the future Pius XII, seem haphazard, without any real awareness of the problems. Solutions were often dependent on the personal views of the negotiators, or the humor of the head of government, and were sometimes determined by the presence or absence in the requests of the Holy See of expressions of praise and approbation for the regime.

This impression coincides with the definition of Mussolini as the *homme qui cherche* given by De Felice in his recent, subtle, and rich biographical research. It seems clear that Mussolini was hardly a statesman, although he was undoubtedly a remarkable politician whose most important decisions "were practically imposed by circumstances or . . . made tactically by degrees in response to outside events" and without "any idea of goals but feeling his way like a true politician." [10] As for his relations with the Holy See, he understood intuitively that he should strive to *nationalize* the Catholic Church so that it would become one of the pillars of the regime. He nevertheless pursued that aim without ideological guidelines, without a knowledge or understanding of the various problems, and at least until the end of 1925, without ultimately wanting anything more than "harmonious relations." [11]

Mussolini explicitly stated all this in his *Autobiography* (still unpublished in its original Italian version). After criticizing the Liberal concept that religion is a private concern, the spirit of anticlericalism, the hostility and "stubborn intransigence" of the Church toward the new Italy, which had exasperated the Church's enemies, he went on to emphasize the dangerous degeneration of political clericalism into the "clerical bolshevism" of the Popularists and asserted that he had never deluded himself into believing that he could settle "a conflict that involves the highest interests and principles." He only wanted "to restore the principle of Catholicism, religious observance, and respect for worship without political controversy," in spite of the fact that the Holy See had not always appreciated his efforts or supported him adequately.[12]

As for the Roman Question itself, he believed that the problem "was not yet ready to be solved and was perhaps insoluble." Fascism might actually have intensified the "historical conflict" between two mentalities and systems that were already locked "in secular opposition" so that it lingered on with all the "inevitable burdens of its antitheses." Although fascism "strengthened and invigorated the national religion," it could never "renounce the sovereign and indefeasible rights of the state." [13]

In conclusion, it seems clear that Italy's policy toward the Church developed with continuity from the period of World War I to the end of 1924. There was a progressive rapprochement between the Holy See and succeeding governments that was evident more in the day-to-day business of government and in unofficial understandings than in questions of principle. One hesitates to call the Church laws that preceded the Concordat "Fascist" except in a purely mechanical and chronological sense.

Neither the solution of the Roman Question nor the regulations governing the activities of Catholic associations in Italy were strictly Fascist in spirit. When all is said and done, they implemented the aspirations and principles of Nationalists and clerical-Fascists with little regard for the views of left-wing interventionists and revolutionary syndicalists.

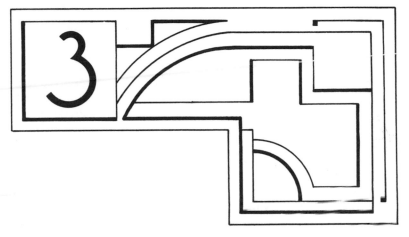

THE
FASCIST MILITIA
AND THE ARMY,
1922–1924 *

The backing of the military was as important to the Fascists as that of the clergy. While the approval of the clergy helped to make the Fascist regime more popular, that of the military gave it the security it needed to set its own house in order and deal forcefully with domestic opponents. Consequently the Fascists always made it a point to reassure the military that fascism would do all in its power to strengthen the prestige and effectiveness of the regular armed forces.

The Fascists never made the tactical error of questioning the

* From Giorgio Rochat, *L'esercito italiano da Vittorio Veneto a Mussolini (1919–1925)* (Bari: Laterza, 1967), pp. 426–442. By permission of the publisher.

authority of the regular army even before the march on Rome when fascism was an insurrectionary movement and the army the ultimate guardian of the status quo. Army officers usually reciprocated by considering the Fascists as a civilian reserve force fighting to strengthen the spirit of nationalism against the allegedly subversive influence of left-wing militants. The many instances of collusion between the army and the Fascist squads before the march on Rome occurred because local commanders personally sympathized with the goals of the squads. Collusion thus developed spontaneously at the local level in spite of the fact that the army high command ostentatiously refrained from engaging in partisan politics.

In other words, the bond between fascism and the military rested ultimately on moral and ideological affinities that transcended specific political issues and disagreements. Basically, the bond consisted of shared value judgments, such as the need for discipline and hierarchy in social relations, reverence for national traditions, the wastefulness of political debate, and the seeming inefficiency of liberal governments. The message that the bond was strong enough to resist the divisive effect of disagreement on questions of detail comes across strongly in this selection by Giorgio Rochat, who is Italy's foremost young military historian. Following a tradition initiated in Italy by the veteran military historian Piero Pieri, Rochat deals with military affairs against the broad spectrum of political and social developments.

In this selection, Rochat examines relations between fascism and the military at the critical moment when the Fascists were trying to organize an independent armed force, the Fascist Militia. Although military leaders did not object to the formation of a paramilitary organization under party control, they did not want the Militia to undermine their own chain of command or threaten the army's role as the sole fighting force in time of war.

The way in which this disagreement was resolved points once again to Mussolini's desire to govern with the consent of traditional vested interests. In this particular case, however, the compromise with the army seriously weakened the political autonomy and effectiveness of the Fascist party. Although Militia units were eventually formed and fought independently in the Ethiopian war and World War II, the Fascist Militia never became as strong and influential in Italy as the SA and the SS were in Nazi Germany. In spite of the fact that the army and the Militia were fully coordinated on paper, relations between the two remained tense. Rumors that army and Militia units actually fired at one another in World War II, whether true or false, are a good indication of the latent hostility between the two organizations. Among the reasons why the Fascists failed to react to the *coup d'etat* that toppled Mussolini on July 25, 1943, the dependent and secondary role assigned to the Fascist Militia is perhaps not the least significant.

■

The Fascists claimed that the Voluntary Militia for National Security (MVSN) was set up after the march on Rome in order to legalize the existence of the action squads by bringing them under the control of the state. According to the opposition, the Militia was established to perpetuate a separate armed force. The intentions of the Fascists were stated plainly. Even before the seizure of power, *Il Popolo d'Italia* had written:

> The Fascist action squads cannot and must not die. For us it would be true suicide because, if force is needed to conquer power, it is even more needed to retain it. The Fascist Militia should, however, be transformed. The squads should cease to belong to the party in order that they may belong to the state. . . . Once the squads are under military discipline, the danger of competition between them and the other armed forces of the nation will cease. . . . Once this volunteer army belongs to the state, it will be our surest guarantee for the future. Woe to those who build on the shifting sands of universal suffrage.[1]

The bulletins of December 1922 announcing that the squads would be organized as part of the National Militia were naturally couched in less brutal language:

45

> We must keep in mind that it is not a question of organizing a new army, certainly not one of praetorian mercenaries at the personal service of the head of government, but of a militia solely dedicated to the highest interests of the country, under the supervision and sure guidance of the prime minister. They will be front line troops, the flower of the army, because they will be recruited among the most sincere Fascists who abound in the numerous action squads. They will be ready for every eventuality, but will be mobilized only at the most critical moments whenever anyone threatens the security of the nation either internally or externally. . . . It will be another giant step toward inserting fascism into the life of the state.[2]

The Militia took shape during 1923. A homogeneous organization was gradually formed, divided into legions (whose reported number varied considerably, from 100 to 180, depending on the source and time of information), grouped into zonal commands, and subdivided, like the ancient Roman army, into cohorts, centuries, and maniples. Militiamen and officers came as a rule from the dissolved action squads. They were normally considered on leave, free to engage in their respective civilian occupations, and were expected to report for ceremonies, drills, or emergencies, which ranged from the repression of antigovernment demonstrations to rescue work in the course of natural calamities. On such occasions they received an allowance. High officers, clerks, and a small number of militiamen who were on permanent duty, as guards in public places or to take care of routine business, received compensations comparable to those paid in the army. Figures on the numerical strength of the Militia are scarce and contradictory: 300,000 men, plus 200,000 reinforcements were anticipated as of August 1923; in February 1924 Balbo claimed that 300,000 bayonet-trained troops were ready; in December 1924 Mussolini spoke more modestly of 139,000 men. On the same date, it was claimed that there were 8,000 officers, of whom 750 were on permanent service. Weapons were reckoned at 50,000 rifles on the eve of the Matteotti crime; another 100,000 rifles were withdrawn from army stores in June 1924. The arsenal also included 250 machine guns, 11 armored cars, and 4 pieces of mountain artillery.

The Militia was in these early years an extremely varied organization, highly influenced by local conditions, of variable efficiency, and difficult to control. Its constitutionality was uncertain and could even be considered illegal: it swore loyalty to Mussolini rather than to the king or the constitution, was at Mussolini's disposal through a command exercised by De Bono, Balbo, and De Vecchi, and circumvented both military and civilian control at the national and local levels. No precise criteria existed for admission or for the distribution of ranks and duties, the latter being granted on the basis of distinction achieved in the squads, political or otherwise. There was no budget (the figure of 25 million lire in annual expenditures is only an approximation), no administration, no staff. The role, duties, and possible uses of this new armed force were far from clear.

The obvious and unconcealed purpose of the Militia was to defend the regime by any means. However, the punitive expeditions and illegal actions committed by the action squads in 1921–1922 could not go on indefinitely. The Militia needed subsidiary tasks that would justify its existence before public opinion, give it a continuous and regular role, while at the same time preserving the aggressive spirit and training of its heroic days. Such tasks could be sought only in military and paramilitary life to which fascism was irresistibly attracted, even at the risk of friction with the army, which was a jealous guardian of its prerogatives. Fascism was confirmed in its military vocation by recent events. The spirit of victory, poorly safeguarded by the army against the disruptive policies of liberal governments, had reasserted itself in Fiume (*in September 1919 the city of Fiume had been occupied by a band of irregulars and patriotic deserters led by d'Annunzio who wanted the city annexed to Italy—Ed.*) and then in the action squads, and had once again animated the entire nation with the advent of the regime. At that point, "the action squads became the Militia. The latter has therefore inher-

47

ited and become the repository of the spirit of victory; from the moral point of view, it is the most important subsidiary of the national army. For if the latter aims at preserving and developing technique, the former aims at preserving and developing the spirit of the armed nation." [3]

An excerpt from a general communiqué issued by the general command of the Militia in September 1923 indicates that the duties of the new force were to extend well beyond the legalization of the squads:

> It is significant that, as part of its duties to defend the revolution, the new Militia has been given the task of maintaining public order, thus taking away from the army a duty which distracted it from its proper functions and goals. But it cannot be denied that the Militia exists above all in order to permeate Italian youth with a new spirit, to train them in the use of weapons, to enlarge the basis which sustains the destinies of the new Italy. . . . The country needs the support of bayonets that sparkle steadily, that speak out because they are made eloquent by the constant training of those who have been fortunate enough to insert them on the tips of their rifles. An army? Yes, an army of volunteers united in pursuit of a single goal with the marvelous army of conscripts. Wars today are not fought by regular armies only, they are fought by nations. The best part of the nation must be held ready for any eventuality because only superior military power can guarantee us tranquillity.[4]

Military circles were not opposed in principle to the Militia. We must keep in mind that, in the general picture, the Militia was accepted as a lesser evil and as a temporary solution even by Liberals and Catholics who understood the new regime's craving for security. The army drew sufficient advantage from its agreement with fascism to be able to overlook some measures that were not to their liking. They would continue to do so in subsequent years, but the initial consensus was more spontaneous. How many officers had dreamed of seeing the army surrounded and assisted by a staunchly patriotic mass organization, capable of educating the young in the cult of traditions, and ready to lend a helping hand in organizing the nation for war! Many looked upon the Militia as a means of realizing that dream. For example, General Pietro Gramantieri, who professed democratic convictions, wrote that whatever judgment one might pass on fascism, one had to agree on one point:

> Strictly from the point of view of national defense, the Fascist military organization offers the possibility of finally achieving, with complete liberty, the definitive organization of the army. . . . Such fearless youth, if well directed, cannot help but have generous sentiments. And if this Fascist force is really devoted to the country, when could Italy be possibly more orderly on a national scale? When could Italy possibly have a stronger army? [5]

Support was not lacking even in the newspapers of the opposition where the partisan character of the Militia was played down in order to emphasize its national and paramilitary aspects, suggesting that it should develop according to the needs of war and the demands of the army.[6]

On the other hand, the military were bound to be displeased as soon as the Militia threatened to set up itself as a rival armed force. Most of all, the military resented the voluntary nature of the squads, which generated disorder, continual squabbling, and loose discipline. Regular army officers were bound to disapprove of the Militia's political character (which was irritating in circles accustomed to despise politics and might also impede its subordination to the military), the danger that the new organization might divert sympathies, funds, and political influence from the army whose appropriations were dwindling, and finally, the potential rivalry between the two officer corps, which were so different in origin and method of selection. In brief, military circles welcomed the Militia for its merits and national ideals, but with a touch of suspicion. And they expected that it would be either strictly political or else would be under regular military discipline and subjected to the army.

The reorganization plan presented by General De Bono, the

first commanding general of the Militia, to the Fascist Grand Council at the end of July 1923 . . . favored the second alternative. The general proposed a reduction of the fighting force to 100,000 men with a rigorous process of selection and maximum recourse to regular army officers (which was already happening in the case of discharged officers). The political character and functions of the Militia were to take second place to activities that would complement those of the army, particularly premilitary instruction. Thus "technicized and militarized," the Militia could have joined the other armed forces of the state under a new ministry of defense, side by side with the army, navy, and air force.[7]

This plan was rejected by the Grand Council on July 25, 1923 when it reaffirmed in no uncertain terms the eminently political character of the Militia with a declaration whose salient points were the following:

> 1. Until the time when the state has become completely Fascist, when the Fascist or pro-Fascist ruling class has completely replaced the previous ruling class in all the administrations and institutions of the state, and until every slightest inclination on the part of anti-Fascist elements to revolt has been irrevocably suppressed, fascism, both at the level of party and government, having created the revolution and assumed all subsequent responsibility for it, cannot give up the armed force of the black shirts.
>
> 2. The black shirts therefore represent the cream of the party, they are the faithful, vigilant, and invincible guard of the revolution that culminated in the march on Rome, an inexhaustible reserve of enthusiasm and faith in the destinies of the country whose symbol is the august person of the king. . . .
>
> . . . . .
>
> 4. The Militia is a great political force. With or without the cooperation of the ordinary police forces, its task is to render impossible any disturbance of the public order, any gesture or seditious attempt against the Fascist government, thereby assuring constant normalcy in the productive and social life of the nation.[8]

The message, as clarified by the Fascist press, was that the Militia would not become a mere military organization, nor would it accept, either in name or in fact, a position subordinate to the army's. As Farinacci wrote, "Our militiamen remain obediently in the ranks because they feel that is the way it should be and because they think that the Militia is the highest form of fascism, a kind of Superfascism. . . . It is not possible, therefore, to make the Militia a military body." [9]

Although the Militia reaffirmed its political character and affiliation, it did not intend to stay out of the sphere of influence that until then had been the exclusive preserve of the military. Its aspirations, as articulated in 1923, may be summed up in three points: maintenance of public order, premilitary instruction, and postmilitary training. Their meaning varied widely. From time to time, the activities of the Militia were understood to be essentially political and at the service of the regime, or generally moral and patriotic, and sometimes even complementary with the army's. The ambiguity persisted in spite of the declaration of the Grand Council on July 25. The ambiguity was encouraged by Mussolini, who did not want to irritate the military and the liberal supporters, and resulted also from the composite nature of the Militia where different tendencies were represented. Thus, maintenance of public order could mean either defending the Fascist government by any means or engaging in basically legal police work. Premilitary instruction was to be limited at times to Fascist youth only, while at other times it was to be compulsory for all Italians between the ages of eighteen and twenty, and variously based on sports, moral-patriotic programs, or truly military exercises, either in conjunction with regular army duty or as a means of shortening its duration. Postmilitary activities sometimes masked the desire to keep the old Fascist action squads in good working order, or establish special units, or even put the Militia in charge of mobilizing the country in case of war.

The aspirations of the Militia found official recognition in two documents of 1923, both, however, of a remarkably general nature and drawn up with evident concern for maintaining good relations with the army which was not begrudged praises and promises. On the question of public order, the Grand Council declared itself as follows:

> With its efficiency, organization, and the high spirit of its volunteers, the Militia completely frees the army from police duties of a political nature in conjunction with the preservation of public order. The victorious army, from which the Militia draws many of its cadres and members and to which fascism is highly devoted, can dedicate itself in perfect tranquillity to its specific task of defending the country against outside attack.[10]

This provision could not displease the military who, in fact, welcomed it, not joining the protests from liberal quarters, because it did not lessen their prestige.[11] On the contrary, the army had always protested against bothersome public security duties, guard details, and outside duties. Presumably, at least some of these would now fall to the Militia. . . .

The Militia's request to assume responsibility for premilitary instruction, on the other hand, aroused open hostility in certain military circles. The existing organization, based on hundreds of independent societies whose activities were coordinated by military authorities, was giving satisfactory numerical results (their membership rose from 50,000 in 1922 to 80,000 in 1923) but was accused by the Fascists of lacking an idealistic drive: "Premilitary instruction therefore lacks a collective soul and a center capable of radiating passion for faith and action." The Militia wanted therefore to take over the training of young men and give them "a strict military preparation capable of imparting the habit of discipline, developing and hardening to fatigue and sacrifice the energies of the body and the spirit." It was not hard for the Militia to show that military authorities had dealt with premilitary training in a haphazard way.[12] The reply came in *Esercito e Marina:* "In our opinion, premilitary instruction . . . should not be removed from the authority and jurisdiction of the ministry of war because it is closely related to regular military training." [13] But . . . the Militia insisted in terms that were unequivocal and slightly polemical toward the army that it be placed in charge of training young men, with particular reference to premilitary instruction.[14] The military argued that there must be close cooperation but agreed nevertheless and the Militia progressively had their own way.

The army, however, scored a complete victory on the third point, postmilitary training. It had already been established in the July 25 meeting of the Grand Council that "In order to make it possible for the Militia, when war is declared, to turn back to the army cadres and privates in top form, individually and collectively, the Militia will be militarily trained with instructions and exercises to be established by the general command of the Militia itself in agreement with the army command." [15]

These brief lines placed the ambitions of the *squadristi* in their proper perspective and restored the army to its function as the only armed force to face the enemy. The withdrawal from the Militia, upon the act of mobilization, of all the men and officers necessary to the army meant for all practical purposes its dissolution for the duration of the war or at least its reduction to purely auxiliary tasks. It also implied that the Fascist squads, or any voluntary formation outside the army, left much to be desired as a fighting force. The peacetime military activity of the Militia was reduced to maintaining the training of its own members only, under the tutelage of military authorities. Although the tutelage would be a mere formality, the Militia's renunciation to set itself up as even a small-scale competitor of the army was a tribute paid by the regime to the military. General Diaz, Mussolini's minister of war, quickly telegraphed his approval to Mussolini, stressing the auxiliary function of the Militia:

> I express to Your Excellency my intense satisfaction with the directives established for the Militia, which consecrate the highly patriotic goals that unite us all in one duty and one faith, facilitating the work of the army as an institution, and keeping firmly

ready the forces which must complement it when national interests require it.[16]

Nevertheless, the Militia could not agree to disband upon the act of mobilization, either totally or in part, without repudiating its much-vaunted warlike vocation. The agreements reached in 1923 were therefore merely provisional and destined to be brought up for discussion again in a very short time.[17]

The "amalgamation" of the Militia, meaning an operation designed to overcome the temporary arrangements of 1923, giving it a definite place among the armed forces of the state and enabling it to march side by side (and in step) with the army, was the opening theme of 1924. The operation, however, was bound to be difficult because it involved an exact definition of the tasks of the Fascist squads and of hierarchical relations between their officers and those of the regular army. A plan drawn up by the army's general staff in January was turned down because Mussolini judged the situation to be premature.[18] The attitude of the military stiffened in response to Fascist demands that, far from being dissolved, units of the Fascist Militia should be assigned specific tasks at the time of mobilization, such as defense of the national territory and the establishment of large units capable of carrying out regular military operations. General Luigi Segato believed that the Militia should be assigned the following tasks:

> To substitute the army whenever possible in patrol duties and the maintenance of public order; help to spread and sustain at a high pitch feelings of patriotism, contempt for danger, discipline, and sacrifice, as well as training in the use of firearms and military drill; provide well-trained men for those units that are demobilized in peacetime in order to strengthen our reserves; train first rate assault troops so that, at least in that respect, we could begin military operations with superiority over our eventual enemy. This is what the amalgamation of the Militia and the army should involve at present. And it is certainly not very little.[19]

The concessions were greater than those made the preceding year, but there was still the most firm opposition to the creation of truly independent units of the Militia for use in war and to the equalization of rank between the two armed forces. The latter problem was particularly felt by army officers and deserves a brief discussion.

The officers of the Militia (almost 8,000, a little more than a thousand of whom were high-ranking officers or generals) were a heterogeneous group.[20] Its composition was not regulated by law, and rank was assigned case by case essentially on the basis of political merits. It is true that many officers came from the army, either from the reserves or from those on leave, but they had been promoted repeatedly, as in the extreme cases of Balbo and De Vecchi, who in a few months had risen from their low ranks as reserve officers to the rank of commanding generals of the Militia, which was the equivalent of an army corps general.[21] Army officers who had advanced after years of study and decades of service and had seen their promotions blocked since 1919 could sympathize with Militia officers only as long as the Militia handled essentially political tasks. They were bound to consider them as shameless opportunists the minute they assumed a military posture. No one envisaged merging the two officer corps, not even the Fascists who had everything to gain by keeping them separate. But the incorporation of the Militia into the armed forces of the country was enough to establish reciprocal obligations of rank and deference, not to mention the problem of preference in mobilizing for war.[22] The military insisted, therefore, that the incorporation of the Militia should involve only a reorganization within its own ranks and not even the slightest redistribution of defense duties which, unless the Militia was to be profoundly altered and strictly subordinated to the army, were to be reserved exclusively for the army. This was stated with extreme clarity in *Esercito e Marina* and occasionally in the political press.[23] Even the government press had to take notice of these attitudes, as was the case with *L'Idea Nazionale* in June 1924:

> The irregular military elements that have come out of the revolution, that is the Fascist action squads transformed into

55

the Militia, and the regular army face each other not with hostility but wary and suspicious. National need stands above both, as personified by the iron will of the one man who orders and demands that the two groups shake hands fraternally and merge to form a single body with a single soul.[24]

The army's lack of understanding toward the Militia had to be overcome. The newspaper recalled the merits of fascism and promised a severe purge of the cadres of the Militia. It pointed out that in the course of two or three years no more than sixty officers had received a rank decidedly higher than that which they had had in the army, and asked the question "is it worth ruining the good relations between the army and the Militia for a question which is of such small importance when reduced to its true proportions?" [25]

The crisis that followed the assassination of Matteotti had a clarifying effect. At the moment when the Liberal opposition loudly demanded the dissolution of the Militia and the resignation of the government, the army reaffirmed its faith in Mussolini (with some slight reservations) [26] and assigned 100,000 rifles to the black shirts.[27] The alliance with fascism proved to be stronger than the differences over the future of the Militia. Once the political crisis was settled, the army had to acknowledge many of the Militia's aspirations, including a gradual merger of the two armed forces. But in the larger context of the agreement between the army and the regime, the political advantages of the merger would more than compensate the army for the sacrifice.

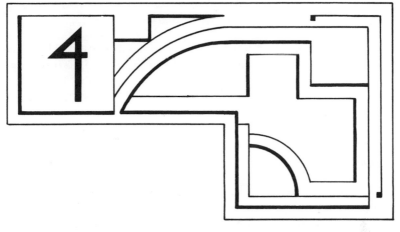

FASCISM IN ITALY:
THE SECOND
WAVE *

Militant Fascists had never accepted the idea that the march on Rome should be the closing act of the Fascist revolution. Disillusioned by the Fascist government's failure to press for speedy, radical change, a number of militants within the party and the militia clamored for the "second wave" of the revolution. The "second wave" came late and in an unexpected manner. It was more the result of fortuitous outside events than of pressure from within. It seems fair to say that without the Matteotti crisis the coming of the "second wave" might have been postponed indefinitely. The crisis, which developed be-

* Adrian Lyttelton, from the *Journal of Contemporary History*, Vol. I (January 1966), pp. 75–100. By permission of the publisher.

tween June 1924 and January 1925, gave the dissatisfied elements an opportunity to challenge Mussolini's politics of accommodation. The extremists confronted Mussolini with an ultimatum that he could not ignore but which he was able to manipulate to his own advantage.

The article by Adrian Lyttelton, a fellow of All Souls College, Oxford, is a concise, thought-provoking discussion of the internal politics of fascism during the Matteotti crisis. Lyttelton's article covers the critical months when all the unresolved internal contradictions and ambiguities of fascism were coming to a head and Mussolini had to adjust his tactics to deal with events which he could no longer control fully. The article needs little introduction because the reader is already familiar with the major currents and personalities appearing in it. But, because the article concludes our coverage of the first phase of the Fascist regime, it may be worth reflecting on the meaning of the closing quotation. Does it suggest that the Fascist radicals were in fact the major beneficiaries of the "second wave"?

■

The Fascist seizure of power was a lengthy process. Beginning in the autumn of 1921 with the piecemeal destruction or absorption of the machinery of local administration, it was finally completed only with the reform of the Chamber of Deputies in 1928. But in this slow process two dramatic "leaps" have always been recognized as decisive. The first, obviously, is the march on Rome; the second is the end of the Matteotti crisis in January 1925. Mussolini's speech on January 3 was taken by the Italian Republic to mark the break between the constitutional regime and the dictatorship. There is an important difference between the two leaps; the march on Rome was the culmination of a steady process of encroachment on the powers of the state, whereas the action of Mussolini in January 1925 was the reversal of what seemed like the fatal disintegration of his power and of the whole Fascist movement, and the initiation of a new phase, the "second wave" of fascism.

How was it possible that eighteen months after the march on Rome the murder of an opposition deputy could threaten the very foundation of Mussolini's power? This harsh question needs to be asked; without the existence of a parliamentary opposition, a partially free press, and a partially free magistracy, the whole Matteotti crisis would have been unthinkable. Moreover, the murder itself was in a sense characteristic of a regime which lacked legal sanctions against its opponents. The Fascist leaders continued to find terrorism necessary, but they were not prepared to assume full responsibility for it. The significance of Mussolini's January 3 speech was that he took this decisive step: "I declare . . . that I, and I alone, assume the political, moral, and historical responsibility for all that has happened. . . . If fascism has been a criminal association, if all the acts of violence have been the result of a certain historical, political, and moral climate, the responsibility for this is mine." [1] Fascism claimed to be a revolutionary movement. But the content of this revolution remained obscure. In his celebration of the anniversary of the march on Rome, Mussolini had boasted that "the fascist revolution had not fallen short of its goal"; but when he came to list its merits, they consisted principally in the things it had *not* done: it had not destroyed the authority of the monarchy, the church, or even parliament: and it had not introduced special emergency legislation.[2]

If the extremists within fascism regretted the absence of repressive legislation, even the moderates, or "revisionists," were concerned at its failure to create an institutional foundation for its exercise of power. At the party's National Council in August 1924 a delegate asked, "What has fascism brought that is new? What is there on which one could base the formula that there shall be no turning back? Nothing!" [3] Before the Matteotti crisis removed the veneer of official optimism such frankness was less encouraged and rarer, but not unknown. Fascism had created one new institution, the Militia; but even that had a somewhat uncertain status and future, continually disputed between those who wished to reduce it to the innocuous role of an auxiliary reserve and training corps for the regular army, and those who wished to accentuate its political character.

The successful elections of April 6, 1924, might seem, however, to have finally legitimized the dominant position of fascism in the state, and, by ending its previously insecure constitutional position, to have made possible that normalization, or return to legal methods, which was the central theme of political discussion. But the end of the provisional period of Fascist government had its disadvantages; it became harder to postpone the basic choices. The question of the character that the Fascist state was finally to assume became an inescapable and actual political problem. Would the new legislature signify, as the liberals hoped, the definitive reentry of fascism into the constitution and into legality? Or would it, instead, be the constituent assembly for the new Fascist state? In the second case, it was not easy to define the plan of the project.

The difficulty of giving fascism a definite shape, its refractoriness to discipline or stabilization, cannot be explained simply by the practical difficulties of implementing this or that reform. Not even the repressive legislation demanded by the extremists would have been capable of immediately satisfying the "revolutionary" demands of the movement; this was made clear by the events of 1925–1926. There was a fundamental contradiction between such a rational and conservative notion as the restoration of the authority of the state, and the irrationalist activism which had inspired the Fascist movement. Ideas of constitutional reform, of any kind of definitive organization, were regarded by this mentality as antipathetic or at least irrelevant. Camillo Pellizzi, a writer who in retrospect has criticized, with intelligence, the failure of fascism to take a technocratic or managerial turning, expressed this attitude with eloquence: "Fascism fought for a principle of authority. . . . Authority: but not that of a written law or a constitutional system." And again: "The genuine fascism has a divine repugnance for being crystallized into a state. . . . The Fascist state is, more than a state, a dynamo." [4]

Nor was this merely the pose of a few intellectuals; the leader of a group of dissidents who revolted against the *fascio* of Pistoia, under the name of the "old guard," explained that "We Fascists must never abandon that dynamism which is one of our most marked characteristics; to remain in the static position which has recently been reached was for us the negation of the Fascist idea." [5] One could speak, in fact, of an ideology of *squadrismo*; in effect, this ideology served to cover and confuse, to mystify, realities which were more simple.

For a real restoration of the authority of the state the first necessity was to reduce the power of the local Fascist bosses, or *ras*. But this was not easy. Mussolini himself desired, in principle, to bring the *ras* under control; he had convinced himself by October 1923, if not before, that it was in his own interest, as head of the state machine, to reestablish its supremacy over the party. This might not appear obvious: for was not Mussolini also the head of the party? However, the party had not yet shown itself capable of controlling the local leaders. The frequency of crises in the central organizations of the party, which were continually formed, dissolved, expanded, contracted, re-named, given greater or lesser powers, is a proof of the difficulty of making the Fascist party into a unity. Indeed, the march on Rome had in a sense aggravated the problem. Previously, a certain unity of action had been imposed on the movement by the necessities of combat; now this centripetal force was removed, and on the other hand the competition for office aroused new rivalries. This was well seen by G. Bottai, the most acute analyst of fascism's internal difficulties: "While homogeneity is more or less possible in parties formed around a rigid and precise program, it is almost impossible in a party whose recruitment stemmed from an atmosphere of passion. While strong feelings are active, it is possible to unite different types of men; calm revives their disagreements." [6]

Nineteen twenty-three therefore had seen an intense struggle for power within the Fascist movement, at both the national and local levels. The central leadership sought to make or break the provincial chiefs; this meant that in turn the more powerful of the *ras* increased their efforts to gain influence at the center. The result was a general increase in confusion and instability. Contemporaries spoke of the crisis of fascism.[7]

The Matteotti crisis began, in a sense, not with the murder of the socialist deputy, but with his speech to the Chamber on May 30, 1924. The idea of the secession of the opposition from parliament, of the "Aventine," and the answering project, on the Fascist side, of a "second wave" of illegal violence or repressive legislation, both date from then. A circular from Cesare Rossi [8] to the Fascist press on the day of the speech ordered the editors to unmask the "concerted plan" of the opposition to prepare for a secession: "These plans are destined to compromise seriously the long hoped for and now achieved normalization of national life, because of the inevitable and legitimate reaction that the Fascist regime will at the right moment unleash." [9] However, the effect of the murder was to make such a reaction impossible. According to his own story, Rossi proposed to Mussolini that he should at once assume responsibility for the crime, as he was to do on January 3, 1925.[10] But Mussolini felt himself, with reason, too weak for such action. The opposition had won a great moral victory; the question was whether they could translate it into political terms. Their failure to do so is notorious; but in order to understand the position of Mussolini and the Fascist movement it is necessary to ask what chances they might seem to have had of success.

The use of force was not wholly excluded. During the moments of greatest political confusion there were possibilities of success for a blow at the center, carried out by a small and determined group, although this solution presented difficulties sometimes too easily ignored. But the most serious danger to Mussolini came from the legal opposition. In retrospect, this appeared doomed by the attitude of the king, but at the time this could not be taken for granted. Mussolini had three dangers to fear. The first was the hostility of the elder statesmen; only the event was to prove the lack of effect on the crown of an alliance between Giolitti, Orlando, and Salandra against fascism. Second, a disintegration of Mussolini's parliamentary majority was not out of the question. When the Liberals, Combatants, and others were subtracted, the Fascists were only a bare majority; and among the Fascist deputies there were a number whose nerve might fail, or conscience revolt, faced with the necessity of extreme measures. Finally, there was danger from the cabinet itself. The broadening of the ministry, with the inclusion of two Liberals, was imposed upon Mussolini by the threatened resignation of four of his ministers, Oviglio, de Stefani, Federzoni, and Gentile.[11] The *Giornale d'Italia* (July 5) claimed that "the dominant elements of the situation are legalitarian; there is a cabinet, that would never approve a revolutionary policy"; later it appealed to the "eight legalitarian ministers." [12] There was a large element of illusion in these hopes. But it is true that Mussolini could count on the absolutely wholehearted support of only one other member of the cabinet, Ciano.

Only these dangers can explain the hesitancy of Mussolini's political strategy. At first the extremists had his favor. It was imperative for him to conserve all the strength he had left, and this implied dependence upon the enthusiasm of the provincial masses and the armed forces of the Militia. The high-water mark of the extremists' success was the Consiglio Nazionale of the party in August. Its resolutions marked the decisive formal break of fascism with the liberal state. However, Mussolini, having achieved his object by uniting the party behind a program of constitutional reform, which had little relevance to the actual political situation, turned to try to regain the lost or wavering support of the Liberals. But the elementary, if often effective, technique of the stick and the carrot was inadequate in the new political situation. The tensions were too great; distrust could no longer be disarmed by promises, and the support alienated by the encouragement given to the extremists in the first phase could be won back, if at all, only by very tangible concessions. Commenting on Mussolini's message to the Fascist party on November 30, the *Giornale d'Italia* (December 2, 1924) explained why its opposition was not irrevocable; between June and the present "there is a whole series of actions and speeches by the right honorable Mussolini himself which are in absolute contrast with the spirit which animated his speech to the Senate in June, or the present letter . . . the Prime Minister in yesterday's document as in his recent speech to the Chamber, appears not as a man of decided conviction, but rather as a man constrained to change tactics in order not to lose power."

There was another important sense in which Mussolini's early line increased the tensions. The Fascists themselves were wrought to a dangerous pitch; this was, of course, necessary, and provided the element of intimidation on which Mussolini counted. However, the new insecurity in the position of fascism made it more difficult than in the past for him to prevent the enthusiasm from boiling over. The first, extremist, phase had also had tangible consequences. The provinces had regained the dominant role in the direction of the party, and Farinacci in particular had become its virtual leader.

For these reasons, by the end of November Mussolini's policy was in ruins; on the one hand, fascism was isolated; on the other, this conspicuous failure to prevent the continued hemorrhage of supporters was sapping the confidence of the Fascists in his leadership, and in consequence the movement was threatening to escape from his control altogether. His only way out of the dilemma was to take advantage of the heightening of tension to proclaim his indispensability as the only man capable of dominating the crisis. A judgment of Massimo Rocca's is relevant here, even though it refers to the situation before the murder of Matteotti; in a conversation with Carlo Bazzi, "we agreed that Mussolini's real guarantee in respect of the monarchy consisted in a latent menace of civil war." [13] It was this menace which Mussolini brought out into the open on December 30, 1924, when he replied to the suggestion of his resignation: "I am ready to resign—but only in order to descend into the piazza." [14] Legal repression was justified on the pretext that it was the only means of averting the "second wave" of illegal violence. In his speech on January 3, Mussolini claimed that "If I had put the hundredth part of the energy that I spent in compressing fascism into releasing it, ah then. . . . But there will be no need of that, as the government is strong enough to cut short the sedition of the Aventine absolutely and definitively." As a pretext the argument deceived no one; but as a threat it had its effect.[15]

If the menace of the "second wave" was finally incorporated into Mussolini's strategy, it does not follow that it was always merely an element in his plans, a carefully solicited orchestration of his main theme. The objection to the threat was not that it was unreal, but that its fulfillment, if it preceded the legal, police reaction, might have fatal political consequences; ministers would resign, and the crown and the army might feel compelled to intervene to restore order. Consequently, it was essential for Mussolini that the government should act first and forestall any general, undisciplined terror action carried out by the provincial Fascists or the Militia. Such an action would probably have caused the downfall of fascism, and in any case would have seriously damaged the Duce's prestige in his own movement. To this extent one can say that the threat of the extremists to take the law into their own hands was really a decisive factor in precipitating Mussolini's decision.

Toward the end of November he was still on the normalizing tack. His intentions were serious enough to arouse stubborn opposition within the party. The communiqué of the Grand Council meeting of November 20 noted that the discussion of Mussolini's new policy directives had been particularly long and animated. Some days later a curious *ballon d'essai* was launched by a member of the party *Direttorio*, Ciarlantini. In an interview with the *Giornale d'Italia* (November 27) he declared, "Fascism is not a phenomenon which can be exhausted by the fortunes of a party. . . . The present formation of fascism may last for one year or five." This cannot have reassured those who believed that Mussolini was preparing to salvage his own fortunes at the expense of his party.[16] The Fascist revolution was declared at an end, and the energies of the movement were concentrated in the appeal for a new amnesty.[17] A general pessimism prevailed, shared even by the Duce's brother Arnaldo. Thanking Michele Bianchi for a present, he wrote that the gift was specially welcome "in these days in which we see the disintegration of a great part of the men and the program on which we had worked and pledged ourselves. I won't hide from you that for months and months I have been living in the gravest distress, condemned to a particularly difficult situation. . . . But the battle is not yet over." [18]

The situation was worsened by an unexpected blow. Balbo, the commander in chief of the Militia, was forced to resign by the disclosures made during his libel action against the *Voce Repubblicana*. Mussolini, himself implicated, accepted his resignation in a comradely letter, which increased the scandal. He had probably decided to replace Balbo by an ex-general of the regular army in any case; but instead of gaining credit for a "normalizing" initiative, he now appeared to have acted only under constraint.[19] Within the Fascist movement, Balbo had great popularity and prestige: the repercussions of his resignation were serious, especially in the Militia, which had an important and distinctive role in the events leading up to January 3.

The Balbo affair accentuated the previous contradictions in Mussolini's policy. To appease conservative opinion it was necessary to give the Militia a national and military role, but this needed the cooperation of the army, which was not prepared to agree without obtaining safeguards. Consequently, Mussolini found himself caught in a crossfire from his military and conservative critics in the Senate, and the powerful vested interest of the Militia officers. The urgency with which influential representatives of the army, such as generals Giardino, Zupelli, and Caviglia,[20] pressed their demands, reflected a serious alarm at the existence of a very considerable armed force which had, in reality, emancipated itself from all effective control. Could even Mussolini be sure of controlling his undisciplined private army?

Even if a successful *coup* remained improbable, it was not beyond the power of the Militia, with support from the rest of the Fascist movement, to create a violent interregnum. Public opinion, Giardino said, was alarmed by the possibility of an armed reaction, "even if limited to a few provinces . . . in the case of political change, or even of a radical purge." The last phrase showed the fear that Mussolini himself would not have the power to discipline the Fascist movement even if he had the will, which was no more than realistic. Consequently, the demand for the purge of the higher ranks of the Militia no longer reflected merely an exclusive professional jealousy, but also the urgent need to bring the corps under control. "The army must always be the strongest force of all the forces which exist in the nation," the general continued. "What guards against even the most unexpected conflict, indeed even the notion of any conflict whatsoever, and therefore assures the peace of civil society, without the actual employment of force, is simply and exclusively the just proportion of forces." The problem was not only one of status but of power.

The opposition of the Militia officers to the new directives, adopted in response to army pressure,[21] can neither be reduced to a mere matter of salary and status, nor seen apart from such pedestrian considerations. Its motives were not only material but psychological (the refusal to abandon political violence as a way of life), sociological (the dislike of impersonal, bureaucratic organization), and political (in common with other extremist Fascists, the belief that the time had come to cut short discussion). This mixture appears in a letter written by the Milanese Militia Consul, Carini; "If instead of consuming liters of ink we took up the *manganello* again . . . how much good would result. With opponents of such a quality the most valid, calm, elevated, convincing argument is worth the same as a dry fig. . . . General Radini has been transferred to Bologna and a brave but completely unknown general is coming here. This way of treating the [Militia] zones like regiments or brigades of the army is a real absurdity, and these provisions will inevitably lead to the death of the Militia—to say nothing else. General Radini is a likable and intransigent *Fascist,* and absolutely OK. He doesn't want to go to Bologna . . . and I think he will finish by offering his resignation. If his example is imitated by others of us and the same kind of attitude is taken up at Bologna, we will see the Militia disintegrate and perish. It is necessary that you should recall this state of affairs to him who has not well understood what the Militia is, and has equally not well understood that we hope that the Voluntary Militia for National Security will remain just that.

"I am writing this . . . with a feeling of true desperation in my heart (and I speak only of desperation because discipline forbids me to mention different feelings) . . . I who for two years have eked out a living with my family on 793 lire and *nothing else* except the modest pension won by twenty-six years of fearless sacrifice. . . . If we act in this way I foresee that at the right moment (which has perhaps already arrived!) the instrument of defense might not respond to the final appeal." [22]

Such a mixture of motives probably lay behind the so-called "movement of the consuls" in December 1924. The culminating event in this story is fairly well known: on the last day of the year thirty or so consuls of the Militia called on Mussolini, with the pretext of wishing him a happy new year, but with the real object of protesting against the changes in the command of the Militia and of warning him that if the government did not act to suppress opposition criticism, the "second wave" would begin.[23]

Much remains obscure in this story: the account of a violent altercation between Mussolini and the spokesman of the consuls has been described as a "pre-arranged comedy." [24] But, at least in its origins, the "movement of the consuls" would seem to have been the product of a genuine dissatisfaction with Mussolini's leadership, and probably envisaged an action of the kind Giardino had feared. One would assume that action against or without the powers of the state would have figured only as a desperate last resort: the intention would rather have been to make impossible a policy of accommodation and compromise by a St. Bartholomew's night of terror, thus compelling Mussolini to throw the government's weight behind the movement.

According to some versions, the movement was organized and led, at least in its earlier stages, by Balbo himself.[25] This is not improbable, but the evidence is not conclusive. Mussolini was acutely nervous of the repercussions of Balbo's resignation among the officers of the Militia.[26] Balbo advised his supporters "to give proof of our discipline one last time. . . . The government of our leader has ordered us not to hold demonstrations either for or against the government itself. We obey, but if even this last message of peace is not accepted by the opposition, let it be known that we are ready to make the war cry of the first days of fascism sound again." [27] The Fascist regional assembly of Emilia elected Balbo chairman; the prefect of Bologna reported that Mussolini's message was "received with notable coldness by the Assembly and there were even some expressions of disagreement." In the heated discussion which followed, "two tendencies were affirmed: one for the possibility of a second wave and the other for normalization. However, in the afternoon that for normalization prevailed. The first tendency was sustained by the representatives of Ferrara and Ravenna who demanded the reconstitution of action squads; the other tendency demanded legislation which would safeguard the claims of fascism. The state of mind of the representatives of some provinces must be seen in relation to the request made by the generalissimo that the present commanders of the Emilian Militia should be maintained. . . . It was affirmed that illegalism can disappear only if the government dictates laws which impress the Fascist spirit as capable of defending the results of the revolution. . . . the Militia, held to be the true and only guard of the Fascist revolution, must include the best *squadristi* as it must be the *squadrismo* of Fascism." [28]

On December 21, 1924, the *Voce Repubblicana* reported "the more or less clandestine meetings of the higher officers of the Militia, presided over by Balbo"; the same paper (December 17) had reproduced a significant telegram from Grandi to Balbo: "Yours received. Remain Ferrara. Keep very calm. Show yourself able to wait in silence. This is what one must do at the moment.

Your faithful friend Grandi embraces you." At this point the indications of Balbo's activity disappear; he was certainly silent, but whether out of obedience or conspiratorial secrecy it is hard to say.

There is no mention of his presence at the meetings of Militia leaders at Ferrara on December 9 and at Bologna on the 10th. According to the vigilant and usually well-informed prefect, Bocchini, the Ferrara meeting dealt only with the difficult personal situation of Consul Forti, one of Balbo's chief friends and subordinates in Ferrara province, implicated in the murder of Don Minzoni. The Bologna meeting, attended by all the consuls of Emilia and Romagna, was presumably official in character; similar meetings were held in other regions on the initiative of the *Comando Generale* to discuss the new directives. Bocchini reported that "the discussion was extremely animated, reflecting the very depressed state of mind not only of officers but also of *capi-squadra* and *militi*. With the exception of the two consuls Borghi and Diamanti, all the others showed hostility to the proposed settlement, noting among other considerations that the Militia in Emilia and Romagna is formed by old *squadristi* who obey none but their present officers because they were once the leaders of the old action squads. Even Consul Zunini, Reggio Emilia Legion, a colonel of the army, fully agreed, indeed threatening resignation." However, the participants agreed to "undergo" the settlement, provided it had "definitive and unmodifiable sanction so as to constitute an irrevocable right for the present officers who will be enrolled," in other words, given security of tenure.[29]

But this request was not so easily granted. Gandolfo's decision to replace all zone commanders who had not attained the rank of brigadier in the regular army left the consuls untouched, but not exactly secure. Although the replacement was officially announced on December 20, the new commanders were not due to take up their posts until January 1. Here is one explanation of why the movement came to a head on December 31.

The zone commanders reacted to their forcible retirement

by turning to clandestine activity. The commander of the zone of Umbria and the Marche, Lieutenant General Agostini, was in a particularly awkward position; the *Voce Repubblicana* (November 29) had revealed that he had organized and personally led an expedition of the *squadraccia Perugina* against the dissident Fascists of Ferrara, in the interests of Balbo. He could expect no help or support from the local leaders of the party, with whom he had quarreled.[30] This quarrel went back to late June, when he had favored the use of force against the opposition. On December 17 the prefect of Perugia reported that Agostini had gone to Rome "to reach agreement with those who find themselves in an identical position, and to regulate his conduct in conformity with theirs"; it was said that he intended to put his command at Mussolini's disposition, but the prefect recommended the government to consider "what other position could be found for Agostini if necessary outside the Militia. This so as not to leave the impression that it is intended to harm or abandon him and to avoid the possible repercussions consequent on such a state of mind."[31]

At this point matters became more serious. With the Giunta episode in the chamber the disagreement between Mussolini and some of the leading members of the party became public. As fascism threatened to split into two or more factions, it was natural that the discontents of the Militia consuls should receive fresh impetus and political backing. According to Montagna, thirteen consuls met at Florence in the days before Christmas, and it was then that the decision was taken to go to Rome on the 31st to demand the "second wave."[32] The *Voce Repubblicana* (December 25) again gives some confirmation; it revealed that "immediately after the Giunta episode in the Chamber, three important and highly secret meetings were held at Ferrara, Bologna, and Florence, each of which was attended by numerous officers of the Militia as well as by several deputies." But the *Voce* went on to give warning that the pretended disagreement between the Duce and the *ras* was a "low maneuver," and that in fact in these meetings provincial fascism had shown itself in perfect agreement with Mussolini, directing criticism exclusively at revisionists, Liberals, and Combatants.

This raises the central question of whether the movement of the consuls was planned in collusion with Mussolini. The *Voce*'s testimony is impressive, but there is one piece of direct evidence to contradict its interpretation. The republican journal refused to believe the report that Mussolini had ordered police surveillance of the secret meetings; however, on the 23rd Mussolini telegraphed to the prefect of Bologna, "Comandante Generale Militia Gandolfo reports to me movement several Militia officers your zone which is said to be headed by Consul Silingardi and lesser figures. Please watch situation discreetly and make understood supreme reasons which impose silence and obedience on all." [33]

It is not clear if or when the movements of the consuls were coordinated from a single center. However, they were certainly extensive. Silingardi and Zappoli, an old Fascist who commanded one of the Bologna legions, conferred with Agostini on the 22nd; the prefect of Perugia added a more urgent note to his earlier warnings.[34] Finally, on the 28th, a meeting of high officers of the Militia of North and Central Italy was reported to have taken place at Florence, with Agostini again present.[35]

It emerges from this account that the movement of the consuls undoubtedly existed as an independent, semi-clandestine conspiracy, to which the prefects and police were not party.[36] However, the problem of Mussolini's relation to the movement cannot be settled so easily. Before evaluating the last act, it is necessary to consider the evolution of the general situation in the Fascist party.

Mussolini's circular to the party on November 30 had been accompanied by stern warnings against indiscipline.[37] The circular itself recommended conciliation toward possible allies, condemned illegalism and the continuance of *squadrismo:* this was nothing new, although it sanctioned the move away from the intransigent line adopted at the *Consiglio Nazionale;* but both the political context and the reception of the message show that these were more than just conventional expressions. Particularly ominous to many Fascists was the suggestion of a purge: "It is necessary to liberate the party from all the elements unfitted for the new settlement; those who make violence a profession." [38]

The reception of the message in Emilia has already been described; it was no better in the two other most Fascist regions, Tuscany and Lombardy. At Florence, the prefect reported that "All the speakers declared acceptance of the message and desire to make act of devotion to Duce but showed state of mind tending to extremism out of fear that opposition parties will gain upper hand. . . . The right honorable Lupi appealed to concord and discipline dissenting from the other speakers. The right honorable Morelli turning to the right honorable Ciarlantini asked him to draw attention to perplexity and sorrow of Florentine fascism and in concluding demanded complete amnesty for Fascists condemned for political crimes. The meeting closed without voting any motion." Meanwhile about five hundred Fascists collected in S. Maria Novella and advanced on the Palazzo Vecchio, where the meeting was taking place, but were turned back by the police; others tried to break into the offices of the Liberal *Nuovo Giornale.* The demonstration was organized and led by the Consul Tamburini, the most influential of the Florentine Fascists; he headed a delegation which was received by Ciarlantini (the representative of the Fascist Party Direttorio), to whom "it manifested extremist intentions, making it known that discipline would not be maintained if some leaders of Florentine fascism were attacked." [39] Tamburini's record was a particularly black one; the Florentine Fascists were extremists out of a sense of self-preservation. But the "parade-ground populism" of Tamburini, in alliance with the armed squads of the *agrari,* represented an organization of great destructive potentialities. [40]

The account of the Lombard regional meeting confirms the rumors of a disagreement between Farinacci and Mussolini. [41]

After the *Popolo d'Italia* had declared that "there are no *ras*. They are fantasies," it cannot have been welcome when the next day Farinacci's leader in *Cremona Nuova* carried the headline "Long live *rassismo*," even if, according to him, the *ras* desired nothing except peace and harmony. On November 30 he had something of a triumph.

"Maggi [Federale of Milan province] although submissive to the Duce said it was necessary to follow a direct path and not a zigzag, not to exalt Farinacci one day and then throw him overboard as had been done during the last days. This mention provoked applause for Farinacci. . . . Farinacci spoke next welcomed by great applause. He said that although having every intention of obeying the Duce, it must be kept in mind that since the opposition aims high and at putting fascism on trial, a policy of force without weakness or compromise is necessary. Teruzzi spoke in the same sense. Finally Arnaldo Mussolini, much applauded, said that the party should be guided by its directorate and not by the government. That this directorate has failed to have a precise political line. That everything must not be demanded from or imputed to the government and that if the party zigzagged the fault must be attributed to the directorate . . . all were concerned to demonstrate their feelings of absolute loyalty by accepting the message. However agreement with the thesis of a strong government has prevailed and a certain preoccupation is to be noted among those present with being abandoned especially by the magistracy which is said to have exceeded in ordering arrests and invoking the intervention of the government to prevent persecution." [42] The speech of Arnaldo Mussolini deserves attention. It was clearly a hastily improvised attempt to shift the responsibilities for failure onto Farinacci and his fellow members of the Direttorio, and as such unconvincing, given that on the same day (November 30) the *Popolo d'Italia* was proclaiming the necessity for the absolute obedience of the party to the government. However, the idea that the party should have a certain autonomy, adopted by Arnaldo so hastily, had serious support. There was a curious apparent convergence between the "revisionist" and the "integralist" or revolutionary points of view; for either, it seemed that fascism, as a political force, could recover its vigor (whether as a legal or a revolutionary movement) only if it regained its independence from the government. Thus the complaint of the revisionist Bottai that the "confusion, rather than connection, between the actions of the party and the government, has caused the party to be corrupted, in ideals and practice, by the necessary diplomacy of the art of government," [43] was taken up by the extremist *Battaglie Fasciste*.[44] Later, the "revolutionary" Suckert's demand that Mussolini should abandon the government and fight the elections "as the head of a revolutionary political movement," [45] can be confronted with de Stefani's letter to Mussolini, protesting against the speech of January 3: "My deep and mature conviction is that fascism should affirm itself in free political competition, freed from the responsibility of supreme power. This will increase the strength of fascism and its training for command. The work begun will be resumed by the will of the Italian people." [46] The sincerity of de Stefani's recommendation is beyond doubt. What legalitarians and extremists really had in common was a distrust of Mussolini's authoritarian and ambiguous leadership, the feeling that he had subjugated the movement to his personal caprices. But it must be asked whether (obviously only up to a certain point) Mussolini himself did not see some advantage in the party's desire for greater independence at this stage; if his right hand, the government, did not know what his left hand, the party, was doing, so much the better. It would make it easier for him to play a double game, as he was so fond of doing.

Mussolini continued to zigzag for some weeks after the regional meetings. It is arguable that he had been preparing to purge fascism and reduce it to the adjunct of a new bloc of order; but the attitude of Fascists and Liberals alike gave little encouragement to the project. This left only one-party dictatorship as a true political alternative: however, Mussolini continued

77

to hesitate before committing himself, and his policy was reduced to a series of expedients. Consequently the crisis of fascism continued to develop.

A serious open division of opinion among the Fascist deputies first appeared over the attempt to pass a new bill for press censorship; the moderates agreed with Liberal criticisms, whereas the extremists demanded that the bill should be passed before Christmas by summary procedures. The withdrawal of the bill was a grave sign of the political weakness of the government, and seemed to be the prelude to disintegration. The crisis appeared irreparable; and at about this time the search for a government that could take the succession became more urgent. Senator Pompeo di Campello, one of the gentlemen of the king's household, approached the Fascist deputy Paolucci and asked him to write to the king, recommending the formation of a "government of national concentration . . . of which all the Prime Ministers would form part, including Mussolini if he accepted, without him if he showed himself intransigent." [47] Paolucci did not ask whether Campello was speaking on Victor Emmanuel's behalf; he was known to sympathize with the opposition.

The Giunta episode brought the split in the Fascist party further into the open. The magistracy requested permission to open proceedings against Giunta, one of the vice presidents of the Chamber, for his part in organizing the attack on the dissident Fascist Cesare Forni. The Fascist deputies staged a demonstration in his favor and when a Liberal, Boeri, showed his disapproval by leaving the Chamber, Mussolini called him back and told him that since he had been elected on the government list, he ought to resign. This unconsidered outburst nearly led to the secession of the Liberals from Parliament; Mussolini retracted, and imposed the acceptance of Giunta's resignation. In the meantime Giunta himself, Edoardo Torre, and others had organized a meeting of the deputies of their way of thinking.[48] Giunta himself backed down and maintained his resignation, but in the Chamber next day the extremists, led by Michele Bianchi, who

was angrily interrupted by Mussolini, made their rebellious attitude plain. The formation of the extremist caucus precipitated a
similar move by the moderates; forty-four deputies met at the
house of Paolucci and agreed, with one exception, to support "a
policy of conciliation and normality within the Constitution,"
and to send a delegation to Mussolini to demand the end of the
Militia's public-order functions, the purge of the party, "greater
respect for the constitutional forces," and the restoration of single-member constituencies.[49] Salandra called a meeting of his
group and it was feared that he would announce his opposition
to the government.[50] At this point it was necessary above all for
Mussolini to gain time and to avoid the threatened convergence
of moderate Fascists and right-wing Liberals; Paolucci relates
that, coming to the Chamber, "I found myself faced with a
masterly *coup:* Mussolini deposited on the bench of the Presidency the bill for the return to single-member constituencies."
This unexpected move disconcerted everyone. It was read as yet
another sign of the disintegration of the government, especially
since Mussolini had evidently acted without consulting the majority of the cabinet: it dismayed the extremists, who took it as
yet another concession to liberalism; but it was successful in disrupting, at least temporarily, Paolucci's following, and in preventing a possible hostile vote by Salandra and his group. However, Mussolini's brusque dismissal of Paolucci himself suggests
that he was already meditating an abrupt change of course.

Mussolini's passage to action was determined, first of all, by
the publication of the Rossi memorial; the comment of the *Giornale d'Italia* (December 31) explains clearly enough why the government could not continue as it was: "We have a Prime Minister inculpated in common crimes. No nation can tolerate that
such a situation be protracted. . . . Whoever helps him today to
subtract himself from the regular course of justice becomes his ac-
complice." But there were also other events which narrowed
Mussolini's choice to two alternatives: resignation or reaction.
The first was the attitude of Salandra, who had resigned from
the Presidency of the *Giunta del Bilancio* on December 26, al-

though his letter was made public only on the 31st.[51] Therefore it was necessary for Mussolini to take the initiative; only an aggressive action could restore confidence and avoid the disintegration of the cabinet. The parallel with the march on Rome is instructive: then the king refused to give special powers to a cabinet which was in crisis. Mussolini's timing, and the efficacy of his threats, enabled him to begin the reaction, on December 30, with the apparent agreement of a united cabinet, and this gave him a great advantage.[52] His maneuver was to have it believed that the repression was underwritten by the Liberal ministers, authorized by Salandra to remain in the cabinet, and then to split the latter's group against him.[53]

Simultaneously the extremist revolt was coming to a head. This was true not only of the movement of the consuls, but also of the activities of the extremist deputies; [54] the discussion of the new electoral law when the Chamber reopened threatened to be the occasion for a revolt against Mussolini's policy. The spokesman of their discontents was Curzio Suckert (Malaparte). An opponent contrasted the revolutionary extremism of Suckert with that of "persons who fear to lose the positions they have conquered by violence," but the distinction, if partially valid on the plane of motive, obscures the convergence possible on the plane of political action. The ambience of Florence, where the most violent *squadrismo* had always found sympathy and encouragement from a certain literary and artistic *bohème,* specially favored such an alliance; and Suckert in spite of the disparity in culture and intelligence could boast of the friendship of a man like Tamburini. In his article "Fascism v. Mussolini?" alongside the assertion that "Mussolini got his mandate from the Fascist provinces . . . a revolutionary mandate . . . hence, the absolute duty of the right honorable Mussolini to realize the revolutionary will of the people," there was the recommendation to the party's deputies that "the immunity which you enjoy should be extended, in just measure, to all Fascists. . . . Either everyone in prison, or no one." [55]

This slogan was the true rallying cry of provincial fascism; it was echoed by Tarabella, if we are to believe the accounts of the meeting, during the consuls' altercation with Mussolini.

In an interview with Mussolini, Suckert explained that the extremist revolt took the electoral reform only as a pretext, or more precisely as the symptom, of "a policy of the liquidation of fascism as a doctrine and as a party." [56] It is also related that the latter replied, "My dear Suckert—if we weaken now, we will never come back, never. Do you understand, yes or no?" [57]

Suckert's exaltation of the revolutionary provinces bore fruit in the *fatti di Firenze* on December 31.[58] Several thousand Fascists from all over Tuscany were brought to Florence for a mass rally; after this had ended, parties of the Militia and irregular squads, armed with shotguns and pitchforks, wrecked the printing presses of the *Nuovo Giornale* and the Combatant weekly, *Fanteria,* and devastated the Masonic lodge, the *circolo di cultura,* and the offices of a number of opposition lawyers. It was the first general punitive expedition directed mainly against middle-class anti-fascism.[59]

The rally was attended by Renato Ricci, a member of the *Direzione*; he "recalled to the Fascists . . . that we are henceforward at the end of the opposition campaign, as the national government has shown that it is taking energetic steps to meet the situation. It is necessary to wait in discipline . . . at the orders of B. Mussolini"; but he then agreed to read a motion expressing the will of the assembly: "The Florentine Fascists, assembled to affirm the precise intentions of the party, faced with the hostile offensive . . . declare their loyalty to the Duce . . . but make their obedience and their discipline conditional on the decisive action of the government, which must be demonstrated, if necessary, by dictatorial action." [60]

The official Fascist version of the events made out that the provincial Federation had taken the initiative in organizing the rally. Farinacci wrote that, "Judging this important event in the quality of a member of the directorate of the party, we should have to pronounce words of regret and repudiation; but we cannot: we would go against our thoughts and our conscience; if our followers rebelled against the *Direzione* of the party and the government in order to defend fascism with devotion . . . the fault is not ours." [61] But such a simple version of the events cannot be believed. The Liberal minister Casati told Salandra "that he knew for certain that the happenings of Florence were organized by Suckert, the envoy of the Palazzo Chigi, or of the *Direzione* of the party, which is the same thing, with the agreement of Mussolini." [62] The source of Casati's conviction is unknown, but clearly his view demands respect. However, it is only in part confirmed by other evidence. Certainly the official version cannot be sustained; Suckert himself wrote that "it is no longer a mystery to anyone that the motion proclaimed by the right honorable Ricci in the Florence assembly . . . and enthusiastically acclaimed by the immense crowd . . . in the Piazza della Signoria, was compiled not at Florence in the seat of the Provincial Federation, but at Rome in the seat of the *Direzione* of the party. This signifies that the *Direttorio Nazionale* itself was with the revolutionary provinces against the normalizing government." [63] But was Casati correct in assuming that the *Direzione* had acted with the prior approval of Mussolini?

To answer this question, it is necessary to return to the "movement of the consuls." One of the accounts relates that Mussolini asked why Tamburini was not among the consuls, whereupon Tarabella gave him a letter from the former, which said that he had started the reaction himself.[64] Now Tamburini's letter does exist:

> To the Duce,
> I am at Florence to prepare and effect the rally that the *Direzione* has requested, otherwise I would be at Rome to wish you well, but also to say to you that now is the hour for the Man worthy of comparison with Napoleon to send all good men to drive out and suppress those in the pay of foreign nations to ruin Italy.
> I, and with me all the Fascists of the province of Florence, have tolerated every insult to ourselves and to the other leaders, *but* absolutely will not tolerate those addressed to you, so the possibilities are two: either you, guided by God, pursue a gran-

diose program, as we hope, or *we* before becoming an object of
ridicule will engage battle because it is a fine thing to win or
die as a soldier. . . . With intransigent loyalty, Tullio Tamburini.[65]

This was a private and unpublished letter, and it is unlikely
therefore that it was written to provide Mussolini with an excuse.
Moreover, evidence of Tamburini's real attitude can be gained
from a letter he wrote to Michele Bianchi several months previously: "If the Duce wishes to be again what he was up till the
Matteotti murder, he will certainly have to send to the devil
some exponents of collaboration and take back the old Fascists.
We wish that at all costs the Ministry of the Interior should be
in the hands of a Fascist, and not of one who mines the ground
under the Duce's feet." [66]

This letter suggests that the governmental reaction, started
on January 30 and entrusted to Federzoni as Minister of the Interior, would have appeared insufficient to Tamburini, even if,
which is doubtful, he knew of the decisions of the cabinet when
he wrote the letter.

It remains to explain the attitude of the *Direzione*. It is possible that, as Casati suggested, they obtained Mussolini's approval for the rally, but did not inform Tamburini. It is also
possible that they were pursuing the tactic of independent party
action. The start of the reaction on December 30 must have suggested that the initiative would in any case meet with retrospective approval.[67]

The precise position of Farinacci is difficult to determine.
Probably, after a period of doubt, he decided to serve as the instrument for regaining the support of the extremist group for the
government. Certainly his recommendation of discipline contained a barely veiled threat: "If Mussolini were disposed to give
way, only then would we rebel and abandon the supreme
hierarchies"; [68] but the next day he argued that the opposition
owed their safety to Mussolini, as "once he had to abandon
power no force could any longer hold back the Fascists and the
nation would be plunged . . . into the horrors of a struggle

whose consequences can be foreseen." [69] One can certainly doubt whether, in his case, the threat of revolt was not mainly a device to impress outsiders with the conviction of the government's moderating function.

There is no evidence linking Farinacci with the movement of the consuls, and there is no reason to believe that their embassy was endorsed by the *Direttorio*. There is, instead, evidence that a dissident group within the party knew of it and tried to exploit it. At first sight, the most improbable aspect of the story is that after their interview with Mussolini, some of the consuls, at the instigation of the deputy Edoardo Torre, went to the house of a prominent member of the Freemasonry of the Piazza del Gesu, Vizzoni, where he proposed to them that they should try to replace the Duce by a leader who belonged to his organization.[70] As a result, Tarabella and Galbiati founded an "anti-masonic order." [71] But the episode seems less unlikely in the light of a reference by Mussolini to "the attempt made by them [Torre and the dissidents of Alessandria] to disintegrate the party *in the whole of Italy.*" [72]

In retrospect, the decisions of the cabinet on December 30 can be clearly seen as the beginning of the drive toward dictatorship. But several of the cabinet, which had refused Mussolini his demand for full powers, probably did not share this view of what they had done; rather they consented, reluctantly, to authorize temporary measures to reduce tension. So Casati and Sarrocchi could nevertheless believe that in exchange for delaying their resignation, they had exacted a promise from Mussolini to employ only legal means of repression.[73] The Fascist ministers Oviglio and de Stefani, who both disapproved of the speech of January 3, had probably the same opinion. Thus the offensive of the extremists, which began in Florence on December 31 and was soon followed up in Pisa, Bologna, and elsewhere, really modified the position and prepared the way for the much more comprehensive repression inaugurated on January 3 and confirmed by the reconstructed, all-Fascist cabinet on the 7th.

However, the illegal reaction of the *squadristi* was second not only in time but in importance to the semilegal repression by the state organs. Suckert protested that "Fascism must recall to its leader that the Ministry of the Interior is the least suitable organ for carrying out a revolution," and appealed to his "friends of the *Direttorio Nazionale . . .* to show that the *Direzione* of the party is not a dependency of the Viminale but a real revolutionary committee, which intends finally to realize, against all comers, the will of fascism." [74] But the Fascist masses had played their essential role in intimidating the king and public opinion and could now be put back in the box: the *Impero* (January 8, 1925) could legitimately accuse Suckert of illogical "demagogy."

Only too much had been gained by the extremists; the reconstitution of the action squads (even if unofficial), renewed immunity from prosecution, the cooperation of the other organs of the state with the Militia; not to speak of the second-stage consequences, the appointment of Farinacci as party secretary and the final advent of the long-promised Fascist legislation. Nevertheless, the events of January prefigured the absorption of the party by the state, and not in the sense that Farinacci or the integralists wished. On the face of it, certainly, the integralists saw their legislative measures enacted; but in practice these resolved themselves into the creation of additional bureaucratic mechanisms, which took their part in the suffocation of the autonomous life of the party, as of the other and worthier currents of national life. The extremist program proved inadequate for the real renewal of the state, even as the Fascists themselves understood it. The "dynamism" of the movement could in reality be maintained only by continued terror; this was the true character of extremism. But after January 3 it lost, along with its last pale pretensions to "heroism," its necessity or relevance.

When the Chamber re-opened on January 12 a Fascist deputy, Maffei, declaimed: "The blackshirts are ready for all the maneuvers of their opponents. They are in a state of complete efficiency." Federzoni interjected, "One *carabiniere* is enough." [75]

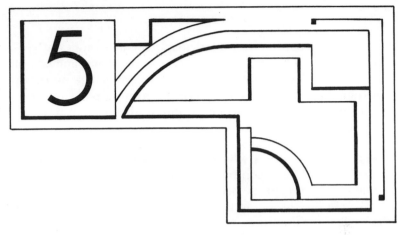

FROM THE
LIBERAL STATE
TO THE
FASCIST REGIME:
THE FIRST STEPS *

Although Mussolini disagreed with the political tactics and goals of many Fascist extremists, he knew that he could not do without their support. In his difficult gambit to be both a reconciler and a revolutionary, he needed the backing of both moderates and extremists. The moderates helped him to win the confidence of conservative sympathizers outside the movement who did not want fascism to move in radical directions. They found the presence of moderate, pragmatic politicians most reassuring. At the same time, Mussolini needed the extremists to keep alive the image of fascism as a revolutionary

* From Renzo De Felice, *Mussolini il fascista* (Turin: Giulio Einaudi, 1968), pp. 55–68. Reprinted by permission of the publisher.

force. The extremists were particularly useful in times of crisis when they could be relied upon to take to the streets and become the government's illegal but effective shock troops against the opposition. The Matteotti crisis marked a turning point in the internal history of fascism because it forced Mussolini to rely more heavily on his rowdy followers.

Once the crisis was settled, Mussolini could not realistically reject those supporters who had remained faithful in fascism's hour of need. The appointment of Roberto Farinacci as secretary of the party reflected the decision to cease all collaboration with non-Fascist groups and to govern the country by relying only on those who accepted fascism without reservations. The appointment is particularly significant because Mussolini personally disliked Farinacci. Their incompatibility, however, could not obscure the fact that they complemented each other politically. After the Matteotti crisis, Mussolini needed Farinacci not only to purge and strengthen the party, which he did, but also as a political foil. With Farinacci in a position of responsibility, Mussolini appeared once again as a necessary political stabilizer. Mussolini's behavior after the Matteotti crisis suggests that he was trying to adjust his customary political technique to changing political circumstances. While before the crisis he had often mediated between fascism and outside interests in an attempt to reconcile differing viewpoints, after the crisis he was determined to eliminate the evidence if not the substance of disagreements by bringing all groups within the official fold of fascism. At that point, fascism could no longer be simply an authoritarian form of government. By trying to represent everything, it was bound to become increasingly more totalitarian.

Renzo De Felice is a professor of contemporary history at the University of Salerno, lecturer at the Istituto di Storia Moderna at the University of Rome, and editor of a new historical review, *Storia Contemporanea*. He is a prolific scholar who, in addition to his many works on fascism, has also written extensively on the history of the Jacobin movement in Italy. His most ambitious work to date is his on-going biography of Mussolini, which so far has covered the life of the dictator through the year 1929 in three volumes. This selection comes from the third volume. In spite of their biographical focus, all three volumes cover a vast range of topics in the history of Fascist Italy.

■

Farinacci's term as secretary of the Fascist party lasted from February 12, 1925 (or, more precisely, from the 23rd when the leader of the intransigents effectively took over the leadership of the party), to March 30, 1926. The collaboration between Mussolini and Farinacci was neither easy nor smooth. Their aims diverged either partially or radically on too many issues. Farinacci was able more than once to impose his views by supporting either in his speeches or in his newspaper *Cremona Nuova* solutions that Mussolini then presented to the government. . . . It was Farinacci who adopted strong-arm methods to eject anti-Fascists from the leadership of the Association of War Veterans; [1] it was he who first demanded insistently and vehemently that steps be taken against the opposition; [2] it was he who generally pushed Mussolini and the government to take increasingly more intransigent frontal positions, not hesitating even to *warn* the king when in June Victor Emmanuel III granted individual audiences to those leaders of the Aventine who were loyal to the monarchy,[3] and who openly polemicized against the Holy See.[4]

On several occasions, however, the secretary of the party seconded Mussolini's moves, paving the way with surprising political smoothness and avoiding difficulties. In April he worked capably behind the scenes in the Senate among the more pro-Fascist senators, more than twenty of whom were granted honorary membership in the party, thus strengthening considerably the government's previously precarious position in the higher chamber.[5] The same may be said of his successful efforts to restrain extremists within the syndical corporations, the Fascist labor unions, who might have created difficulties for the government at that particular moment.[6] Nor can we overlook his backing of

89

Minister of Finance Alberto de Stefani's policies, in spite of the fact that he did not approve of him and that he was being attacked more or less openly by other intransigents.[7]

Above all, Farinacci succeeded in restoring a measure of discipline to the party, salvaging some real or potential dissidents, drastically purging the stubborn ones, and preparing the ground for the party's reorganization by starting to review its members and halting recruitment.[8] It cannot be denied that under Farinacci the party experienced an organizational and numerical resurgence.[9] During 1924 the members dropped from 782,979 to 642,246; in 1925 they numbered 599,988, but an upswing brought them to 937,997 in 1926, 1,034,998 in 1927, and 1,051,708 in 1929.[10] Obviously, the reorganization and strengthening of the party were not achieved without rocking the boat and without some lively arguments.[11] Not all problems were solved (instances of chronic dissidence and, above all, of silent drifting away from the party continued for several years). In general, however, these shocks and polemics were not too serious, an indication that Farinacci's efforts deserve to be judged more positively than negatively.

At least during his first months in office, Farinacci for various reasons won support even among non-intransigent Fascists. For instance, his nomination was welcomed by Giovanni Gentile, the chief philosopher of fascism and former minister of education under Mussolini, who probably hoped that a more intransigent Fascist policy would save his reform of the school system, which was under attack by Fascist fellow travelers and was poorly defended by Minister of Education Pietro Fedele.[12] And in the long run (by October) even Bottai once reluctantly allowed himself, if not to praise him, at least to recognize his political merits.[13] As for former Nationalists, while Farinacci tried in every way to play the role of the anti-Federzoni (*Luigi Federzoni was minister of the interior from June 17, 1924 to November 6, 1926, and a strict law-and-order man who opposed the violent tactics of the intransigents—Ed.*), he won nevertheless the support of some, particularly those who had not been Nationalists from the very first (such as Roberto Forges-Davanzati), or those who were not willing to search for new forms of political and social organization that would break with tradition (as was the case, up to a point, with Alfredo Rocco).[14]

For all intents and purposes, Farinacci began to move the party in the direction favored by Mussolini, who summed it up well in his letter of May 14, 1925, to Farinacci:

> It is time to say *enough* to the splintering of fascism with a reserved circular or oral instructions (preferably the latter). It appears that integralism, revisionism, extremism become the substantives and poor *fascism* a mere glued-on adjective. These distinctions are completely idiotic and I reject them. In fascism there are only leaders and followers. I bring to your attention an article in this morning's edition of *Impero* (*an extremist Fascist newspaper in Rome—Ed.*) in which a defeatist imbecile announces nothing less than "the complete failure of the Fascist Revolution." He deserves to be identified and punished as we used to punish defeatists in wartime.
>
> I am glad that in this morning's edition of *Idea Nazionale* Forges has deplored that many *semi-cultured* youngsters should be saying that the revolution is "standing still" when instead it moves on as formidable as ever. I wouldn't want the party congress of June 21 to turn into an idiotic jeremiad for that boring species of *weeping willows* which I fearfully see sprouting on the holy soil of fascism.
>
> I assure you that, in that case, I will uproot all *weeping willows* . . . even if they should be a whole forest.
>
> Finally, whoever works seriously and *hard* in the party and in the government on behalf of fascism and the nation has a right to be spared the lamentations of the impotent and disillusioned.[15]

However, from a general political perspective, and in relation to their respective long-term goals, Mussolini and Farinacci stood for essentially different things. The former believed that the reorganization and strengthening of the party should be carried out with regard for the unquestioned and absolute priority of the state over the party; the party, like the Militia and the syndical corporations, should remain an instrument in the service of the state.[16] In this respect, Mussolini's views resembled those of Federzoni who, while publicly equating "the propelling action" of an autonomous party "that is not directly responsible to the sovereign state" with the "achieving, disciplinary, harmonizing work of the government," in reality relegated the party to a wholly subordinate role.[17]

Farinacci, instead, envisaged a party that would play a prominent role in the life of the country, capable of guiding and representing all other forces and groups, from the syndicates to the government, encompassing the state itself. Aware of Mussolini's views, Farinacci did not state this policy in explicit and drastic terms, but it did run through his most significant actions and emerged occasionally among his collaborators. It was typically evident, in its very tortuousness, in an article written by R. Forges-Davanzati on the eve of the national party congress of June 1925:

> The Fascist party is simply the compact nucleus of fascism and must be the most jealous procreator of fascism in view of the fact that a Fascist government does not yet mean a Fascist state and that the corporations have not yet been fully assimilated by the regime.[18]

The secretary of the party tried in every way to influence government policy along these lines, urging it to conform to the intransigent course on which he had launched the party, to avoid the influence of opportunists and transformists . . . whose main concern was to avoid defections and disagreements with fellow travelers like Federzoni (the minister of the interior, who was Farinacci's most resented Fascist, was being closely watched by Attilio Teruzzi, a reliable henchman whom Farinacci had been able to place at Federzoni's side).[19] Farinacci believed that these fellow travelers were dangerous fifth-columnists determined to prevent the rise of a true Fascist state.[20]

Repeating Mussolini's statement that a battle had been won on January 3 but that it was now necessary to win the war, Farinacci argued that the victory had to be won not only against the opposition but also and above all against the non-Fascists who supported fascism. "The supporters," he said, "are an obstacle to the rise of fascism." [21] Victory would be achieved only by "legalizing Fascist illegality." He was obviously referring not to the restoration of normalcy, but to acquiescence and endorsement by the government of every request and "retaliatory" act committed in the name of "revolutionary" fascism. He was consequently absolutely opposed to the idea of holding new elections in the more or less near future even on the basis of single-member constituencies. As he wrote on March 26, the new electoral law ought to be a "sword of Damocles" in Mussolini's hands; [22] new elections could perhaps be held in 1928 or 1929 but not earlier.[23] His knowledge that Mussolini agreed with this request explains why . . . he did not discuss the merits of the new law and that he upheld it in spite of the fact that, like most intransigents, he did not consider it truly Fascist, believed that it would be mostly for the benefit of fellow travelers, and considered it a harmful consequence of Mussolini's transformist tactics.[24]

Farinacci's behavior as secretary naturally reflected these attitudes and expectations and involved him in a whole series of clashes and disagreements with both Mussolini and Federzoni. Lively confrontations occurred whenever Farinacci took violent and intransigent stands that threatened to undermine Mussolini's efforts to win the support of fellow travelers, who had strayed during the Matteotti crisis, and heal the scars which the preceding months had left on public opinion and the political class. Two incidents are particularly worth remembering because they reveal what Mussolini expected of his party's secretary. The first occurred immediately after the publication by the high court of the Senate of its sentence against De Bono in response to the charges leveled against him by Giuseppe Donati. (*In December 1925, Donati, who was the editor of the Catholic newspaper* Il Popolo, *placed formal legal charges against De Bono for complicity in the Matteotti crime. The Senate subsequently dismissed the charges, but only for lack of evidence—Ed.*) Farinacci, who took exception to the sentence, violently attacked General Zuppelli who had presided over the investigating commission. The incident made a great impression everywhere and endangered relations with the president of the Senate, Tommaso Tittoni.[25] Mussolini then intervened with this telegram to the prefect of Cremona, Farinacci's hometown:

> Issues of *Cremona Nuova* are to be confiscated whenever, as in the Zuppelli affair, direct references to representative personalities may provoke individual reprisals or embarrass the government as is the case now.[26]

The second incident took place a little more than ten days later. Speaking in Catania, Farinacci had let himself go into one of his extremely violent diatribes against the "enemies" of fascism, going as far as stating that the murder of Matteotti had been a blessing for fascism. Mussolini reacted instantaneously by ordering the press to ignore the questionable parts of his speech. He then gave a curt reply to Farinacci's protest:

> I am the one who ordered Stefani (*the semi-official news agency—Ed.*) to drop your phrases which are worthless for having been repeated a thousand times. I deny that the Matteotti crime is responsible for the success of fascism. Such statements can be extremely dangerous, and they are no less dangerous when they are said in self-praise. The truth is that fascism has pulled through successfully in spite of the Matteotti crime. Everything else is fine.[27]

Other clashes occurred over Farinacci's twofold policy in the provinces. On the one hand, he strengthened the party by eliminating every sign of dissidence, including minor groups or tendencies that opposed his intransigent policy. On the other hand, and here obviously Mussolini and Federzoni could not agree, he sought to strengthen local party officials against the representatives of the government. Furthermore, Farinacci tried, more or less underhandedly, to reconstitute the armed squads (in the summer of 1925 they were to be found in Rome, Civitavecchia, Trento, Trapani, Albenga, Florence, Mantova, and Reggio Emilia, and others were emerging ever more numerously in the subsequent months), whose task was to "restrain" the "subversives" and "react" against their "provocations"; in simple words, they were to do what the extremists claimed the government was not doing: eliminate all forms of opposition, including legal ones. *(The author quotes Federzoni to the effect that, because of Farinacci's encouragement, the squads were once more a nuisance in 1925–1926* [Italia di ieri per la storia di domani, *p. 100ff.]— Ed.*)

We have already seen in the preceding volume that, even though it was difficult to implement, the subordination of the party to the state was a fixed point of Mussolini's policy. As for the reconstruction of the squads, Federzoni had given instructions several months before to prevent it and the command of the Militia agreed. We can see why Farinacci's efforts along these lines were followed with apprehension by the ministry of the interior, which tried to obstruct them by periodically issuing circulars and instructions to the prefects, urging them to take action against the "residues of Fascist illegality," to prevent repeated acts of violence, and to work in every way to break up the squads. For instance, in response to "repeated acts of violence by Fascists against members of subversive parties, homes, clubs, public places, newspaper stands," Federzoni urged the prefects on May 28 to "put an end to this state of affairs and . . . restore order everywhere." Anticipating objections from the extremists or from Farinacci on their behalf, he added that even retaliatory actions "were in no way justified because it is a principle of civil society that only the state can deal with crime and because the state does intervene promptly and energetically." As in other instances, a copy of this circular was sent to Farinacci, accompanied this time by a letter from Federzoni. *(The author quotes a lengthy excerpt from a letter in which Federzoni urged Farinacci not to interfere with government efforts to restore law and order in the provinces, particularly in certain areas of the Romangna and Venetia where Fascist squads had been most active.*[28] *—Ed.)*

Mussolini did not intervene at first, probably because he did not want to alienate the intransigents, or because, as usual, he found it convenient to have the extremists around even as he claimed to be in favor of peace. He could then always ingratiate himself with public opinion or with the supporters of fascism by eventually eliminating the extremists. But by October when, as we shall see further on, Fascist violence in Florence went beyond the limit, thereby alarming public opinion (as well as the king), particularly since there was a possibility of further violence in Turin, he was compelled to intervene directly and take a stand against Farinacci. In the meantime, Federzoni had already ordered the dispersal of all the squads. Following up this order, Mussolini telegraphed Farinacci on October 13, renewing it and reproaching him that among the squads "there are many unsavory characters whose misdeeds have been fully documented in recent newspaper stories." He then went on to say:

> I will not tolerate squads of any kind and I will not tolerate that resolutions of the Grand Council be questioned. . . . Whenever the prestige and authority of the government are involved I will not be questioned and I will employ all means. My order is clear. . . . All squads are to be dissolved at any cost, I repeat, any cost. The time has arrived to make a necessary distinction: Fascists with Fascists, criminals with criminals, exploiters with exploiters. Above all, we must practice moral, I repeat, moral intransigence.[29]

Going beyond the particular incidents that provoked them, these quarrels point to how widely Mussolini's and Farinacci's policies diverged; they also explain why their collaboration, indispensable to both after January 3, not only wore out in little more than a year (as soon as Mussolini strengthened himself in power, finding wider and more reliable support than the Fascist intransigents could give him), but also gave way to a disagreement as obvious as it was irreconcilable that was destined to run like a red thread through all the subsequent vicissitudes of fascism. . . . Running somewhat ahead, it may suffice to say that Mussolini not only would not entrust Farinacci with any significant political post either in the party or in the government after his removal as party secretary, but would repeatedly try to destroy him politically and to have him expelled from the party outright (he would not succeed because the *ras* of Cremona continued to enjoy great prestige among the old-timers of fascism and because his criticisms of the regime were based on facts that could not be entirely denied). As for Farinacci, all we need to say is that he ultimately became the champion of many Fascists who were opposed to the regime, both on the "right" and on the "left," acting as their spokesman, considered as "the other man" who, for better or worse, could not be ignored.

Having said all this . . . there are still two points to be made about their disagreement. The first refers to its basic political and historical significance; the second concerns Farinacci's reasons for never trying to topple Mussolini from power and take his place.

As for the fundamental significance of their disagreement there can be little doubt: beyond all its minor motivations, it was essentially political. As long as the regime lasted, it was Farinacci who represented the political aspirations and disillusionments of "revolutionary" fascism as it existed before the march on Rome; he represented the fascism of the middle and lower middle classes that drew most of its support from the new landowners, who had appeared in the years immediately preceding and following the war, who were striving to prevail politically as an autonomous force and were competing against other groups to assert their own role.[30] Although Farinacci did not entirely avoid politically expedient contacts and entanglements with powerful economic interests, he represented nevertheless those elements who were most genuinely Fascist but who were also the weakest.

For that kind of fascism to prevail, it would have had to assume the leadership not only of the lower and middle bourgeoisie, but also of all the other social groups interested in bringing about a substantial political and social renewal of the country, particularly the agricultural and industrial proletariat. It could not do this for both subjective and objective reasons. Subjectively, because the country's middle and lower bourgeoisie was, and felt, too weak and divided to accept other and more homogeneous social groups as equal allies, particularly because it was scornful of them and had considered them enemies for several decades and was afraid of becoming their victim. The fight that the intransigents waged against the syndical corporations to deny them autonomy is indicative of their fears. Objectively, they could not succeed because the violent political and class struggles of the preceding years had left behind such a heritage of hatred, blood, and reciprocal rancor that, even if "revolutionary" fascism had been able to develop a policy other than mere intransigence against all other social groups, only small segments of the lower and middle bourgeoisie and the proletariat would have followed them. Such were the grounds for the basic weakness of Farinacci and the intransigents, for their disillusionment and entrenchment behind an intransigence as sterile as it was charged with repressed cravings for revenge. Depending on circumstances, these cravings would manifest themselves in the future as sudden, savage explosions of violence, as imperialist outbursts, or (especially after Hitler's rise to power) as demands for an alliance with other European Fascist "revolutionaries," or as an acceptance of new pseudo-revolutionary myths such as racism, etc.

Finally, the presence of the intransigents also brought about the strengthening of countervailing political forces, not only among anti-Fascists and fellow travelers, but also of Mussolini's personal influence and the influence of all those Fascist groups who were established in the agencies of the regime. Once Mussolini had agreed to transform the "Fascist revolution" into a large-scale transformist-authoritarian enterprise (it is impossible to say whether he did this deliberately or in a gradual and unpremeditated way) based on a general compromise between various interest groups, with forceful repression being reserved only for the most stubborn opponents, it was clear that he no longer had any use for Farinacci's kind of intransigence. All interest groups found, if not harmony, at least a form of coexistence based on the recognition of mutual spheres of influence, on the Duce's personal mediation, and in growing state intervention in large sectors of society. Farinacci's intransigence must have struck him as being completely out of step with his politics; it was unacceptable and had to be rejected in the most decisive way because, as long as no external enemies threatened the regime, the intransigents were the only group capable of undermining Mussolini's precariously balanced political edifice.

We now come to the second possible aspect of the conflict between Farinacci and Mussolini, the theoretical possibility that Farinacci might try to take Mussolini's place. In reality, however, neither the intransigents as a group nor Farinacci individually could ever be anything more than simple rebels: they could neither oppose the "system" nor come to power. There were many reasons for their passiveness: their isolation in the country, their lack of support in the army (on this particular point it is worth emphasizing that Farinacci's contacts with the military personalities of the regime were never political in nature and resulted from divisions within the military establishment), the "system's" and Mussolini's ability to win over individual members and groups among the intransigents and spread dissent among the others. Most of all, the intransigents remained isolated because they lacked outstanding personalities and clear ideas. Most of them were always ready to complain, rebel, and engage in sudden violence, but were unable in the final analysis to act decisively, particularly if that meant risking what little power they had at the local level (which meant a great deal to many of them), their prestige and well-being. . . . Hence the frustrations which within a few years rendered the old-style Fascists innocuous. Some left the party disillusioned and disgusted or accepted their own removal passively. Others accepted the situation as it was, limiting themselves to occasional outbursts and sudden hopes that they would soon "get even." [31] At the end, only a minority was still struggling; they represented a lingering mood but were numerically insignificant and without political prospects,[32] unless one takes seriously their continuing polemics against the absorption of the Fascist party and the co-opting of fascism by the state.[33]

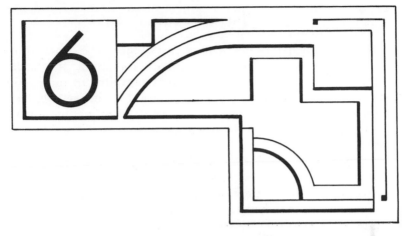

THE RISE OF THE FASCIST STATE, 1926–1928 *

Far-reaching constitutional changes accompanied the passage of the Fascist regime from authoritarian liberalism to totalitarianism. The passage from one phase to the other did not occur without considerable exploration and debate of possible alternatives. A crucial question that should be kept in mind at this point is whether the Fascist regime could not in fact choose from several possible forms of totalitarian government. Indeed, there was no lack of theoretical alternatives, all having legitimate ideological roots in the variegated intellectual terrain from which fascism had sprung. To simplify matters somewhat,

* From Alberto Aquarone, *L'organizzazione dello Stato totalitario* (Turin: Giulio Einaudi, 1965), pp. 73–92. By permission of the publisher.

of the two principal components of Fascist ideology, namely revolutionary syndicalism and conservative nationalism, it was the conservative nationalist alternative that prevailed in the period of constitutional reform. The Fascist state that emerged between 1926 and 1928 owed far more to the conservative nationalist Alfredo Rocco than to the revolutionary syndicalist Edmondo Rossoni.

The following selection by Alberto Aquarone deals with the nature and consequences of the decisions that were actually made rather than with the question of possible alternatives. Aquarone makes it clear that Fascist constitutional reforms increased the power of the central government, strengthened the police, and suppressed political dissent. While it is true that many constitutional reforms took the form of compromises struck behind the scenes by rival factions representing different concepts of what the Fascist state ought to be like, it is also undeniable that the Fascist state emerged with a new authority to regulate public and private activities which had not previously been within its purview.

Alberto Aquarone was born in 1930. He graduated from the University of Rome and is currently professor of modern history at the University of Pisa. His special interest is public administration, and his books deal with such diverse topics as eighteenth-century America, the period of national unification in Italy, and Italian fascism.

■

Between 1926 and 1928 the Fascists took over the executive posts in the public administration, particularly on the staffs of the ministries of internal and foreign affairs. This onslaught was labeled *ventottismo,* or 1928ism, because it became most conspicuous in that year, while its principal protagonists were named *ventottisti,* or 1928ers.[1] The experiment, according to the Fascists themselves, did not yield good results. Here, for example, is the opinion of Yvon de Begnac, the more or less official biographer of Mussolini:

> The writer of these pages has met these "chosen ones" everywhere. Completely ignorant of our history and culture, they have attained a rank that is far above their social education. The present writer has seen Fascist consuls, consul generals, and ministers who are objects of ridicule in foreign cultural circles and who, because of their lack of preparation, discredit the very revolution they have used to obtain their lucrative jobs. And let us not speak of the Fascist prefects. Some of them behaved very well, but the majority of these political functionaries, as soon as they were put into office became firm reactionaries against the interests of the proletariat. As a result, we have witnessed the paradox of Fascist prefects fighting against Fascist party officials (*federali*) because each group felt that its slice of power was too small.[2]

On the whole, however, the "fascistization" of the state bureaucracy came about not so much by the introduction into its ranks of strictly Fascist elements drawn from the upper echelons of the party and the squads as by the gradual and sometimes halfhearted acceptance of the regime on the part of those who were already in the bureaucracy. In 1929, Michele Bianchi, who was then the undersecretary of the interior, declared while speaking to the Chamber on his ministry's budget that since 1922 twenty-nine prefects had been drawn from the party, a figure which certainly cannot be called impressive. The prefects who had been retired in that same period numbered eighty-six, most of whom had been replaced by regular career men.[3] It is also symptomatic that even in the most typically Fascist ministry, that of corporations . . . , the executive posts remained the monopoly of the career bureaucrats. In 1936, ten years after it was set up, all its director generals, inspector generals, and division heads were officials who had joined the state administration before, and usually long before, the march on Rome.[4]

The first Fascist law of a truly constitutional nature concerned the attributes and prerogatives of the head of government. This law merely gave legal sanction to the *de facto* concentration of political power in all its forms in the hands of

Mussolini. The relative bill was presented to the Chamber on November 18, 1925. It determined and defined the constitutional position of the president of the council of ministers, making him the head of government in name as well as in fact, sole depository of the crown's trust, and the principal channel through which the sovereignty of the state was to be manifested. It declared that the king exercised executive power through his government, that the government consisted of the prime minister (who was also the head of government) and of his ministers who were nevertheless distinct from him, that he was no longer a *primus inter pares,* or first among equals, as in the liberal tradition, that the head of government, who was appointed and subject to recall by the king, was responsible to the latter for the general direction of the government, that the ministers, who were appointed and subject to recall by the king upon the recommendation of the head of government, were responsible both to the king and the head of government for all the acts and measures of their respective ministries. It also established that the number, organization, functions, and duties of the ministries were determined by royal decree on the recommendation of the head of government who, also by royal decree, could take charge of one or more ministries, in which case he could delegate part of the functions of the same ministry to an undersecretary of state.

For the purpose of making parliament totally subservient to the executive branch, particularly to the head of government, the bill also established that no proposal could be placed on the agenda of the two houses without the consent of the prime minister, who could also request that a bill rejected by either house be put to the vote once again after three months had elapsed from the first vote. As Rocco made clear in his report, this provision aimed at "eliminating the disadvantages arising from the custom which had prevailed for a quarter of a century to enact only the bills of a particular session, which means that a bill rejected by either house can only be presented again in the following legislative session." [5] The new political and legal prerogatives of the president of the council of ministers were bolstered by stiff penal sanctions against anyone who threatened the life of the head of government either by word or deed.

The bill, while affirming the twofold responsibility of the head of government to the king and of the ministers to the king and the head of government, said nothing at all about the responsibility of the cabinet to parliament. "Concerning relations between the head of government, that is to say the government itself, and parliament," wrote the minister of justice, "they are essentially political and therefore elude a legislative definition. The bill does not even attempt to define them and does no more than set forth, in Article 6, some rules to strengthen the position of the cabinet and protect it against the excessive use of purely political debate and the pitfalls of procedural issues." [6] In spite of this omission, the new system obviously ruled out any responsibility of the government to parliament. It was equally clear that any discussion of whether the parliamentary system was being abolished was utterly pointless.[7] The irrelevance of parliament became perfectly clear when the Chamber approved the bill without debate. There was a brief debate in the Senate where one lonely voice, that of Gaetano Mosca, spoke out against the consolidation of Mussolini's personal power.

> The proposal might be worth consideration if it clearly stated that parliamentary government was to be replaced by constitutional government. The report which accompanies the bill states instead that the office of head of government is unlike that of the former German chancellor in that he does not remain in power only as long as the king wishes to keep him there. It actually states that the chief of state, the king, will keep him in power until such time as the economic, political, and moral coalition that sustains the cabinet disappears. The meaning was clear as long as the economic, political, and moral coalition which supported the cabinet, and sometimes dissolved it, manifested itself through the votes of parliament. But if this coalition is no longer represented by parliament, we must then ask who represents it. Basically, the king is being denied the freedom to choose his government and parliament the freedom to influence the choice by its votes. It would be an unanswerable riddle were it not for the fact that we can read between the

lines of the report and the bill. I have already mentioned that this time I would speak with some passion because we are witnessing, let us say it frankly, the end of a system of government. I would never have believed that I would be the one to deliver the final eulogy of parliamentary rule.[8]

A complementary law was passed on January 31, 1926, No. 100, to define the rules whereby the executive branch could issue decrees having the force of law.[9] According to the inner logic of every authoritarian regime that is grafted onto a representative and parliamentary system, the law sought to reinforce the position of the government over that of parliament by redefining their respective spheres of legislative jurisdiction in favor of the former.

Clearly, a reform in this area was long overdue, and sooner or later any government would have had to take steps to remedy the extreme confusion and cumbersomeness that had hindered the legislative process for a long time. . . . It would be misleading to say that the bill in question aimed solely and exclusively at asserting the power of government over parliament, particularly because that power had already been abundantly confirmed. The Fascist dictatorship did indeed wish to prominently legalize the government's pre-eminence in introducing legislation, but, like any other regime, it also wanted an orderly legislative process with more rigorous control on the great body of minor legislative provisions. Long before the advent of fascism, the bureaucracy of the various ministries had found it expedient to issue decrees having the force of law. These bureaucratic decrees were often scrutinized by the two houses in a perfunctory way, and sometimes were not scrutinized at all, unlike the royal decrees that had to be examined, and almost always were meticulously and substantially examined by the council of state and other technical advisory groups.

The principal objective of the law of January 31, 1926 . . . was to extend the scope of royal decrees and restrict to a minimum the jurisdiction of legislative decrees, the latter being subjected to precise regulations which until then had been missing.

A serious infraction of the traditional principle that legislative acts not ratified by parliament could not contravene a law passed by parliament occurred when the law of January 31, 1926, provided that the executive branch could retroactively modify laws regulating matters that were put under the jurisdiction of the executive branch by the new law. On the other hand, laws which would be promulgated in the future would not be subject to modification by royal decrees.

(*The author points out that the government was never able to enforce these provisions of the law of January 31, 1926. The bureaucracy first ignored, then successfully resisted Mussolini's efforts, and legislative decrees continued to proliferate.—Ed.*) The conclusion of this protracted and troublesome wrangle throws considerable light on the legislative and administrative practices of the Fascist state. The law of September 4, 1940, No. 1547, recognized the practical inapplicability of one of the fundamental directives of the law of January 31, 1926, No. 100, and provided that . . . the organization, duties, and personnel of public administrative bodies could be regulated by royal decree, even when these regulations modified previous legislative acts [10]— which is precisely what had been suggested by the cabinet as early as 1931 . . . for the purpose of legalizing a *de facto* situation.

It was quite natural that, once the Fascist government had become committed to erecting a totalitarian state, it should give a high priority to destroying local autonomies, particularly the autonomy of municipal governments, which were one of the last strongholds of the opposition now that it was being pushed to the margins of national politics. After all, the conquest of the municipal administrations had been one of the political aims of fascism even before the march on Rome. Now that it was entrenched in power both at the center and at the periphery, it was once again a question of wanting to legalize what had already happened and of depriving the municipalities of the last vestiges of local autonomy.

The first step was taken by introducing a special administrative system for the city of Rome. The question of administrative reform for the capital was an old one. The recognition that such a reform was needed cut across political lines. The problem had been discussed in 1923 by the technical council on public administration. At the meeting of the grand council on March 17 of that year, Giovanni Preziosi had presented the technical council's plan for the administrative reorganization of Rome. The plan envisaged setting up a state agency to deal with municipal problems and charged with governing the capital. The general idea of the plan was approved by that group.[11] The royal decree of October 28, 1925, No. 1949, transformed the muncipality of Rome into the governorship of Rome, with full authority over all municipal services and functions. The new administrative unit was headed by a governor who concentrated in his own hands all administrative and legislative functions and was assisted by two vice-governors who were also appointed by royal decree. (*The author briefly describes the administrative structure of the new city government.—Ed.*) The experiment began poorly. In November 1926, a little more than one year after his installation, the first governor, Filippo Cremonesi, resigned under circumstances that gave rise to all sorts of rumors. Undersecretary of the Interior Giacomo Suardo had to step in by sending the prefects, including that of Rome, a telegram in the name of the minister of the interior (who was then Mussolini himself) in which he cautioned them as follows: "I warn Your Excellency that newspapers absolutely must publish nothing concerning crisis in the governorship of Rome except what will be revealed through the official government news agency, Stefani, abstaining from any comment. Unheeding newspapers will be confiscated." [12] The reactions of the public, as duly reported by police informers, may be summed up in the following comment: "This is the sad result of the dictatorial innovation on the governorship. . . . While in the past the assessors were under the control of the elected municipal council, today they no longer stand for anything." [13] (*The author goes on to describe how, as a result of the incident, the governorship was*

reformed. The number of advisers was reduced and the preroga-
tives of the governor defined more clearly.—Ed.)

In the meantime, the municipal reform had been applied
throughout the kingdom by creating the new office of *podestà*.
Elections and the separation of power among different agencies
gave way to appointment from above and concentration of power
in a single body. At first the reform was limited to municipalities
with a population no greater than 5,000 inhabitants. According
to the law of February 4, 1926, No. 237,[14] the administration of
these municipalities was entrusted to a *podestà* who was appointed by royal decree to a five-year term, and who was also
subject to recall by royal decree upon the request of the local
prefect to the ministry of the interior. The *podestà* took over all
those functions that municipal and provincial law had previously
conferred on the elected mayor, the municipal executive committee (*giunta*), and the municipal council (*consiglio*). He was assisted, wherever the prefect thought it advisable, by a municipal
advisory board (*consulta*) composed of no less than six members,
one-third of whom were to be chosen directly by him and the
other two-thirds appointed by him but nominated by business associations, labor unions, and local organizations. The prefect
could also decide which organizations were to be represented and
to what share of the total representation they were entitled. The
consulta was a purely advisory body. The *podestà's* decisions
were subject to review by either the executive committee of the
province or the prefect, depending on their nature.

Subsequently, with the royal decree of September 3, 1926,
No. 1910, the office of *podestà* was extended to all the municipali
ties of the kingdom.[15] When the decree came up for discussion to
be converted into law, the report of the committee in the Chamber stated the following:

> Once again, in this serious issue, which involves the na-
> tional administration, fascism has progressed gradually, first
> trying out new arrangements where they were most needed and
> waiting for good results before applying them to the large cen-

ters of the nation. It was argued that the office of *podestà* was feasible in small municipalities which, because of their limited population, could not easily develop their own ruling groups, but that cities and large towns could produce their own capable administrators without government intervention. Instead, both in the small municipalities and the large centers, the ruling classes are incapable and mediocre as long as they are chosen from below by electoral methods which favor the least respectable elements and the least justifiable ambitions. Cities as well as towns know the venom of political feuds which divide and embitter, drown out the intelligent and those who are animated by selfless devotion, and favor the rise of mediocrities and demagogues. The new national spirit makes it mandatory for us to clear the large centers of their elective elements and reform the administration by appointing commissioners who will concentrate in their own hands all those responsibilities that were scattered in the defunct municipal councils. The law which we are asked to approve is therefore nothing more than the legalization of an existing state of affairs which has already proven itself and which conforms to the new spirit of the land.

We hope that, by extending the office of *podestà* to the larger municipalities, we will eliminate, wherever they still linger, the seeds of discord that are rooted in the more or less secret desire to gain a municipal seat, and that we will free the mind of the Italian people from the disease of politics as the sole objective of life. The citizens who used to waste their time in saving the municipality every five minutes will put it to better use in the other countless worthwhile pursuits that are possible in this world, the towns will be more tranquil, the administrations will proceed more expeditiously, and in this field as well, fascism will then have achieved one of the goals that most effectively assure the future of the nation: unity of command.[16]

A circular dated September 10, 1927, from the ministry of the interior to the prefects set forth the rules that were to govern the selection of the municipal advisory boards. According to the royal decree of September 3, 1926, their members were to be chosen from lists prepared by the officially recognized syndical associations of the municipality, by the prefect in those towns with a population no greater than 100,000 inhabitants, and in all other instances, jointly by the ministry of the interior and the ministry of corporations. In accordance with a practice typical of the corporative state, it was established for reasons of "uniformity" that the representation of the employers should be numerically equal to that of white- and blue-collar workers. Within this last group, however, at least one-third of the positions were to be reserved for intellectuals, including professionals and artists. As a result, the representatives of blue-collar workers were definitely in the minority.[17] The same principle was reaffirmed by the royal decree of October 27, 1927, No. 2059, which regulated the selection of municipal advisory boards in municipalities with populations exceeding 20,000 inhabitants.[18]

The reform of the provincial administrations that was enacted with the law of December 27, 1928, No. 2962, finally completed the destruction of local autonomies and fully subordinated all self-governing bodies to the government.[19] Nevertheless, considering the limited power that the provincial administrations had always had, that particular reform did not significantly affect local politics and administration. Finally, the year 1928 also witnessed a reform of provincial executive committees, based once again on the criterion of eliminating electoral procedures and making them docilely obedient to higher commands.[20]

The extension of the powers of the prefects was closely related to all these legislative initiatives. The principle was endorsed by the council of ministers on October 9, 1925, as a means of strengthening "the surveillance and coordination of the various branches of the state administration to assure political unity."[21] The relative bill was presented to the Chamber by the minister of the interior on November 27 and became law No. 660 on April 3, 1926. It provided that the prefects were to summon, normally once a month, together or separately, the heads of the various provincial offices to be informed in detail on the general performance of their services and to issue appropriate orders. The royal prosecutors of the provincial courts could also be invited to attend whenever matters within their jurisdiction were being discussed.[22] Furthermore, surveillance over the personnel of various state agencies within their jurisdiction was expressly

111

entrusted to the prefects, with the exception of employees in the administrations of justice, war, navy, air force, and the railroads.

According to what Federzoni has written in his memoirs, the extension of the powers of the prefects was sought and obtained by him primarily for the purpose of preventing the continuous interference of Fascist party officials in the political and administrative affairs of the provinces, which under Farinacci's secretariat had reached alarming proportions.[23] It is indeed probable that this was one of the reasons behind the reform, particularly in view not only of Federzoni's long-standing efforts in that direction while he was minister of the interior, but also of the fact that the greatest threat to Mussolini's personal power no longer came from the anti-Fascist opposition, which had been definitely routed and rendered powerless, but rather from the attempts at autonomy and criticism within fascism itself.

The measures adopted by the government during this period to gain totalitarian control of public affairs had to include a fundamental reorganization . . . of the two professions that were most closely tied to political activity: law and journalism. In spite of the increasing risks, the members of these professions had been and continued to be among the most determined opponents of fascism.

It was on April 4, 1925, that Rocco, the minister of justice, presented in parliament a bill to regulate the professions of lawyer and prosecutor. With some modifications, the bill became law No. 453 on March 25, 1926. Without going into a discussion of its many technical and organizational provisions, we may simply mention that the bill established a superior legal council, half of whose members were elected by the local councils of lawyers and prosecutors, and the other half, chosen from the lawyers attached to the court of cassation, the highest regular court of appeal in the Italian legal system, were appointed by royal decree (at the recommendation of the minister of justice). The superior legal council was given final jurisdiction over the registration and cancellation of names from the professional rolls of lawyers and prosecutors and over disciplinary matters. The elective character of the local legal councils was retained, but the minister of justice was granted power to dissolve them after having consulted with the council of state. Later on, Article I of the royal decree of May 6, 1926, No. 747, which spelled out the relationship between the measure in question and the law of April 3, 1926, No. 563, on labor relations, stated the following:

> Any person who has behaved publicly in such a manner that conflicts with the interests of the nation cannot be listed in the rolls of lawyers and prosecutors, and everyone who is so listed must be deleted from the rolls.

Thus, because of the extremely broad wording of the measure, anyone could be prevented from exercising the legal profession who had in any way expressed his dislike for the regime. In practice, however, this measure was applied leniently and there were numerous cases of lawyers who were able to excercise their profession in spite of the fact that they had expressed their lack of sympathy for the regime. The decree containing the above-mentioned regulations also formulated the oath that, with the law of March 25, became obligatory for all lawyers and prosecutors. The wording was sufficiently palliative with its customary reference to the "best interests of the nation" that it could be interpreted as not implying complete identification with the Fascist regime.[24] Nevertheless, the government's intention to consider the oath a purely political act was made clear in a circular dated October 16, 1926, which Rocco sent to the general prosecutors attached to the various courts of appeal: "The obligation to take the oath . . . is also incumbent on lawyers who are already registered and have taken the oath according to the old formula. The renewal of the oath must occur within three months after the new law goes into effect." [25]

The reorganization of the lawyers' councils as foreseen by the new measure was never carried out, partly because the rapid establishment of the syndical associations of lawyers and prosecutors introduced quick changes in the legal profession (*after April 1926 all employers, workers, and professionals had to belong to officially recognized trade and professional associations.—Ed.*) As a result, the special royal commissions, which had temporarily replaced the dissolved councils, remained in effect until the royal decree of November 22, 1928, completely reformed the system created in 1926. The reasons given were that the system of 1926, "while it may have answered the needs of an embryonic syndical structure, was inadequate for the notably improved organization of the present, and above all, no longer conformed to the concept and the legal-social organization of the Fascist state inasmuch as it made the councils purely an expression of class interests, often leaving the state a powerless spectator that could not even exercise the supervisory role attributed to it by the law." [26]

The independence of the legal profession, already thus curtailed, underwent further restrictions: the lawyers' councils were permanently transformed into royal commissions whose members were appointed by the government in part directly, in part upon the recommendation of the local professional associations. These commissions could be dissolved by the authorities whenever they did not function properly or for other serious reasons, while the appointment of one or more of their members could be revoked at any time. As for the superior legal council, it was transformed into a body nominated exclusively by the king. Later on, with the royal decree of November 27, 1933, No. 1578, all professional associations and royal commissions were abolished. Their powers, including the custody of the professional rosters and the disciplinary functions over those registered therein, were transferred to the syndical associations in the various occupations.

Questions dealing with the press and the journalistic profession were even more sensitive and vitally important. And in this field, fascism did not hesitate to resort to force even before applying any legislative pressure. All during 1925 an intense campaign of intimidation, violence, confiscation, and suspension was waged against the opposition press, which was finally reduced to silence. On the one hand, the squads stepped up their attacks against those newsstands that continued to sell the newspapers and periodicals of the opposition until most vendors were forced to desist.[27] On the other, the police also intervened with ever-increasing frequency, issuing warnings, confiscating, ordering suspensions. In Turin, following an order from the prefect, *La Stampa* was forced to suspend publication from September 9 to November 3, while practically every issue of Gobetti's *La Rivoluzione Liberale* was confiscated.[28] Zaniboni's attempt on the life of Mussolini on November 4 gave the government a pretext to crack down still more severely on the opposition press. The *Avanti, La Giustizia, La Voce Repubblicana,* and *L'Unità* were suspended. *Il Mondo* and *Il Risorgimento* underwent daily confiscation.[29] *La Rivoluzione Liberale* ceased publication on November 11, after Gobetti had received an injunction from the police chief of Turin to end all journalistic activity "in view of the clearly anti-national course" which he was pursuing. As is generally known, that same month also witnessed the ouster of Luigi and Alberto Albertini from the *Corriere della Sera. (Senator Luigi Albertini became an outspoken critic of the Fascist regime after the murder of Matteotti. The Fascists prevailed upon the owners of the newspaper to dismiss Albertini as editor in chief. —Ed.)* That newspaper had also been subjected to warnings and confiscations. Luigi's farewell message appeared in the November 28 issue. It was followed by the exodus of a large number of that newspaper's most illustrious editors and contributors, such as Francesco Ruffini, Carlo Sforza, Mario Borsa, Luigi Einaudi, Giuseppe Giacosa, and Augusto Monti. The Italian press was by now almost completely muzzled when, to put the finishing touch on the year that had seen its death struggle, law No. 2307 was passed on December 31, 1925, with new rules for periodical publications that completely legalized their subjugation.

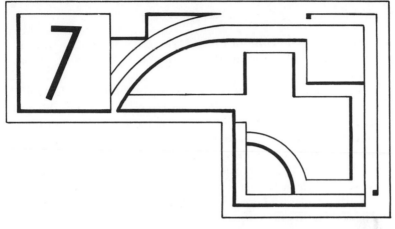

FASCIST REFORMS
AND THE
INDUSTRIAL
LEADERSHIP *

A fatal political weakness of intransigent Fascists like Farinacci was that they had few constructive ideas to offer. Theirs was the restlessness and fanaticism of people who know that they want change but can suggest nothing more positive than removing all vestiges of dissent and concentrating power in their own hands. Their program consisted mostly of a list of grievances. Lacking a coherent view of society and firm ideological convictions, they were rebels rather than revolutionar-

* From Roland Sarti, *Fascism and the Industrial Leadership in Italy, 1919–1940: A Study in the Expansion of Private Power Under Fascism* (Berkeley: University of California Press, 1971), pp. 69–78, 94–104. By permission of the Regents of the University of California.

ies. They were therefore of limited use to a regime that, once secure in power, sought to justify its monopoly of power by proposing a new social order.

If the regime was able to develop a blueprint for social reform that was coherent at least on paper, it was only because fascism could fall back on ideas that came out of revolutionary syndicalism and integral nationalism. Although revolutionary syndicalists and Nationalists seldom agreed on specific proposals, they did agree that there was a pressing need to develop new ways of dealing with the familiar phenomenon of class conflict and with problems of economic management. They also shared a contempt for liberal politics and believed that political institutions should represent the needs of production rather than the collective wishes of individuals. In the political jargon of the time, these aspirations were translated into demands for the creation of syndical and corporative institutions.

Before the government could legislate these new institutions it had to convince those economic groups that were well entrenched in the existing political system that they ought to go along with the experiment. No economic interest group was better entrenched than the industrialists, who in 1919 had formed a powerful national organization called the *Confederazione Generale dell'Industria Italiana* (CGII), better known in Italy as *Confindustria*. Because it had an independent basis of power, the industrial lobby was in a position to oppose those demands for change that threatened entrepreneurial autonomy. The industrial leaders thus found themselves in the midst of political controversy. The following selection examines how the Fascists dealt with their opposition. The fact that the industrialists managed to preserve most of their traditional prerogatives and broaden their access to government indicates that Fascist totalitarianism was not incompatible with the expansion of private power.

■

THE EMERGENCE OF THE SYNDICAL STATE, 1925–1926

Major constitutional changes occurred after January 1925. As far as the relationship between organized industry, labor, and government is concerned, the changes marked a continuation rather than a radical departure from what had evolved before the Matteotti crisis. Far from being fully absorbed into the Fascist state as the idea of totalitarianism implies, organized industry managed to retain a degree of autonomy. If the Fascist state turned out to be considerably less totalitarian in practice than it was in theory, the reasons are to be found in Mussolini's political techniques and in the resistance and resourcefulness displayed by outside groups, foremost among them the industrialists.

Mussolini approached the question of institutional change more as compromiser and arbitrator than as committed reformer. He acted more as the manager of a corporate enterprise than as a political leader pursuing well-defined objectives. By January 1925, he understood the need for change because most of his followers were determined to have it so and because there was no other way of solving the political crisis. The *ras*, the leaders of the Fascist Militia, syndicalists, intellectual revisionists like Giuseppe Bottai, and nationalists like Alfredo Rocco and Luigi Federzoni, all wanted change, although they were by no means agreed on the nature of the change. Mussolini responded to these demands in September 1924. He appointed a special Commission of Fifteen, later replaced by a Commission of Eighteen (nicknamed Commission of Solons), to study possible constitutional reforms. Aware that Fascist labor organizers were particularly dissatisfied over the lack of support from the top (two of them, Tullio Cianetti and Arnaldo Fioretti, who would soon play important roles in the Fascist labor movement, even considered the possibility of merging with the CGL in the summer of 1924), Mussolini began to take more of an interest in social problems and addressed several workers' rallies.[1]

On January 23, 1925, the Fascist Grand Council issued a statement deploring the fact that some employers were allegedly sabotaging the work of the Fascist syndicates and commented that these problems will be solved permanently by major institutional changes.[2] Such statements annoyed and alarmed the industrialists. There is no evidence that they objected to the demise of the liberal state on philosophical or moral grounds, but they were afraid of reforms carried out by elements hostile to private enterprise and implemented without the advice and consent of the business leadership. The reforms before the Matteotti crisis had been introduced with the consent of the industrialists; after January 1925 there seemed to be a danger that the new reforms might be carried out against them. Olivetti had gone on record in December 1924 as being in favor of politically unaffiliated labor organizations, a view which could not please the Fascists at a time when they thought of allowing only Fascist associations to operate freely. The CGII review *Rivista di Politica Economica* featured articles criticizing Fascist plans to introduce compulsory membership of workers and employers in government-sponsored associations.[3]

The Fascist answer to the industrialists' criticism was a series of strikes that were practically authorized by Mussolini and by the Grand Council. The most spectacular was the steel strike of March 1925, which was joined by the Socialist Industrial Federation of Metal Workers. For a few days, it looked as if the unity of the labor front had been restored. The Fascists eventually pulled out of the strike after having obtained a modest wage increase, because by that time the strike had served its political purpose. The industrialists were reminded that socialism was still a force to be reckoned with among industrial workers. A few weeks after the strike, Benni remarked how the industrialists had recently heard voices which had been considered silenced forever.[4] The strike also demonstrated that the Fascists could, if they chose to, make life difficult for all industrialists, a realization that undoubtedly helped to reconcile the industrial leadership to the idea of a Fascist *Gleichschaltung* of Italian society.

Neither side wanted to prolong the tension indefinitely. Having made their show of force, the Fascist leadership decided to hold out the olive branch. The minister of the interior, Luigi Federzoni, called in Benni and informed him that the government had decided that the CGII and Rossoni's Confederation of Syndical Corporations ought to work together more closely. Calm would be restored by making sure that strikes would be initiated in the future only as a desperate last resort. Benni informed the members of the CGII that no individual employer could declare a lockout in the future without the approval of the CGII.[5]

By April 1925, when Benni and Federzoni had their conversation, it was clear that the impending political reforms would not be as radical as the industrialists had anticipated earlier. The Commission of Solons was dominated by conservative Fascists. It followed Rossini's wishes by recommending the elimination of non-Fascist syndical associations, but it did not specify what the function and power of the officially recognized Fascist associations would be. The syndical law of April 3, 1926, provided that only the officially recognized syndical associations had the right to conclude lawful labor contracts. The industrialists did not want to go that far but, on the whole, they could not be dissatisfied with the reforms recommended by the Commission of Solons. The reform essentially broadened the powers of the head of government and restricted those of parliament. It made the government more authoritarian and the industrialists had never objected to authoritarianism. They were concerned primarily with making sure that the new order developed with them rather than against them. They cooperated. In Benni's words, "An act of courage was therefore needed by which, overcoming all the absurd scruples that still manifested themselves here and there, we would break all contacts with non-Fascist organizations." [6]

The act of courage was performed when the CGII and Rossoni's confederation signed the Vidoni Palace agreement on October 2, 1925. Article 3 of the agreement specified that all labor contract negotiations would take place between the CGII and its affiliates on the one hand and the Fascist syndicates on the other. Non-Fascist labor unions were excluded from collective bargaining. The Fascists had to pay a price for this concession. The Vidoni agreement provided for the abolition of all workers' factory councils. That did not particularly displease the Fascists because most factory councils were still under Socialist control (a Socialist council had been elected by Fiat workers as late as September 1924), but Rossoni was angered when the CGII refused to recognize Fascist workers' trustees (*fiduciari di fabbrica*) with which he hoped to replace the factory councils. Benni insisted that the Vidoni agreement must broaden the authority of management. Mussolini made it clear that he agreed with Benni: "only the hierarchy of management should exist within the factory; therefore, we shouldn't even talk about trustees." [7]

The industrial leadership wanted to strengthen the authority of management within the factory and the authority of the CGII over individual firms. This was the message of a CGII circular issued a few days after the signing of the Vidoni agreement. Those industrialists who still did not accept the CGII were warned that their associations would be replaced by more cooperative ones.[8] Olivetti, who had been the most stubborn opponent of the Vidoni agreement, commented that "we must loyally admit that if the monopoly [over labor negotiations] represents a gain for the workers, it can also be advantageous for the industrialists and for the CGII." [9]

One thorny issue left unsolved by the Vidoni agreement concerned the introduction of compulsory arbitration of labor disputes. The government made it clear that it intended to ban strikes and lockouts on the ground that, as expressions of class interests, they failed to take into account national needs. Only officially recognized workers' and employers' syndicates were authorized to conclude labor contracts legally. To become the officially recognized syndicate, an association of workers or employers had to demonstrate its "capacity, moral acceptability, and national loyalty" to the satisfaction of government officials. Whenever these officially recognized syndicates failed to agree on the terms of a collective labor contract, the matter was settled by the compulsory arbitration of specially constituted labor courts.

The industrialists, who had accepted the Vidoni agreement

with hesitation because they feared it might lead to more comprehensive regulation of labor relations, were determined not to yield on the question of compulsory arbitration. They began by raising specific objections designed to show the impracticality of compulsory arbitration. Could the government really guarantee the observance of arbitrated labor contracts? Were there enough competent arbitrators to staff the labor courts? Where were they to be found? [10]

When the matter came up for discussion in parliament in conjunction with the bill which eventually became the syndical law of April 3, 1926, Benni undertook the task of warding off compulsory arbitration. He attacked the principle of compulsory arbitration while the bill was still in committee. To overcome his stubborn resistance, the other members of the committee decided to grant his request that industry be specifically excluded from the jurisdiction of the labor courts. The battle was then transferred to the floor of the Chamber where Benni justified the exclusion of industry on the ground that no one but an experienced industrialist could judge the economic feasibility of a labor contract and stated unequivocally that the extension of compulsory arbitration to industry would mean economic chaos throughout the land.

There were obvious weaknesses in Benni's reasoning and Rossoni moved in to expose them. He pointed out that Fascist labor leaders were too aware of the real needs of production and too reasonable to make excessive demands. Benni was in an uncomfortable political position. If he persisted in his refusal to accept compulsory arbitration for industry, he would in effect be suggesting that he had no faith in the Fascist syndicalists, which could be construed as a slur on the entire Fascist regime. He rose to the challenge with tortuous verbal dexterity. Industry would accept any reform sponsored by the regime in the certainty that fascism could not possibly advocate anything contrary to the national interest. However, precisely because fascism stressed the importance of authority, order, and legality, industry could not approve of new agencies (the labor courts) which bypassed the authority of the state and undermined the basis of law and order. He concluded with the verbal somersault that the industrialists would follow Fascist directives "with daring prudence" (*con ogni audace prudenza*).[11]

The lines were drawn and this time the industrialists were at a disadvantage. The opposition included not only most Fascists but also the representatives of agricultural and commercial employers who resented the special treatment demanded by the industrialists. Alfredo Rocco, the minister of justice who sponsored the bill and who had initially supported the industrialists, confessed that he was unhappy over the exclusion of industry from the jurisdiction of the labor courts. But the industrialists' most serious disadvantage was that this time Mussolini was not on their side. Their demands were so one-sided that Mussolini could not support them without antagonizing many followers and tarnishing the image of impartiality which he cultivated. He made his position quite clear:

> I am not the secretary of the corporations but there has never been a major labor problem . . . which I have not examined and sometimes solved. Under the circumstances, I believe that the CGII can and will take this step, if for no reason than the advantages will outweigh the disadvantages.[12]

This time the industrialists had to yield. Industry had to accept the principle of compulsory arbitration, although Olivetti was able to salvage a great deal. At his suggestion, parliament agreed that collective labor controversies should be reviewed by the highest syndical associations before being turned over to the labor courts.[13] This right of preliminary review gave the CGII the opportunity to settle most collective labor controversies outside the courtroom. By 1937, only forty-one collective labor controversies had reached the labor courts, only sixteen of which were settled by court decisions.[14]

The fact that the Vidoni agreement and the syndical law of 1926 were received by some industrialists with reservations cannot obscure the advantages which the industrial leadership derived from these measures. The CGII became the official and exclusive representative for all industrial employers vis-à-vis labor and government. We shall see in the next chapter how, as a result of this official recognition, the CGII extended and tightened its control over entrepreneurial groups that were still beyond its reach. It also entrenched itself more securely into the institutions of the Fascist state. As the official representative of industry, it was entitled to a permanent seat in the Fascist Grand Council, in government planning agencies, and after the parliamentary reform of 1928, in parliament itself. Furthermore, although the official recognition meant that the CGII would operate on a level of juridical equality with other employer associations and with labor syndicates, it exceeded the others in influence and prestige.

On the basis of the syndical law, workers and employers were organized separately in twelve national syndicates, one for each group in industry, agriculture, commerce, banking and insurance, land transportation and inland navigation, sea and air transportation. An additional association for professional workers, artists, and intellectuals brought the total to thirteen. The CGII was unquestionably the most powerful. After the government officially recognized it on September 26, 1926, as the exclusive representative of industrial employers, its new functions as a public agency complemented its continuing activities as a private pressure group. The industrialists continued to choose their own leaders who in turn ran the CGII without interference. Labor contracts concluded by the CGII or its members were legally binding on all industrial firms. Freedom of contract was a thing of the past. Now the CGII enjoyed both the administrative autonomy of a private organization and the juridical authority of a public institution.

Juridically speaking, the syndical reform was a great innovation because it attenuated the traditional distinction between private and public institutions. In this sense, it approached one of the original goals of fascism. The CGII, however, remained the citadel of private business; it was nominally subject to the same government controls that applied to other syndical associations but, unlike them, it was strong enough to resist the demands of government officials and Fascist radicals. Organized industry was in the state but not of the state. The aspirations of revolutionary syndicalists, fascist revisionists, and integral nationalists were frustrated once again. All these groups envisaged a corporative state in which production was regulated by representatives of capital and labor organized side by side within the corporations where they would work together under the guidance of the state. The syndical reform assigned workers and employers to separate associations (the syndicates) which were authorized to deal only with labor problems. The enactment of the syndical reform meant that the realization of the corporative state was postponed indefinitely. The idea of corporativism was kept barely alive by a provision of the syndical law authorizing the formation of mixed associations of workers and employers, provided these mixed associations would not jeopardize the existence of the syndicates. The reasons for keeping the corporative principle alive will soon become apparent. The royal decree of July 1, 1926, which specified how the syndical reform was to be implemented also provided for the creation of a Ministry of Corporations and a National Council of Corporations. The presence of these two agencies enabled the regime to speak as if corporativism was already a working reality in spite of the fact that until 1934 there existed only one economically insignificant corporation for artists and intellectuals.

The concept of corporativism failed in 1926 for several reasons. The nebulousness of the concept strengthened those opponents who had specific objections. Olivetti was one of them. He opposed the corporations on the ground that the workers were allegedly still too immature and irresponsible to be given any say in the management of production (this was probably his way of saying that they were still under Socialist influence). He also feared that the establishment of mixed associations would mean the permanent removal of craftsmen and industrial cooperatives from the CGII.[15]

Only a few Fascists were seriously committed to the realization of the corporative state in 1926. Some integral nationalists and Catholic intellectuals were committed to corporativism on intellectual grounds but lacked significant support in the party or in the country at large. Rocco, who of all former nationalists was perhaps most closely identified with fascism, was too much of an evolutionist and too sympathetic to big industry to insist on the enactment of meaningful corporative reforms at that particular moment. The one Fascist leader who put up a brave struggle was Rossoni, but he was virtually isolated and was soon to succumb to a coalition of anti-Rossonian Fascists and to Mussolini's pent-up resentment of his growing power and prestige. For most Fascists, corporativism was still little more than a slogan, a nebulous cause to which many paid lip service and few gave serious thought.[16]

Fascist ideologists began to differentiate clearly between syndicalism and corporativism after the syndical reform. Because the syndical state was an accomplished fact and corporativism could not be renounced, Fascist theoreticians had to devise a system that would give each a logical function. The most authoritative view, worked out by Bottai and endorsed by Mussolini, was that the two were complementary. Syndicalism was now declared to be a necessary pause on the way to the corporative state. Eventually, the syndicates would be absorbed by the corporative state, thereby crowning the Fascist revolution.[17] All was sufficiently vague to serve several purposes. The distinction between syndicalism and corporativism now helped to prolong the myth of the continuing Fascist revolution and to justify the regime's ineradicable social ambiguity. Disgruntled Fascists who felt the syndical reform had not gone far enough could look forward to the next round when the ambiguity would be dispelled.

Given its antecedents, the Fascist regime could follow no other course. Obviously, the distinction between syndicalism and corporativism was not the result of a spontaneous process of ideological clarification within fascism. Fascist social doctrines developed as they did because the regime was unable and unwilling to resolve its internal contradictions. Having come to power with

127

the consent of powerful outside groups, fascism could hardly disregard their wishes once in power. The industrialists were the socioeconomic force that resisted the revolutionary tendencies of fascism with the greatest success. Fascist economic and social reforms, therefore, were as much a product of industrialist caution as of the revolutionary aspirations of Fascist innovators. The industrialists were never strong enough to dominate fascism but they were always sufficiently influential to remain in the ring for the next confrontation. They accepted the syndical reform partly because it was a necessary step to strengthen the regime, which to them was a necessary barrier to socialism, and partly because it was otherwise convenient for them to do so. The industrial leadership found the reform advantageous because it gave them new opportunities to discipline industry and because it gave them a better vantage point in the public administration from which they could continue to influence the course of Fascist reform and the formulation of public policy.

■

INDUSTRY AND THE ADVENT OF
THE CORPORATIVE STATE

The industrialists' determination to protect managerial authority affected the corporative reform that had been postponed *sine die* by the syndical compromise of 1926. We have already seen that the Ministry of Corporations was set up without the corporations. The corporations had remained a vague reference in Article 3 of the syndical law to the effect that the syndicates might be linked by means of "central connecting agencies" staffed by representatives of labor and management. None was actually set up because, as Benni and Olivetti explained in the Chamber, management could not agree to giving the workers a voice in production.[18]

Subsequent steps to realize the corporative state stopped short of seriously challenging the authority of management. The Charter of Labor promulgated by the Fascist Grand Council in

April 1927 was hailed in Fascist circles as the Magna Carta of the Fascist revolution. In reality, there was little in that document to justify the claim. In its final form, the charter reflected a compromise between the CGII and Rossoni, with the industrialists gaining most of their points. Business interests in all sectors of the economy joined forces under Benni's direction to make the charter a statement of general principles rather than specific provisions on wages, working hours, fringe benefits, and social security as Rossoni would have preferred.

The industrialists' battle was more than half won once it was decided that the charter would be issued in the form of a general social manifesto. When it came to phrasing the charter, Benni argued that it must assert the "purely Fascist principle" that every individual has a specific function in society and that "the function of the industrialist is to organize and manage production." [19] He won his point but not as fully as he would have preferred. The charter promised respect for managerial independence but also stated that management was ultimately responsible to the state, which could regulate production whenever the public interest required it to do so. The ambiguity was absolutely necessary. Since the regime had to satisfy both traditionalists and innovators, to clarify that point would have meant disrupting the social balance that sustained the regime.

As the pressure to clarify the meaning of corporativism increased in the early 1930's, the industrialists lost no opportunity to thwart the plans of those Fascists who still hoped that something qualitatively new might emerge from the Fascist revolution. The most radical expectations were voiced by a professor of philosophy at the University of Rome, Ugo Spirito, during a well publicized colloquium that took place in May 1932 in Ferrara. Spirito defended the daring proposition that private property should be abolished and that ownership should be vested in the Fascist corporations. Such "proprietary corporations" would then assume full responsibility for production, thereby putting an end once and for all to the historical conflict between private and public interest.

It is not surprising that the revolutionary implications of Fascist doctrine should have been enunciated by an academic intellectual. Everyone involved in the realities of power was too busy manipulating and compromising to follow Fascist postulates to their revolutionary conclusions. Olivetti, who participated in the Ferrara colloquium, rejected Spirito's suggestions in no uncertain terms. But even Bottai, who had a reputation for intellectual independence and who favored the evolution of a new system of property relations, felt Spirito had gone too far. Specifically, Bottai rejected Spirito's contention that the corporations should supersede the syndicates. He had opposed Rossoni's brand of syndicalism on the ground that it exasperated those class antagonisms that fascism was supposed to transcend. Now that the labor syndicates were under more moderate leadership, Bottai felt they had a useful role to play. He argued that as long as capital and labor retained any vestige of their class mentality, the separation of workers and employers simply reflected a fact of life.[20]

On this last point, Bottai and the industrialists were in agreement. Business had learned to live and work with the syndical system and had little desire to take another leap in the dark. The decision, however, was not up to them. Fascism could not afford to renounce the myth of the continuing revolution. To halt its progress, particularly at a time when most Fascists felt the need for some spectacular gesture to deal with the economic depression, would have ended the complicated give-and-take that held the regime together. Most industrialists therefore resorted once again to the well-tested strategy of flexible resistance. The one industrialist who went too far in opposing the new experiment was Olivetti and his intransigence cost him his post as secretary of the CGII (Mussolini forced his resignation in December 1933). Probably exhausted by years of hard work, and increasingly antagonistic toward Mussolini whose demagogic, plebeian ways clashed with his austere self-restraint, Olivetti at the Ferrara colloquium committed the blunder of expressing his opposition to the principle of corporativism. Most of his colleagues worked quietly but effectively to limit the regulatory power of the corporations over production. They insisted that corporative agencies have purely advisory functions, that they respect the legislative prerogatives of parliament, that labor negotiations remain in the hands of the syndical associations, and that all corporative decisions be subject to review by Mussolini. The twenty-two corporations that were finally established in 1934 conformed to all these criteria.[21] In July 1932, probably to reassure the industrialists, Mussolini took over the Ministry of Corporations from Bottai.

But the industrialists were not simply interested in rendering the corporative experiment harmless, they also wanted to use the corporations to facilitate the restructuring of the system of production to their greater satisfaction. One of the specific functions of the corporations was to promote cooperation between the different sectors of production. Benni agreed that this would be highly beneficial: "Our vision of the economy is a Fascist vision, an integral vision; agriculture, banking, and commerce stand at industry's side." [22] Most corporations covered large cycles of production. The corporation for textiles included the agricultural groups that produced the fibers, the manufacturers who processed them, and the commercial organizations that marketed the finished product. Other corporations, such as those for building construction, machinery, chemicals, and public utilities included only industrial and commercial groups. The arrangement was designed to reconcile the need for economic planning with the desire of the various economic groups for some autonomy.[23]

We need to examine now why the industrialists preferred the corporative approach to economic planning. Their attitude toward corporativism can hardly be understood without taking into account the impact on their thinking of the great economic crisis that followed the crash of the American stock market in October 1929. The effects of the crisis were not immediately evident in Italy because the Italian economy was already experiencing a recession as a result of the deflationary policy adopted by the government after 1925. Apologists for the regime, including numerous industrialists, took advantage of this coincidence to

boast that a Fascist economy was immune from the cyclic disturbances of capitalism. When the period of grace proved to be
short-lived, the government began to experiment with various
forms of economic interventionism in a flurry of poorly coordinated moves strongly reminiscent of the early days of Roosevelt's
New Deal.

The industrialists were now faced with a serious dilemma.
They could not afford to refuse public assistance, nor did they
want to risk public regulation of production by accepting public
assistance. Their aim was as clear as it was difficult to achieve: to
have public assistance without public regulation. Their reaction
was therefore both bold and oblique. On the one hand, Benni
called upon the industrialists to save themselves by adopting la-
bor-saving techniques, scientific management, and rationalization
of production. On the other, he asked for a massive infusion of
public funds into the private sector to rescue the firms that were
on the verge of bankruptcy.[24] The idea was to justify keeping
control of production in private hands in spite of industry's need
for large-scale public subsidies by showing that industry was still
sufficiently strong and vital to clean its own house.

Government responses to the crisis included the vast subsidies Benni had called for. The public rescue of private initiative
was carried out by the *Istituto per la Ricostruzione Industriale*
(IRI), a government agency set up in January 1933 to provide financial assistance to industrial firms. . . . At this point we should
mention that although in the long run it was IRI that changed
the character of the Italian economy, the industrialists were initially more worried about other forms of economic interventionism. Much to Benni's chagrin, there were many influential Fascists who argued that the government should intervene directly
to encourage the concentration of ownership and management
and the rationalization of production. The idea was not new. Industry and government had worked together to rationalize production since the mid-1920's. One reason why the industrialists
had supported Mussolini's policy of monetary deflation after 1925
was that they hoped a temporarily declining level of profits

would drive many marginal producers out of business to the advantage of the larger and supposedly more efficient firms. But deflation could not be pushed beyond a point without the risk of driving every producer into bankruptcy. That point was reached in 1927 when Mussolini decided to stabilize the currency at his famous *quota 90* (to be precise, at the exchange rate of 92.46 lire to the pound sterling) against the advice of many businessmen who feared that stabilization at such a high exchange rate would entail a drastic loss in exports.[25]

After business had accommodated itself with some difficulty to *quota 90*, it looked as if further changes in the structure of production would have to be initiated by direct public intervention, which most industrialists wished to avoid. In the government, Belluzzo and Bottai were in favor of industrial cartels as a way of reducing fragmentation of ownership and management. The idea was taken up by Arnaldo Mussolini, the dictator's influential brother, who argued that producers should be required by law to join cartels whenever total participation was in the national interest. The suggestion was unacceptable to industry for a number of reasons. To have such government sponsored *consorzi obbligatori* (compulsory cartels) would be an admission that the industrialists were incapable of managing production efficiently without outside leadership. The very principle of the separation of private and public initiative was at stake. There was widespread fear in industry that compulsory cartels would pave the way to complete public regulation of production. Benni therefore rejected the idea in no uncertain terms in spite of the fact that Arnaldo Mussolini was generally known to speak for his brother.[26]

The industrialists wanted to save the principle that cartels should rest on the voluntary participation of their members even though they were prepared to admit that compulsory cartels might be desirable under exceptional circumstances. Not only did voluntary cartels reduce the risk of public regulation, they were also a convenient means of regulating competition. Of course, voluntary cartels seldom led to significant improvements in the methods of production. They usually took the form of price agreements whereby prices were pegged at a sufficiently high level to assure the survival of even the least efficient producers.[27]

Ironically, the CGII was instrumental in promoting passage of a law that authorized the government to form compulsory cartels. In spite of its formal stand in favor of voluntary membership, the CGII was always ready to favor compulsory cartels on pragmatic grounds. When the leading firms in steel insisted that the particular needs of their sector made it imperative that all producers belong to cartels, the CGII agreed with them. In fact, the CGII appealed to the government to prevail upon a few non-participating firms to join two sales cartels. Having intervened successfully, the government felt the need to legitimize its intervention by passing an appropriate law. Bottai argued in parliament that because many industrialists frequently disregarded the principle of voluntary membership in practice even as they upheld it in principle (and he mentioned names and instances when strong-arm tactics had been used to coerce individual firms into joining), it was incumbent upon the government to make sure that cartels were run in the national interest.[28] The law on compulsory cartels passed in June 1932 but the CGII saw to it that it remained a dead letter. When the two steel cartels expired in February 1933 they were renewed on a voluntary basis with the participation of all firms, an indication of the CGII's suspicion regarding compulsory cartels.[29]

There was the possibility that those who favored public regulation of production might seize upon the proliferation of voluntary cartels as an excuse to demand more stringent controls over production. The industrialists need a legal umbrella that would legitimize the regulation of competition on the basis of private price and production agreements between businessmen. They found that umbrella in corporativism. They discovered the usefulness of the corporative principle of the *autodisciplina delle categorie* (collective self-regulation by businessmen within the various corporations). Now that the ubiquitous cartels curtailed the independence of managers at the factory level, the industrialists preferred to talk about collective rather than individual self-regulation. Leading business and political personalities argued that the corporations were fascism's answer to capitalism and socialism and that the practice of collective self-regulation within them struck a happy balance between the atomism and unpredictability of free market economies and the bureaucratic inefficiency of centralized systems.[30] This rhetoric cannot obscure the fact that corporativism was a useful smoke screen to disguise the retention of economic power in private hands.

As most of the twenty-two corporations cut across several sectors of production, it naturally made it easier for previously competing groups to reach mutually acceptable agreements. Although the activities of the corporations have not been studied in sufficient detail, there are indications that they served the industrialists' purpose. One-third of the cartels registered in 1937 were formed after the enactment of the corporative reform. Manufacturers, landowners, and commercial dealers discovered the advantages of coordinating their pricing and marketing policies. Agrarian-industrial cartels included those between beet growers and sugar refiners, producers of textile fibers and textile manufacturers, dairy farmers and manufacturers of dairy products. The best example of an industrial commercial cartel is the sales cartel in cotton formed in June 1932 between several thousand manufacturers and dealers. In March 1934 this cartel was authorized by the government to assign fixed quotas of raw materials to its members, to determine how much each participant should produce, what share of the market he was entitled to, and at what prices he should sell. When in April 1936 these powers were extended to all cartels provided they would submit to the Ministry of Corporations an annual statement of their activities, the cartels became the regulators of production. Decision-making powers were taken away from local managers and vested instead in the business elites that represented the dominant firms. Because the cartels always assigned raw materials, production and market quotas on the basis of a firm's past share of the market, the proliferation of cartels acted as a powerful brake on the entire economy. Acquired positions were perpetuated and newcomers excluded from the market. As a result, there were large numbers of small firms struggling to emerge, confined to a gray zone of semilegality, at the mercy of bureaucrats, and whose workers were underpaid, insecure, and beyond the reach of social security programs.[31]

The corporative agencies supposed to supervise the work of the cartels could never do so effectively. The staff of the Ministry of Corporations was overwhelmed by the avalanche of reports from the numerous cartels. When the corporations began in 1935 to take over the task of supervision, their investigating boards discovered that the reports were not sufficiently detailed to make the investigations meaningful. The investigators also discovered that supplementary data was difficult to come by even though they were authorized by law to request all necessary clarifications. When the corporation in steel and machinery decided after hearing numerous complaints to look into the activities of some forty cartels that were nominally under its jurisdiction, its investigators were unable to reach any conclusion on the basis of the information available. The fact that workers and employers had equal representation on the boards of the various corporations meant that debates could go on indefinitely if either side was determined to stall for time.[32]

The failure of the corporative state to establish effective controls over the cartels reveals how Fascist totalitarianism functioned in practice. The industrialists were fond of describing the cartels as totalitarian, perhaps as a semantic effort to disguise their coercive basis. The cartels, however, were totalitarian only in the sense that they severely restricted managerial autonomy at the factory level. They were not totalitarian in the sense that they disciplined private power in the public interest, however that elusive concept may be defined. The corporative principle of the *autodisciplina delle categorie,* as practiced by the cartels, was ultimately incompatible with the regime's totalitarian aspirations. The incompatibility became clear as soon as the regime tried to mobilize the country's natural and human resources for war. With that effort, we move into the period of autarky, or the pursuit of economic self-sufficiency, as a necessary prerequisite to a more independent foreign policy.

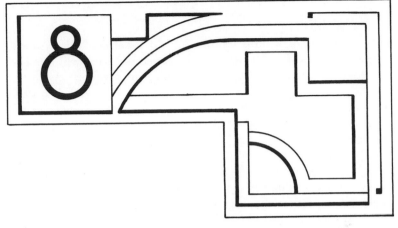

THE
LIVING STANDARD
OF
ITALIAN WORKERS,
1929–1939 *

As far as organized labor was concerned, the liberal era formally ended in Italy on April 3, 1926, when the syndical law was enacted. Although anti-Fascist labor organizations had been steadily losing ground since fascism's advent to power, they had been able in the early years of the regime to maintain a substantial following among the industrial workers of the north. By prescribing that only government approved labor unions had the authority to conclude legally binding labor contracts, the syndical law made it impossible and pointless for the

* Cesare Vannutelli, "Le condizioni di vita dei lavoratori italiani nel decennio 1929–39," *Rassegna di Statistiche del Lavoro*, X, 3 (May–June 1958), pp. 97–108. By permission of the publisher.

anti-Fascist labor unions to continue to function. The syndical reform thus left Italian workers no choice but to accept the Fascist labor syndicates as their sole bargaining agents. As far as labor was concerned, freedom of association had ceased to exist in practice if not in theory. The following selection discusses the consequences of this state of affairs for labor and for the economy as a whole.

Both the workers and their Fascist representatives were soon confronted by severe challenges arising both from political and economic developments. As the author points out, the Italian economy experienced a severe setback long before the crash of the Wall Street market in October 1929. Labor had to face this prolonged crisis with the double disadvantage of being represented by a leadership that was not of its choice and of not being able to go on strike because strikes and lockouts had been declared illegal by the syndical law. Fascist labor leaders, particularly those who were sincerely interested in the well-being of the workers, soon discovered the limits of their power. Because they were appointed and remained in office at the discretion of Mussolini and top party officials, they could not ignore political pressure. And since political priorities often conflicted with the needs of labor, they were torn between loyalty to the party and to the workers.

Cesare Vannutelli discusses the consequences of this dilemma. He is a statistician and an expert in problems of production and labor relations, who has held top executive posts in the Institute for Industrial Reconstruction, the government holding agency that controls the public sector of the Italian economy. The article is based on a report that Vannutelli presented at the University of Strasbourg in the course of a colloquium held on March 24–27, 1958. The article is particularly interesting because it makes enlightening use of statistical data in dealing with issues that have generated passionate debate. Vannutelli's figures give a quantitative picture of how labor fared under fascism and also indicate how Fascist labor leaders sought to reconcile political priorities and social needs. To what degree were they successful?

What was the role of labor in the Fascist economy? Were the sacrifices made by the workers a result primarily of the economic crisis or of the politics and ideology of fascism? How did fascism try to justify its image as a socially revolutionary movement? These are some of the major questions that should be kept in mind while reading Vannutelli's article.

∎

In order to place my topic in its proper setting, it seems advisable to begin with a brief summary of the development of the Italian economy during the decade in question, if for no other reason than that events of a political nature in that period stamped upon our economy characteristics different from those found in most other countries.

In the first place, I should like to recall that, while all the countries of Western Europe and the United States . . . experienced in the period between 1922 and 1929 a phase of exceptional economic expansion, Italy in 1929 found itself in a different situation. A severe deflationary policy had been put into effect in 1927 in an effort to revaluate the currency and raise its exchange rate in relation to the stable currencies of the world. The rate of exchange between the lira and the pound sterling (the dollar was not yet the widespread monetary standard that it is today) was aggressively fixed at *quota 90* on December 21, 1927, by the Italian government, which set the exchange rate at 92.46 lire to the pound sterling. Fascist propaganda popularized that rate by dubbing it *quota 90*. Since the rate was set unrealistically high for reasons of political prestige and with a complete disregard for economic considerations, the resulting disparity between domestic and international prices put an end to the expansion of industrial production, which in the preceding years had benefited from the restoration of order at home and from the favorable international situation.

It can only surprise us today, permeated as we all are by Keynesian doctrine (variously understood and shared), that an important country such as Italy should deliberately pursue a deflationary policy leading toward the cessation of trade and a loss of employment. One possible explanation is that John Maynard Keynes' *A Treatise on Money* was not published until 1930 and that his earlier writings that set forth his theories (in however confused a manner) were certainly not read either by Mussolini or his economic advisers at the time.

The seriousness of the crisis of adjustment that followed such a policy is revealed by the drop in wholesale prices, whose index fell from 129 in 1926 to 100 in 1929, a drop that was not much less, as we shall see, than the one that occurred when the world crisis began to affect Italy at the end of 1929. That Italy was able to recover quickly from the blows of this deflationary policy was due only to the favorable economic conditions that prevailed in 1928–1929. It is nevertheless certain that Italy entered the period that concerns us in a weakened condition, unprepared to sustain the additional blows that followed the crash of the stock market on Wall Street.

All the countries that felt the great crisis experienced a collapse in the prices of raw materials, an increasing imbalance between costs and prices, the accumulation of stock in hand, the reduction of industrial production, a rise in unemployment, and a reduction in foreign trade.

Table I summarizes some of the most significant economic indexes for the period under examination. They show that wholesale prices dropped from 100 in 1929 to a low of 65 in 1934, the cost of living from 102 to 78, manufacturing production from 90 to 80, and industrial employment from 90 to 71 (a decrease considerably greater than that shown by production). The national income, which brings together and sums up the component elements of the economic situation (expressed according to the value of the lira in 1938), dropped in these same years from 124.6 billions to 118.5 billions, reaching a low point of 116 billions in 1931. The average annual per capita income decreased from more than 3,000 lire in 1929 to 2,829 in 1934, making it a loss of nearly 8 percent in a period of four years.

It was not easy, as we well remember, for the world economy to overcome this crisis. Today we can admit that its principal causes and fundamental characteristics . . . were not understood at that time. We were still debating a point that today seems anachronistic: Was the crisis due to "overproduction or underconsumption"? People are attracted by simple ideas and welcome simple slogans. A phrase that gained currency in Italy at that time expressed still another thorny dilemma: "Was the crisis *in* the system or was it a crisis *of* the system?" It was meant to suggest that the phenomenon of "poverty in the midst of plenty" (still another slogan) was not simply due to a malfunction within the self-balancing mechanism of the economy, but rather to the inherent incapacity of the system to function properly, and to indicate that it might be necessary to do away with the economic system that until then had been generally accepted in Italy. These were the first signs that a new economic orientation was developing, designed to undermine the prestige and dominant economic role of private initiative and entrust to the state the direction of the economy.

But fascism was not then (or better said, was not yet) a movement inspired by socialistic ideologies, and Mussolini had forgotten (but he would remember it later) that he had been a Socialist leader. A new formula was therefore coined, that of the "corporative economy," which on the one hand claimed to transcend class struggles, and on the other to transcend the need for a policy of government intervention by insisting that operational decisions were to be made by taking into account the "higher interests of the state" as represented in the decision-making agencies by the leaders of the party.

The corporations were established in 1934, just as the economy was beginning to revive. Although they did not play a decisive role in shaping economic policy in subsequent years, it nevertheless seems likely that the corporations served to slow down the economic recovery. In Italy, the recovery that was strikingly initiated by the American New Deal, in a world still suffering from the preceding crisis, had a slow and painful start.

The subsequent acceleration in the rhythm of recovery and economic development was due to factors that were political rather than economic in nature, or to be more explicit, that were connected with the war.

On the one hand, war operations against Ethiopia mobilized industry, which had to intensify its productive efforts in order to satisfy the needs of the campaign. On the other, the economic sanctions decreed by the League of Nations against Italy—as a result of which a large group of European and non-European countries stopped acquiring products of Italian manufacture for nine months, bringing about a drastic reduction in our exports and, therefore, in the availability of funds to pay for the importation of raw materials and products finished abroad—encouraged and provided technical justifications for the policy of autarky (the pursuit of national economic self-sufficiency).

Italy had already been forced to curtail imports because of the deficit in its balance of payments . . . a result of the losses in its export trade that were attributable to the great crisis. Controls on currency exchanges had been introduced in 1934, and in February 1935 imports had been subjected to quotas. The sanctions aggravated the need for the policy of controlling imports and gave additional encouragement to the policy of autarky, whose principal characteristics were the following:

    a. expansion of production in those sectors requiring minor monetary outlay
    b. importing, whenever possible, raw materials rather than finished or semi-finished products
    c. increasing domestic production of raw materials that were being imported and searching for substitutes

The consequences of this policy were numerous. Partly as a result of the demands of war, a notable expansion occurred in the mining, metallurgical, and chemical industries, in naval construction, and in the production of hydroelectric power. Other industries (textiles, building construction) were necessarily sacrificed. Shortages of many products became a source of complaint, and consumers did not always like available substitutes.

In spite of the fact that many industries producing substitutes began to develop at that time and survived later on their own right in a free market society, technological development in general was arrested because of the difficulty of renovating plants and machinery (licenses were required for the construction or renovation of industrial plants). Finally, costs of production in Italy diverged from those in other countries partly for the technological reasons mentioned above and partly because domestic production, protected by import quotas, no longer had to compete on the domestic market with products manufactured abroad, while exports were supported by bounties and subsidies.

After the Ethiopian War, additional reasons for persevering in the new economic course emerged from the so-called "non-intervention" in the Spanish Civil War and the preparations for World War II.

Monetary policy during this period abandoned the deflationary course pursued until 1929 and in part up to 1934. Price supports for agricultural products were adopted, salary increases permitted, and fixed rates for currency exchanges ceased to be a major concern because of the spreading conviction that the laws of the state could replace the laws of economics.

The wholesale price indexes rose from 65 in 1934 to 100 in 1938 and to 104 in 1939. The cost of living indexes behaved in an analogous fashion. Production rose from 80 in 1934 to 100 in 1938 and to 109 in 1939, while employment rose even more: from 71 in 1932, to 75 in 1934, to 100 in 1938, and to 103 in 1939. The national income, however, did not show such a substantial increase: between 1934 and 1935 per capita income regained the level of 1929, proceeding then at a moderate pace up to 3,360 lire in 1939. During these ten turbulent years, per capita income increased therefore by 10 percent. I would like to point out that today, 1958, the index for manufacturing production is more than 100 percent higher than that of 1938, while the per capita income, expressed in 1938 lire, is 4,242, which is 33 percent higher than that of 1938 and 50 percent higher than that of 1934.

The statistics on unemployment also clearly reflect the gen-

Table I. Economic Indexes for Italy
During the Decade 1929–1939

Years	National income in 1938 lire		Indexes of manufacturing production	Indexes of industrial employment	Wholesale price indexes	Cost of living indexes
	Total in millions of lire	Per capita		(1938=100)		
1929	124,621	3,079	90	90	100	102
1930	116,024	2,845	85	88	90	99
1931	116,019	2,823	77	80	78	90
1932	120,575	2,916	77	71	73	87
1933	119,369	2,868	82	72	67	82
1934	118,523	1,829	80	75	65	78
1935	129,672	3,075	86	85	72	79
1936	128,280	3,022	86	86	80	85
1937	137,995	3,228	100	94	94	93
1938	137,877	3,201	100	100	100	100
1939	145,115	3,360	109	103	104	104

eral situation as we have described it. The number of those registered at job placement offices, which rose to about 300,000 in 1929 (having reached this number as a result of the crisis of revaluation from an average of about 110,000 in 1925–1926), increased to over 1,000,000 (with peaks above 1,200,000) on the average for the years 1932–1933, falling to 960,000 in 1934 when the forty-hour week was first introduced, falling further to 740,-000 in 1935 and to 700,000 in 1936 partly as a result of the mobilization for the war in Ethiopia. The number rose to about 710,000–720,000 in the years 1937–1938, dropping then below 700,000 in 1939, partly because of the resumption of production but mostly because of new conscriptions.

We may doubt that these statistics give a true picture of the extent of unemployment in the country. Their reliability is particularly questionable in view of the fact that during this period the task of compiling the statistics was handled by two different agencies (the National Institute for Social Security from 1924 to 1933 and the central offices of the placement agencies after 1933). Furthermore, the failure to publish any such statistics after 1935 makes it extremely difficult to obtain uniform data.

Nevertheless, regardless of how close the data may be to the actual number of unemployed, the trend is quite clear: the crisis created a very serious situation that was subsequently alleviated by the adoption of the forty-hour work week, by conscription, and by the resumption of production.

It should also be mentioned that . . . the demographic circumstances of the period lent themselves to easing the burden of unemployment. The labor market in those years only had to absorb the smaller numbers of those born from 1915 to 1918, the war years. The larger labor force produced by the increased births of the 1920–1925 postwar period reached the labor market from 1938 to 1940 when they were quickly absorbed by the military draft. The failure to achieve a more substantial reduction of unemployment is attributable to the fact that emigration was interrupted. . . .

There is no need to discuss the organization of labor and the course of collective bargaining. . . . I only wish to point out that during this period the labor movement was incapable of pursuing an independent course of action on the question of wages because of the intrinsic nature of the labor movement and its subservience to the political directives of the party. We must nevertheless keep in mind that in the early part of the period in question, which coincided with the crisis, the adverse economic conditions of the country offered no possibility for independent action on the question of wages. When the situation changed, steps were taken to improve wages insofar as political considerations permitted.

But, above all, I must emphasize that the very lack of power to work directly for salary increases encouraged the labor movement to pursue other compensatory goals.

In the first place, the techniques of collective bargaining

were effectively and significantly developed. Labor unions took on the task of regulating minutely detailed aspects of labor relations by introducing new bargaining agencies . . . and expanding the scope of labor contracts.

In the second place, in the subsequent period of economic recovery labor contracts often provided more extensive social security benefits and expanded the scope of salary compensation. Efforts in this direction were so intense and widespread that they can only be understood . . . as attempts to compensate for the inability to take up the question of wages. Unable for political reasons to deal directly with wages, the unions tried and largely succeeded in introducing and expanding additional and complementary forms of compensation. I refer primarily to family subsidies (introduced in 1934), sick pay (developed from 1928 to 1938), the system of year-end bonuses (1938), paid national holidays (1938), and the extension of severance pay (in varying amounts) to blue-collar workers (the custom of giving it to white-collar workers was already well established in Italy). Aside from the family subsidies, which must be discussed separately, these measures prepared the ground for further developments. As a result, Italy today has a unique salary structure whereby salary, instead of being paid simply according to the duration or the results of the work done, is retained in part by the employer to be disbursed under special circumstances. The firm thus acts as a kind of savings institution for the employees, acting on their behalf by setting aside a part of their salary that is earmarked for special purposes or for the termination of relationships. . . .

As for family subsidies (they were first introduced at the request of the labor unions and subsequently prescribed by law), they had the twofold purpose of adjusting salary to family size (either by taking the place of general salary increases or lessening salary reductions) and acting as incentives to population expansion in conjunction with the official policy of the regime. Special prizes for early marriages and births were therefore added to the family subsidies. The interesting thing that many people, particularly outsiders, may not be aware of is that this policy of population expansion had no noticeable results: in the early years of the Fascist regime (1921–1925) the birthrate in Italy was 29.8 per thousand, while at the end (1936–1940) it was 23.1 per thousand, excluding the war years. Today we are below 18 per thousand.*

(*The author explains that he will approach the crucial question of salary levels by discussing why hourly earnings were often different from the official hourly rates provided by national labor contracts. Another point that must be taken into account in order to understand what the actual earnings of the workers were is the number of hours that they actually worked.—Ed.*)

In the period of deflationary policy, the first reduction of wage rates was stipulated in October 1927 by the various trade unions. The agreements reduced contract wages from a minimum of 10 percent to a maximum of 20 percent. But this was not the only reduction of contract wages. In December 1930, the various workers' and employers' confederations agreed to a wage reduction of 8 percent for blue-collar workers. In an effort to make reductions roughly proportionate to purchasing power, the salaries of white-collar workers were reduced by 8 percent up to a monthly salary of 1,000 lire, and by 10 percent for the exceeding amount. A further reduction of 7 percent, which was also negotiated by the confederations, occurred in May 1934. The percentages of wage rate reductions were applied in each instance to the preceding rates so that their effect was cumulative.

If we look at the figures for hourly earnings shown in Table II (as in the case of Table I, I have retained the base of the original sources), we will see that they not only reflect the total reduction of approximately 16 percent that resulted from the two separate reductions introduced between 1928 and 1934, but that they also indicate the downward course of earnings in the intervals between these particular reductions. It has already been ob-

* The slight increase in the birthrate in the years 1938–1940 was due to the fact that the wave of postwar babies was reaching the age of reproduction.

served that the trend in earnings tends to accelerate and emphasize that in rates. It should be remembered that during that period the practice prevailed (ineffectively opposed by the labor unions) whereby firms fired their workers in order either to rehire them at the minimum hourly wage whenever they had risen above it, or rehire them at a lower grade. All this may help to explain why wage losses exceeded the officially negotiated reductions.

But, as we have already stated, the overall earnings of the workers also varied according to the number of hours worked. During the crisis, from 1929 to the end of 1934, the system of working short time was widely adopted because firms preferred to keep the firing of personnel to a minimum by putting their employees on a reduced schedule. We can see from Table III that the average monthly time schedules of industrial workers were reduced from 182 hours in 1929 to 172 hours in 1934. As a

Table II. Indexes of Nominal and Real Earnings for Industrial Workers

	(1928=100)				
Years	Indexes of hourly earnings	Indexes of monthly earnings	Cost of living index	Index of real earnings hourly	monthly
1929	99.5	100.6	101.6	97.9	99.0
1930	98.6	95.8	98.4	100.2	97.4
1931	92.9	87.7	88.9	104.5	98.7
1932	91.0	84.9	84.9	107.1	100.0
1933	88.6	85.6	81.4	108.8	105.1
1934	85.7	81.9	77.2	111.0	106.1
1935	84.3	74.5	78.3	107.6	95.1
1936	89.5	78.1	84.2	106.3	92.7
1937	100.5	91.0	92.2	109.0	98.7
1938	107.6	95.1	99.3	108.3	95.8
1939	117.8	104.6	103.7	113.4	100.8

Table III. Average Monthly Hours by Industrial Workers

Years	Hours	Years	Hours
1929	182	1935	159
1930	175	1936	157
1931	170	1937	163
1932	168	1938	159
1933	174	1939	160
1934	172		

result, the index of monthly earnings for these same workers was nearly 20 percent lower in 1934 than in 1929.

We should also take into account the fact that in the meantime the cost of living was getting correspondingly lower. If we compare the indexes of nominal earnings with the cost of living indexes having the same base, we see that the buying power of hourly earnings was somewhat higher in 1934 than in 1929, while, because of reductions in the number of hours actually worked, the buying power of monthly earnings was practically the same (statistical variations in the order of 3 percent or 5 per cent cannot be considered meaningful).

An important decision was taken in Italy in 1934 in connection with working hours: an agreement reached in October of that year by the syndical confederations tentatively established the forty-hour work week, subsequently confirmed by legislative order. This provision did not aim at improving the living conditions of employed workers . . . but rather at reducing unemployment. The reduction in the work schedule was not accompanied by an increase in hourly rates. The final result was a further drop in monthly earnings, which was partially compensated for by the simultaneous introduction of family subsidies. As the work hours dropped, employment rose somewhat (as may be seen from Table I), while average monthly earnings (excluding family subsidies) declined and buying power fell decisively below the 1928 level.

We may mention at this point that Italy then took the initiative to propose to the International Labor Organization an international agreement to reduce the working hours based on the same criteria and for the same goals. In spite of the fact that, for various reasons, neither the employers' nor the workers' associations in the various countries belonging to ILO supported it very strongly, an international agreement was actually concluded (No. 47, 1935). It was not, however, ratified by any country, including Italy. There were several reasons for the failure to ratify the forty-hour agreement by the very nation that had proposed it. The main one, however, seems to be that in the meantime the political and economic situation had changed significantly as a result of the outbreak of military hostilities in Ethiopia and their already mentioned repercussions on the economic policy of the country. The number of working hours kept rising in those industries that were involved in supplying the military. If this did not appreciably influence the averages given in Table III, it was because the number of working hours dropped further in those industries that suffered the most from the economic sanctions and from the policy of autarky.

In the meantime, salaries were rising. Agreements stipulated by the trade organizations between July 1936 and February 1937 increased salary rates by amounts varying from 4 percent in the textile industries to 11 percent in the machine industries. Taking into account the number of workers in the various sectors, the average increase turned out to be around 10 percent. A later increase was decided on in May 1937, this time by contract between the confederations. The increases were of 10 percent for those industries that had had increases above 10 percent by the previous agreements, 11 percent for those that had had increases from 9 percent to 10 percent, and 12 percent for those that had had lower increases. This agreement, therefore, tried to equalize the salaries resulting from the earlier discriminatory increases. A new across-the-board increase of 10 percent came in March

1939 with only a few exceptions (for instance, in the public services where prices were frozen, the increase was only 8 percent). On the whole, these cumulative increases brought up salary rates by about 34 percent in the period 1936–1939.

The increase in hourly earnings was greater. The index rises from 84.3 in 1935 to 117.6 in 1939. The increase of about 40 percent may be due, in addition to the reasons already given, to the fact that employment rose in those industries, like machinery, where salaries were above the average. . . . Average monthly earnings also rose almost proportionally. However, since the cost of living also rose, the buying power of monthly earnings (excluding family subsidies) barely regained the level of 1928. The economic and social policies followed in the whole decade had done nothing more than restore to the Italian workers, on the eve of the new world conflict, their previous standard of living. (*The author goes on to say that in 1958 the purchasing power of contractual wages was 20 percent above that of 1938, minimum salaries were much higher, working hours were about the same or only slightly higher, and it was understood that further reductions in working hours should involve no reduction in earnings.—Ed.*)

Until now we have considered the course of salaries but we must also keep in mind that, in addition to the salaries, there were also those forms of compensation discussed earlier that must be taken into account once again in order to assess their impact on the standard of living of the workers.

I should like to pause once more on the family subsidies, which were originally and still are today in part a form of wages, in spite of the fact (as I myself would argue) that they are closely connected to the system of social security. (*See Vannutelli's essay "Allocations familiales et salaires," in* Journées internationales d'études sur les prestations familiales [*Bruxelles, 1952*].—*Ed.*) Family subsidies were introduced in Italy by collective bargaining in October 1934 in conjunction with the introduction of the forty-hour week to compensate for the reduction in weekly earnings for those workers with family responsibilities. The practice of granting family subsidies remained and was consolidated as a substitute for wage increases even after the system of reduced hours was practically abandoned. The subsidies, which at the beginning were granted only after the birth of a second child, were soon extended to cover the first child (1935) and were also granted to white-collar as well as blue-collar workers. Family subsidies were then used in 1939 to circumvent a salary freeze that had been legislated in conjunction with the outbreak of military hostilities in Europe. The freeze was circumvented not only by increasing by 50 percent the amount of subsidies for children, but also by introducing a subsidy for the wife (and for the parents) as a means of supplementing the income of workers with a family to support regardless of the size of the family. Additional subsidy increases, granted in April and June 1941, doubled the benefits.

In addition to the family subsidies, there were many achievements in various areas of social security. . . . Improvements were registered in the area of health insurance, introduced first in 1928 by collective bargaining and legislated only in 1943. Labor contracts provided health insurance for professional workers by geographical district, thus improving on what some large firms had already begun to do on their own by establishing company insurance programs. We must keep in mind, however, that this insurance provided economic aid (equal to 50 percent of the salary) only to workers who were absent from work because of illness. It was only later, in 1939, that it was extended to provide medical care (doctor's visits and drugs, limited however to the generic variety and excluding the so-called proprietary drugs), and it was later still, in 1940, that medical assistance was extended to members of the family.

In the traditional areas of social insurance, the only innovation was the introduction in 1927 of insurance against tuberculosis. Total payments under unemployment insurance did increase, however, because of the growing number of unemployed workers. As for disability and old age insurance, a substantial reform occurred only in 1939 (at the very end of the period that we are considering) when the eligibility age was lowered (with payments being also lowered accordingly) and the benefits were made payable to the survivors.

There is no better way of estimating the value of the benefits conferred by social security than to look at the incidence of its costs on the average salary. Leaving aside the details of costs and administration, we must relate the burden of contribution to the sum of the benefits enjoyed or accruing to the workers. In 1929, employers contributed an amount equal to 5.75 percent of the average salary of Italian industrial workers toward the cost of social insurance, health insurance, and accident insurance. The workers contributed 3.25 percent of their salary as their share of the cost of social and health insurance. The first substantial increase in the cost of social insurance followed the adoption of family subsidies in 1934 when the employers' share rose to 10 percent and the workers' to 4.5 percent. At the end of 1939, following the reform of social security, the expansion of medical assistance, and the first massive increase in family subsidies, the quotas borne by employers and workers were 19.50 percent and 8.30 percent respectively. The most substantial increases in costs came later, when family subsidies were increased even further during the war and employers were required to take over the contributions that they had previously withheld from the workers' salaries. Today, 1958, the employers contribute a sum approximately equal to 45 percent of the paid salary while the workers contribute 4 percent.

On the whole, although social legislation was exceptionally broad during that period, the practical and financial benefits were much more modest. Contrary to the exaggerated claims of those who argued that the regime was ahead of everyone else, its achievements in the field of social insurance were considerably behind those in other countries, particularly in the British Commonwealth. But most important, what was missing was the concept (already accepted elsewhere) of establishing a comprehensive system of social insurance. The various mechanisms for insurance and assistance were set up on different principles, different rules, and administered by separate agencies, thereby creating the technical and legal necessity for a reform of social security which, unfortunately, still has not been enacted in Italy. All of which may come as a surprise if we stop to think that the regime had the means, had it only thought of it, to capture the imagination and the support of the working masses by establishing a more comprehensive and systematic network of salary supplements, as is clearly envisaged today . . . by those who carry the principle of the welfare state to its ultimate conclusions.

The statistics on consumption for the Italian population as a whole indicate clearly and conclusively the repercussions of the policies discussed above on the standard of living. (*The following figures are drawn from two publications issued by the* Instituto Centrale di Statistica, Compendio statistico 1956, *and* Indagine statistica sullo sviluppo del reddito nazionale dell'Italia dal 1861 al 1956 [*Rome, 1957*].—*Ed.*):

1. The consumption of meat (average availability per capita) was approximately 20 kilograms annually in 1921–1925, rose to almost 22 kilograms in 1926–1930, only to drop below 20 kilograms in 1936–1939 (today, after an even greater reduction as a result of the war, it has barely reached the same level).
2. The consumption of sugar was about 8.5 kilograms per person in 1926–1930, and fell to less than 8 kilograms in 1930–1939 (today we exceed 16 kilograms).
3. The average daily consumption of fats was close to 70 grams per person in 1926–1930, and fell to almost 60 grams in 1930–1939 (today we have barely surpassed that level).
4. The consumption of carbohydrates was about 450 grams daily per person in 1926–1930, and fell to about 400 grams in 1934–1936 (today we are once again in the vicinity of 450 grams).
5. The daily calorie intake was about 2,800 in 1926–1930, and fell to about 2,600–2,700 in 1936–1940. Today, after the subsequent reductions resulting from the war, we have barely sur-

passed 2,700 (but, as is well known, the significance of the calorie intake figure is open to doubt).

6. Of the population's total consumption, the proportion destined for food fell from 49.5 percent (1925–1930) to 45.5 percent (1936–1940), while the proportion destined for other goods and services increased from 30.4 percent to 34.1 percent (according to a well-known law of economics, this is a sure sign of a qualitative improvement of consumption and of a better standard of living). Today, 1958, our prospects have improved significantly, the amount of consumption destined for food being 46.3 percent and that destined for other goods and services being 39.8 percent. The difference between the percentages given above and 100 is the percentage spent on alcohol, tobacco, and housing.

7. The total expenditure for private per capita consumption (all figures are based on the purchasing power of the lira in 1938), which was 2,545 lire annually in 1926–1930, fell to 2,479 lire in 1931–1935, rising only to 2,522 lire in 1936–1940. Today, 1958, still on the basis of 1938 lire, private per capita consumption reaches 3,345 lire annually.

All this makes it clear that the 1929–1939 decade did not witness a substantial improvement in the standard of living of the Italian people, a conclusion that was also implicit in the previously cited figures on national income and wages.

■

For more than ten years, in Italy as in most other economically developed or developing countries, we have been experiencing a period of high prosperity. We almost take for granted the steady and often rapid rise of all the indexes measuring economic growth such as national income, employment, salaries, and perhaps even prices! Those of us who are used to dealing with statistics and who want to measure the rate of progress more accurately have even had to adopt the method of calculating the annual rate of growth instead of using a simple number that relates to a base year. Some of us living in this climate of progress may be astonished to learn that the economy was stagnant for more than a decade.

This may simply be one of those realizations that astonish only the so-called "man in the street" and that come as no surprise to anyone who looks at current events in historical perspective. But there is no doubt, in my opinion, that one of the fundamental differences between the state of mind and daily behavior of today's population, with specific reference to Italy, and the attitude and behavior of the people in 1929–1939 is precisely this: that while today we live in progress, work for progress, and wait for progress, living, working, and waiting in that period were more for preservation than for progress.

I am very much aware of the danger involved in this as in all generalizations, and I wish to caution you that the observations which I make in the attempt to capture the prevailing mood of the working population in Italy at the time transcend the particular events and circumstances that are still largely controversial. But there is no doubt that during that period the fear of unemployment, the generally stagnant state of the economy, and the pressure of party discipline on the conscience and behavior of individuals, weakened the spirit of initiative, repressed ambition, and often suffocated the will to act.

There were, as I have already mentioned, some exceptions to this attitude: scientific research, its practical applications, and industrialization continued along their established direction. Under the protective cover of the policy of autarky there were some important developments in machinery and chemicals, communications, and in the infrastructures of business and production. But it is nevertheless true that even with autarky (or, rather, precisely because of autarky), industrial production did not develop as rapidly as it did in other countries. In fact, instead of pursuing a program of more rapid industrialization, the regime boasted that it was promoting a romantic "return to the soil" and hindered urbanization, ignoring that economic and social progress consists of reducing the number of people involved in primary activities and proportionately increasing the number engaged in tertiary activities.

Nor can we forget that, precisely because of autarky and the fear of unemployment, technological progress was arrested in many sectors of the economy because industry lacked the incentive to lower costs and reduce manual labor. Public works projects were often awarded on the condition that certain types of new machinery not be employed in order to provide jobs for workers. Basically, the concept of productivity was not part of the autarkic mentality of fascism. Productivity in Italy increased an average 3.8 percent annually in 1901–1925, 0.8 percent in 1925–1940, and 3.5 percent in 1940–1952.*

In such a situation, there could be no widespread sense of progress, evolution, and free enterprise. There could only be a desire to preserve acquired positions, to retain one's job, and not to rock the boat.

But since there were then, as there always are, spiritual cravings, ambitions, and expectations that could not be denied, fascism tried to compensate for the absence of competitive impulses by fostering the illusion, particularly among the young, that Italy was at the forefront in every field of human endeavor. By so doing, it propagated some gross misconceptions, such as presuming to be ahead of other countries in social programs, industrial progress, transportation, economic theory, and political institutions. Most of all, it encouraged the desire for conquest that brought us to the Ethiopian adventure (a frightful historical and political error whereby we committed ourselves to an anachronistic colonial policy with a delay of nearly one hundred years behind the other powers) and eventually to the world war whose wounds have barely healed.

I thus conclude my rapid survey of living conditions among Italian workers in the period 1929–1939. This survey has glossed over many aspects of the question and, in certain respects, has

---

* These figures are taken from Colin Clark, *"Lo sviluppo dell'economia italiana,"* Moneta e Credito, vol. VII (1954)—*Ed.*

been deliberately polemical because, in order to generate debate, one must say things that invite disagreement. I realize that some of my historical perspectives are one-sided and some of my categorical assertions require closer scrutiny and qualification.

My hope is that this gathering will either agree with or, if necessary, rectify the following conclusions that are based on a comparison of income and employment trends in Italy with those in other countries:

1. Italy suffered more than other countries from the repercussions of the world crisis in 1930–1932 because its economy had already been weakened by the preceding crisis of adjustment to the revaluation of the currency.
2. Unlike other countries, Italy could not benefit from the subsequent recovery stimulated by the American New Deal because of the policy of autarky.
3. Consequently, Italy's economic development has lagged behind that of other countries, and this lag has been overcome only in part by the political and economic policies pursued since the war.

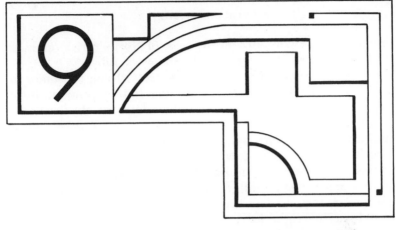

THE ECONOMIC
AND POLITICAL
BACKGROUND
OF FASCIST
IMPERIALISM *

Italy turned to colonialism long before the rise of the Fascist regime. In 1869 a private shipping company from Genoa bought a sparsely populated territory on the Red Sea, which the government subsequently acquired and transformed into the colony of Eritrea in 1890. In 1889 the government also established a protectorate over the entire Benadir coast on the Indian Ocean and gradually consolidated its hold over it until it eventually became Italian Somaliland. Finally, in 1911–1912 Italy seized from Turkey the adjacent regions of Cy-

* From Enzo Santarelli, *Storia del movimento e del regime fascista* (Rome: Editori Riuniti, 1967), II, pp. 161–171; 221–230. By permission of the publisher.

renaica and Tripolitania on the coast of North Africa opposite Sicily and joined them to form the colony of Libya.

Italy's colonial drive met unexpectedly strong resistance in 1896 when the Ethiopians arrested the Italian penetration of their country by defeating an Italian force at the battle of Adowa. Although it was a major setback for a country of limited military resources such as Italy, it was the psychological rather than the military consequences of the defeat that had the most lasting and shattering impact on Italian society. The battle of Adowa precipitated a bitter political controversy at home where the government was attacked from the left for being imperialistic and from the right for failing to take the necessary steps to avenge the national honor. Adowa remained a sensitive political issue for years to come, mostly because a vocal minority of disappointed nationalists kept its memory alive and used it to discredit the entire system of liberal politics. According to these nationalists, political liberalism meant divisiveness at home, indecisiveness in government, and timidity in foreign affairs.

Alienated nationalists thus anticipated by many years the Fascist critique of liberalism. When fascism came to power, it found a colonial tradition, a sense of frustration, and an anti-liberal rhetoric that helped to legitimize and popularize Fascist imperialism. The Fascists boasted that they had finally given the country the kind of determined and energetic leadership that could fulfill Italy's thwarted colonial mission. The Fascist attack on Ethiopia in October 1935 was therefore perceived in Italy as the logical culmination of a historical trend. There is little doubt that when Mussolini announced on May 9, 1936, that the Ethiopian capital had fallen and called upon the Italian people to "greet after an absence of fifteen centuries the reappearance of the Empire over the fateful hills of Rome," Mussolini and fascism had reached the apogee of power and popularity in Italy.

In the following selection, the Marxist historian Enzo Santarelli recognizes that the existence of traditional colonial aspirations broadened the appeal of the war beyond Fascist circles. At the same time, he also argues that the Ethiopian war was much more than an anachronistic recrudescence of old-fashioned colonialism. Going further, he even claims that there was more behind it than Mussolini's undeniable desire to increase his personal prestige with a spectacular show of force. More fundamentally, fascism sought in Ethiopia a solution to problems which could not be resolved domestically. It was not simply a question of diverting public attention from the pressing economic problems of the moment. The war in Ethiopia, according to Santarelli, was an effort to restore a sense of direction and credibility to a regime that had reached a political impasse.

Looking at the international situation, Santarelli sees the Fascist attack on Ethiopia as an extreme instance of the general tendency of capitalist societies in the 1930's to become more exclusivist and expansionist. Even in his treatment of international diplomacy, Santarelli is on the lookout for connections between domestic developments and foreign policy. Although the approach is by no means novel, it is one that relatively few diplomatic historians follow. Their reluctance is perhaps due to the fact that documents explicitly linking domestic and foreign policy decisions are scarce. Possible relationships are sometimes suggested by the fact that outwardly unrelated developments occur in close sequence or are inferred by a highly selective and interpretative use of the available evidence. By its very nature, therefore, the process raises certain questions that the reader ought to keep in mind. When the connections between domestic and foreign policy are not explicitly documented, how can we separate fact from conjecture? What is the evidence that might indicate that political and business leaders agreed on the desirability of pursuing an aggressive policy of political expansionism? Does the fact that certain interest groups gained economically from the consolidation of a war economy necessarily mean that they actively promoted it? Were private interests enthusiastic about Fascist imperialism or did they simply make the best of policies that were not entirely to their liking? These questions are not intended to discredit the idea that there are indeed important links between domestic considerations and foreign policy. They are suggested simply to emphasize the need for caution and for continued effort to understand all aspects of foreign policy.

■

Mussolini turned to Africa hoping to find there the opportunity for a show of force that would impress the world and increase the international prestige of Italy and fascism. Concerned as he was with scoring a quick victory at the first opportunity, he envisaged only the demagogic aspect of establishing an empire and strengthening Italy's presence in Africa. Marshal Enrico Caviglia noticed this attitude and, after the campaign had been concluded, jotted down in his diary that, while the diplomatic, economic, and financial preparations had been neglected, the propaganda buildup had been exaggerated to the point that it had been self-defeating. Nevertheless, in spite of Mussolini's indifference, it was precisely the existence of a colonial tradition that enabled him to win the support of important groups. Once again, the conservative sectors of Italian society misunderstood the nature and objectives of fascism, not because they were naïve but perhaps because they sensed that their interests coincided with those of fascism. Thus, the king and the dynasty were completely won over to the new course. Victor Emmanuel, who during his first trip to Eritrea in September 1932 had manifested his opposition to the idea of a conflict with Ethiopia, changed his mind after having visited Somaliland near the end of 1934. He obviously "let himself go with the current." [1] Career officers, colonial governors, officials in the ministry of foreign affairs, former Nationalists who were still politically active, journalists and propagandists, were also generally favorable to the idea of colonial expansion. The *mal d'Africa* (lure of Africa), which fascism had revived and turned into a propaganda device, certainly had its traditional and dynastic aspects. We shall soon see, however, that in addition to the dynasty the most authoritative circles among the Italian clergy also developed an interest in colonial expansion in Africa.

In spite of its *fin-de-siècle* overtones, the Ethiopian adventure sponsored and conducted by fascism grew out of specific circumstances. Italy was caught in the squeeze of the European crisis, with Germany intent on reestablishing its presence in central and eastern Europe (the problem of the *Anschluss* being the obvious consequence of that new tendency) and England attempting to preserve the existing balance of power in the Mediterranean, its economic position on African markets, and free access to its empire.

Italy's conflict with Ethiopia thus developed into a war at a time when the great imperialist powers were already beginning to clash. The restlessness of Japan, who had already trespassed against China, and of Germany, whose eyes were on Austria, were already evident. In 1935 Ethiopia was no longer the sealed, victorious country that it had been in 1896; it was under pressure and exposed to infiltration from various quarters. It was now trying to circumvent the threat of territorial conquest from Italy by granting economic concessions and concluding diplomatic agreements with other countries.

The years 1930–1934 were critical ones for Italy. Both at home and abroad, fascism was seeking political solutions that would fulfill the regime's promises and solve the economic problems of the country. At home, it was in the process of developing new social and administrative institutions, establishing a balance between Mussolini's personal power and that of the party, and formulating new doctrines. The policy of population expansion, nationalist ambitions, the first indications of a racist policy, the advocacy by what was still a small, extremist minority of an imperialist mission, all begin to point to a possible solution in Africa. As early as 1931, with unemployment high in the country, representatives in the Chamber began to suggest that fascism could fulfill its mission and solve the economic crisis by settling people in Africa outside the territories of the existing colonies. A few writers took up the notion that the regime could consolidate itself by setting up a colonial empire. The policies pursued in oversea territories, the heritage left behind by Italian explorers, the Catholic tradition of missionary work, the ideology of nationalism, all began to converge toward the same objective. Interest in colonial affairs revived, with a marked preference for African questions. The earlier tendency to think mostly in terms of commercial expansion toward the countries of the eastern Mediterranean declined noticeably. The first symposium on colonial studies, held in Florence in 1931, was an important landmark with its repeated references to the colonial achievements of fascism, topped by the reconquest of Libya, whose hinterland Italy had lost effective control of during World War I, and the economic development of Somaliland.[2] Developments in the great colonial empires were analyzed with an increasingly pro-Italian bias. Fascism exerted a clear-cut, dominant influence. A vast network of organizations, agencies, and institutions worked steadily on public opinion and succeeded in stimulating considerable popular interest in the Italian parts of Africa, meaning not only Libya, Eritrea, and Somaliland, but also those parts of Africa that had been part of the Roman empire, had adopted Christianity, and had been unsuccessfully claimed by Italy after its unification (particularly French Tunisia). That was the Africa where Fascist Italy wanted to reassert itself. The old idea of radically revising the colonial map, first raised by fascism in its early days, gained more popularity. The fact that the French and British colonial empires were in a state of crisis seemed to strengthen Italian aspirations. This revival of colonial ambitions was anachronistic, going as it did against the historical trend. At the same time, however, the gains of fascism in Europe, the emergence of economic nationalism everywhere, and the intensification of trade rivalries throughout the world, made the policies, claims, and aspirations of Fascist Italy seem more credible. A racist tone and orientation emerged occasionally before the Ethiopian venture got under way by linking together the two policies of population expansion and colonialism, as had been done earlier by Enrico Corradini, a leading spokesman for Italian nationalism around the turn of the century.[3]

Interest in Ethiopia increased in 1933–1934 because of general economic and political developments within Italy. The Fascist regime and the industrial syndicates decided in 1933 that the best way to reduce unemployment was to shorten the work week to forty hours without adjusting hourly rates of compensation. The "Fascist Saturday," an innovation similar to the "English Saturday" already adopted by the Labour party, was introduced concurrently to take up the hours of forced unemployment. Salaries thus suffered a general reduction, which in turn enabled employers to reorganize production and face the sluggish market situation. By that time, unemployment had reached nearly one million, the highest in a long time, and the indexes of production and profits reflected the gravity of the national economic plight.

It was at that point that the political and business leadership turned to Ethiopia and joined the worldwide race to reach new markets and sources of raw materials. The United States and its capitalist groups were oriented toward South America and beyond (Henry Ford embarked on a vast project to monopolize the production of natural rubber by acquiring huge tracts of land in Brazil and Malaysia). Japan turned to the northern regions of the Republic of China in order to consolidate its own colonization of Manchuria and exploit their natural resources.

Ethiopia was variously affected by the race to gain control of new sources of raw materials and markets, which was designed to artificially stimulate the domestic economies of the colonial powers. Italy was actually a latecomer in this respect. It was preceded by Great Britain, Japan, and the United States. Once in the race, it was hampered by the traditional suspicion of the government in Addis Abeba, reinforced at that time by the new policies of Emperor Haile Selassie. A Japanese commercial delegation, which included representatives of the most powerful Japanese *zaibatsu*, or financiers, the Mitsui family, visited Ethiopia in 1932. Political and economic ties between Japan and Ethiopia were established in 1933–1934. In 1933 the American firm of J. G. Wite also sent representatives in the region of Lake Tana. Addis Abeba invited England to negotiate concessions in the Lake Tana region in 1935. Almost simultaneously, a Swiss firm was authorized to build a road from the Upper Sudan to Addis

Abeba. An Anglo-American oil trust was authorized in the summer of that same year to drill for oil and exploit deposits in large areas.[4] It became urgent once again to take up the old question of the waters of Lake Tana which, being one of the sources of the Blue Nile, affect the cultivation of cotton throughout the Sudan and Egypt. The question had been discussed by London and Addis Abeba in 1902 and in 1919 and 1925 the Italian government had recognized it as being of special interest to the English. It was now complicated by the arrival on the scene of American and Japanese financial interests (a Japanese society to study Ethiopian problems was set up in 1934). The issue was who would control western Ethiopia, with Italy trying to gain the objective by constructing railroad lines in Upper Eritrea and extending them in recent years almost to the border with Sudan. It was a crucial contest whose outcome would affect Ethiopia's capacity to play a role in the political and economic affairs of the African continent. Rivalries were intensified by the existence of plans for investment and expansion, which, while they seldom materialized, led nevertheless to sharp and bitter confrontations.

Italian interest groups took steps . . . to oppose outside influences and strengthen their own positions. The object was to gain control of land suitable for settlement, cotton fields, mineral resources, roads, and waterways. Also part of the picture were unemployment and population growth, foreign competition and expansion of production, particularly in view of the fact that trade with Africa seemed to be on the rise. The preparations for the undertaking in Africa and the gigantic expedition overseas quickly transformed the economic situation at home (with an army of 400,000 soldiers and 100,000 workers it was the largest colonial expedition in history). By the summer of 1935 the number of workers unemployed had dropped by 250,000 below what it had been one year before and the trend was still continuing. It was expected that even the soldiers occupying the colony would eventually become workers and settlers. The recruits, at least the "voluntary" recruits of the Militia who were organized in separate units fighting side by side with those of the regular army,

170

were mostly unemployed workers from the south. Industrial profits, which began to recover slowly in 1932–1933, rose substantially as mobilization got under way (eventually about one million men were mobilized at home and in the colonies). Textiles, machinery, heavy industry in general, and food processing began to produce once again at full capacity. The index of metal production went from 72 in 1932 to 106 in 1936, machinery from 70 to 120. Agricultural production received a boost from consumption related to the war. The net profits of business corporations, which in 1931 were less than 0.08 percent of paid-up capital (in 1932 they actually registered a loss of 1.38 percent), rose in 1933 to 2.18 percent. In 1934 they went up to 4.10 percent, in 1935 to 5.74 percent, and in 1936 to 7.28 percent. Industry expanded, more workers were employed, the country was hard at work. New economic problems did develop, but the worst of the crisis was definitely over.

With the economic crisis behind and military operations concluded, certain interest groups turned to the new colonial market with the expectation that it would provide unprecedented opportunities for employment and profits such as the Italian bourgeoisie could never have realized in the parched colonies of the pre-Fascist period or in the trade with Mediterranean countries or eastern Europe. The "riches of Ethiopia" were wildly exaggerated, in precisely the same manner that those of Tripolitania, which lies in the northwestern part of Libya, had been twenty years before when it was conquered by Italy in 1911–1912. Groups like Fiat, shipbuilders, contractors for the vast public works, and capitalist groups interested in obtaining agricultural and mining concessions did go into business and, being conveniently backed until 1940 by the government and public subsidies, made some quick profits out of this Fascist venture. While subsequent developments in Italy and the rest of the world prevented these capitalist groups from consolidating their position in the Italian colonies, commercial, industrial, and agricultural companies were set up after the undertaking was well under way to form a short-lived network of enterprises designed to exploit the new territories and their resources. Unfortunately, the Ethiopian economy could not complement the Italian economy because it also lacked iron and coal. It required more investment capital for equipment, settlement, and the development of mineral, hydroelectric, and agricultural resources than Italy could possibly provide without outside help. For this reason, foreign capital had to be occasionally called in.

In 1933, while the Ethiopian problem was still open to various solutions, Mussolini appointed Count Luigi Orazio Vinci as the new ambassador to Addis Abeba. Vinci was a minor diplomat whose career had developed mostly during the Fascist period. His appointment indicated that the already precarious relations between the two countries were deteriorating further. As far as the Ethiopians were concerned, the recall of the Marquis di Paternò, who represented Italy's old liberal policies, was an alarming development. When Count Vinci presented his credentials, the young emperor Haile Selassie, who had recently come to the throne animated by the desire to reform and innovate and who surrounded himself with western advisers, replied to the formally correct greetings of the Italian ambassador with a stern reminder "of the spirit of friendship happily inaugurated by your predecessors on the basis of the accords of 1928 and confirmed by the League of Nations." Within a short time during 1933 and 1934 the frontier incidents registered by the Italians jumped quickly to seven, while only eight had been counted during the entire five-year period from 1928 to 1933.

There were three problems in particular that prevented good neighborly relations: the ill-defined border with Somaliland . . . which led to the complete Italian occupation between 1925 and 1930 of the territory traditionally assigned to Italy; the failure to construct a highway from the port of Assab in Eritrea to Dessye in Ethiopia with a free trade zone for the Ethiopians at Assab . . . ; and finally, Italy's increasing economic activities in the Ethiopian region of the Tigre, on the border with Eritrea, and Ogaden, on the border with Somaliland. The first sign of the impending conflict came when Ethiopian and Italian troops clashed on December 5, 1934, in the vicinity of Walwal in the Ogaden, located some one hundred kilometers beyond the traditional border with Somaliland but garrisoned for some time by Italian colonial troops. It was simply one of many frontier incidents provoked . . . by local raiders or by the movement of more or less illegal caravans. But the tension created between the two countries by the new political policies of Rome enabled Mussolini to skillfully transform the incident into the pretext for war. Ten days after the engagement at Walwal, the Italian government rejected the Ethiopians' request to submit the dispute to arbitration as provided by the treaty of 1928. It agreed to it later but only in order to gain time and seek a diplomatic accommodation, particularly with France. The maneuver was successful and Ethiopia withdrew its request that the League of Nations should intervene. The Italian government also rejected the idea that an inquest should be held to determine whether or not Walwal was in Somaliland's territory, which after all was the central point of the dispute. The Italian foreign ministry was thus able to prevent recourse to arbitration in spite of the fact that it had agreed to it in principle. It was the tactic of "maneuvered defense followed by a counteroffensive," as described right after the war by General Emilio De Bono, but applied for the time being to diplomatic affairs while Italy was openly going ahead with massive military preparations.[5] (*De Bono was in charge of military operations in Ethiopia until November 16, 1935, when he was replaced by General Pietro Badoglio.—Ed.*)

A close look at the policies that led to the war with Ethiopia reveals the existence of various and uncoordinated considerations both at the domestic and international levels. As far as Italian nationalist aspirations are concerned, there are two separate strains that stand out from the events of 1932–1934 . . . leading to the Walwal incident. On the one hand, we have Mussolini's policy, which could not be transformed into the kind of traditional colonialism based on a compromise solution that would have given Italy a large sphere of economic influence without leading necessarily to territorial conquest. On the other, we have the policy inaugurated by the treaty of 1928 and favored by Raffaele Guariglia and Grandi that aimed at avoiding a disruption of the European balance of power . . . but which was quickly rendered obsolete by the rapid course of events and, most of all, by mounting Fascist pressure. It is interesting to note in this context that, regardless of their practicality or sincerity, the efforts made by the Italian ambassador in Addis Abeba to strengthen Italy's commercial, economic, and political influence were very short-lived. As early as April 1934 the foreign ministry spelled out the limits that could not and should not be exceeded by Italian diplomatic action: "At the moment, our trade with Ethiopia lacks a sound economic basis. For the most part, our goods cannot compete on that market with foreign goods. Large scale ventures in Ethiopia based on concessions, etc., are too risky to attract our private capital, which is already reluctant to travel abroad. We must also take into account that the political climate in Addis Abeba is certainly not favorable for us. . . . Therefore, efforts at economic penetration can only be initiated and paid for by the government. This is the reason that we prefer to work through SANE and SAPIE (*two government agencies operating in East Africa—Ed.*)" Furthermore, the old tariffs dating back to the days of Prime Minister Francesco Crispi were still in force, excluding Ethiopian trade from Eritrea and Somaliland. Both the ministry of foreign affairs and the ministry of colonies were therefore interested in promoting Italy's "offensive penetration" of the various regions of the Ethiopian empire in order to bring about its political disintegration from within.[6] At that point, the situation had become critical. Italian capital, both public and private, lacked the strength and determination to compete within Ethiopia by peaceful means. It chose instead the alternative of conquest, absolute control, open warfare, and colonial exploitation of the resources and territories of Africa. The gist of that policy was expressed in Mussolini's speech on the "historical objectives" of fascism, which he pronounced before the second quinquennial congress of the regime that was held after the diplomatic, military, logistical, and propaganda preparations had begun.

(The author goes on to describe how during 1932 Mussolini took pains to emphasize that Italy's interests were not limited to any specific geographical area. At the same time, he tried to profit from England's precarious diplomatic position and the weakness of the League of Nations. On England's advice, Ethiopia took refuge behind the provisions of the "treaty of friendship and arbitration" concluded by Italy and Ethiopia on August 2, 1928, and of the covenant of the League. The stage was thus being set for the confrontation that would take place when fascism finally resorted to war.—Ed.)

It was against this background that the opponents of fascism closed ranks at the peace congress of Brussels to form a united front of all the revolutionary and democratic forces opposed to Fascist aggression. German revanchism had not yet asserted itself but would soon intensify even against Italy. In 1934, however, it was Mussolini who prevented the annexation of Austria by Nazi Germany by mobilizing Italian divisions on the Austrian border. It was only at the beginning of March 1935 that the government of the Third Reich announced to the European powers that it would no longer observe the restrictions of the peace treaties and would proceed to reestablish an air force and double the size of the German army.

It was at that very moment that the Ethiopian crisis entered its most critical phase and, following the official appeal of the Ethiopian government to the League of Nations, became an international issue. As in the case of the Libyan war in 1911–1912, the war in Ethiopia disrupted the international settlement that had come into being after World War I by initiating a chain reaction leading from one local conflict to another and culminating within a few years in World War II. Although few people in Europe and elsewhere in the world may have realized it at the time, with the opening of hostilities along the Mareb River border between Eritrea and Ethiopia on October 3, 1935, the great powers entered into a new phase of open warfare, of diplomatic skirmishing whose long-run consequences could not be anticipated, armament races, and opposing alliances. After the first violent jolt administered by Japan to the League of Nations and the withdrawal of Nazi Germany from the League, Mussolini gave the League its final blow. The settlement created by the peace treaties of 1919–1920 suffered irreparable damage for the first time. Balance of power relations . . . underwent fundamental change in the very center of the European system. Left without the protective cover and platform of the League of Nations, England drew closer to France, which in turn drew closer to the Soviet Union. Italy found itself drawn into the orbit of the more dynamic imperialism of Nazi Germany. After a lengthy period of preparation, Mussolini had made up his mind with fatal consequences for the future of Europe and world peace.

■

After Ethiopia, the hope (or illusion) of a peaceful return to a policy of stability, consolidation, and work was not realized. The regime entered instead into the critical and descending phase of its parabola. Far from abating, the restlessness that had impelled Mussolini into the African campaign developed into an irresistible attraction for international adventure. The conquest of Ethiopia contributed to making power relations in Europe fluid, unstable, and difficult to readjust. As a result and simultaneously with Italy's initiative, Hitler's Germany denounced the Locarno treaty and occupied the Rhineland. Breaking with the tradition of Weimar Germany, it began to rearm openly and rapidly. It eventually overcame the impasse over Austria by concluding an agreement with Vienna on July 11, 1936, with Mussolini's blessings. As for France, the agreements between Mussolini and Laval, which had given Italy freedom of action, were superseded by international developments and by political changes within the country. (*Mussolini claimed that in January 1935 French Foreign Minister Pierre Laval secretly agreed to give Italy a free hand in Ethiopia. Laval subsequently denied ever having encouraged the Italian government to launch a military invasion of*

Ethiopia. Laval, who became prime minister in May 1935, fell from power in January 1936 and was followed in June by the Popular Front anti-Fascist government of Leon Blum.—Ed.)

Within Italy, the Ethiopian campaign had noticeable repercussions on the economy, the state of public opinion, and the expectations of the political leadership. Its reverberations on the public administration, finances, and production continued to affect all major government decisions long after the war had ended. On March 23, a month and a half before the occupation of Addis Abeba, Mussolini convened the national council of corporations at the Capitol. The League of Nations had voted on October 11, 1935, to impose economic sanctions on Italy in an unsuccessful effort to halt the Italian attack on Ethiopia. Reacting against the imposition of these economic sanctions and to the economic difficulties of the moment, Mussolini outlined a "regulatory plan for the new economy of Italy." The assumption behind the plan was "that the country would inevitably have to face the test of war." It must therefore achieve "maximum economic self-sufficiency in the shortest time possible." It thus became extremely urgent to solve the problem of raw materials (fuel, minerals, textile fibers). All key industries related to "defense" were to be given "special status under state control," particularly in view of the fact that the government had already taken a first step in that direction by reorganizing and expanding the Institute for Industrial Reconstruction. In line with developments elsewhere in Europe, the Chamber of Deputies would be replaced by a chamber of fasces and corporations, which in turn would grow out of the existing national council of corporations. The new economic policy of autarky would carry further earlier efforts to expand the "limited industrial potential" of the country as revealed by the war. Responsibility for the new policy would rest with the corporative institutions already in existence. The policy of autarky thus established both short- and long-term goals for production and became an official goal of the regime, which transcended the immediate requirements of the war in Ethiopia.

The occupation and conquest of Ethiopia and the aspirations and policies of the regime involved the capitalist groups of the country in many ventures that had to be coordinated and directed once the war was over. The national budget had been seriously undermined by war expenditures and by the sanctions. According to the figures and estimates provided by Francesco Coppola D'Anna, the deficit rose from 2,119,000,000 lire in the fiscal year 1934–1935 to 12,687,000,000 in 1935–1936, reaching 16,230,000,000 in 1936–1937. The intensification of financial and economic difficulties and of problems of production and currency exchange against a background of worsening international relations encouraged the regime to begin manipulating monetary exchanges (an undersecretariat for exchanges and currency was set up in December 1935 under the direct supervision of the head of government), turn its attention to the problem of inadequate oil supplies, proceed with the electrification of the railroads, exploit systematically deposits of coal and lignite, manufacture artificial textiles, and expand agricultural production including that of cotton.

The national research council, the banks, industry, government, the corporations, and the press, all jumped on the bandwagon with an enthusiasm and rhetorical outbursts that occasionally bordered on the ridiculous. Although it was not until 1937 that the policy of autarky turned into a full-fledged effort to prepare the national economy for war, the trend was already clear in 1936. Aside from the naïve and exaggerated claims of the regime's propaganda and from several specific technical errors attributable to excessive eagerness and a demagogic mentality, the development of the national economy was vitiated from that point on by the overexpansion of basic, war-related industries, particularly engineering, oil, chemicals, and the hydroelectric sector. Popular consumption of foodstuffs and textiles suffered accordingly. With industry becoming the dominant sector and the expansion of public enterprise favoring the greater concentration of production, the profits of the large financial groups rose rapidly. Following this realignment of interests groups and methods of management, the bonds between political and business groups grew stronger, the economic and corporative bureaucracy expanded, industry moved after 1937 into completely new areas of investment and production often under the control of government agencies, new labor groups appeared, and a general race after quick profits developed both at home and in the colonies. The political process and the state of public opinion were adversely affected as it became clear that Fascist methods were increasingly and hopelessly corrupt. The cost of living rose, the lira was devalued, and unsuccessful efforts were made in July and October 1936 to raise salaries to their pre-war levels.

When the world economy was shaken in 1937 by a new economic crisis emanating once again from the United States and the likelihood of war and armament races increased, fascism and Italian capitalism turned to autarky as a last-ditch effort to face the escalation of international conflicts and resolve by more or less forcible means the weaknesses and contradictions of the system. The growing gap between profits and wages, production and consumption, brought to the surface once again vehement social resentments. Corporativism revealed its inadequacy as a social doctrine, and Mussolini could think of nothing more effective than to raise once again the old diversionary goal of shortening the "social distance" between the various groups of producers. In Mussolini's own words, the "fact of war" became "the basic criterion of public policy within the national economy."

Although the possibility of a general war became stronger as a result of the outbreak of civil war in Spain in July 1936, it would be inaccurate to say that no other alternative existed immediately after the Ethiopian war. The regime wavered between two different courses of action, depending on the opinion that happened to prevail at any given moment and the dissimilar aspirations of various interest groups. Faced by serious social problems made even more urgent by the economic crisis, the government reacted by sending surplus manpower on spectacular but inadequate and risky mass migrations to Libya, Ethiopia, Germany, and Albania. The limited possibilities of the colonies in east Africa and the tensions persisting in the Mediterranean and central Europe exploded the myth that national problems could be solved by encouraging mass settlements outside of Italy. The years immediately following the war in Ethiopia witnessed nevertheless instances of forced migration organized by the state in response to economic pressures. The colonization of the eastern regions of Libya, long in the making but somehow accelerated, intensified, and "democratized" by Italo Balbo, did respond to military requirements in the vicinity of the Egyptian border but also helped to relieve the pressure of landless workers particularly in Emilia and Venetia. About 60,000 Italians settled in Libya from 1937 to 1939, forming there a small "army of rural infantrymen." [7] The undertaking had its spectacular aspects and inspired the social and ideological propaganda of fascism in connection with the "geopolitical" reappraisal of the importance of the *quarta sponda,* Italy's "fourth coastline," as the Libyan coast was often described. . . . and the autarkic orientation of the national economy. But the colonization of Libya (like the gradual revision of the earlier policy of massive settlement in Ethiopia, the opening of new job opportunities for migrating peasants and workers in Germany where industrial production was expanding, or in Albania which in 1938–1939 was being turned into a military base, an economic colony, and a place for settlement) was neither a policy of peace nor of war. It was a halfway measure that reflected the larger ambiguity of the regime's policies in the three-year period 1937–1939 both in the area of domestic and international affairs.

After the success in Africa, Mussolini's diplomacy seemed to be briefly pursuing the possibility of establishing a more favorable balance of power. Fascist foreign policy continued throughout 1936 to waver between England and Germany. The restoration of normal relations was the first objective. The League of Nations took the first step by repealing the sanctions against the government in Rome on July 15. The second objective was to gain recognition of Italian sovereignty over Ethiopia. The first important country to recognize it was Germany, while England and France hesitated instead for a rather long time. Mussolini seemed ready to reach an agreement with England based on the mutual recognition of the two countries' interests in the Mediterranean. At the same time, he continued to pursue his old policies in spite of the fact that the atmosphere had been made more tense by the recent conflict. In the course of an interview with the *Daily Telegraph* at the end of May, Mussolini indicated that he was aware of the still impending dangers: "I urge you to repeat and convey to everyone that Fascist Italy wants peace and will do all in its power to preserve peace. A war in Europe would be disastrous for Europe." Meeting with Austrian Chancellor Kurt von Schuschnigg on June 5, he suggested that Austria seek an understanding with Germany and made it clear that he had no intention of clashing a second time with Hitler.

Hitler by that time was seizing the initiative against the League of Nations and the western powers. Hitler had been very much impressed by the final phase of the Ethiopian war and by Mussolini's determination. . . . With the Rhineland occupied and Italy showing itself ready to yield or at least be conciliatory on the question of Austria, an alliance with Italy could be useful against the western democracies, particularly England. In the meantime, Blum had replaced Laval in France and Mussolini hoped to play on English fears of Germany to conclude an agreement that would give him greater freedom of action in the Mediterranean. This diplomatic game . . . led to the understanding of January 2, 1937, whereby Italy and England agreed to maintain the status quo in the Mediterranean. The British were in a quandary. On the one hand, they regretted the failure of the League's sanctions, but on the other they feared that Germany might rearm and reassert itself too quickly. On July 17, 1937, Chamberlain's government finally decided to reach an understanding with Hitler on the question of naval rearmament.

While the international situation was becoming more complicated and sensitive, some of Mussolini's power began to slip into the hands of new collaborators, particularly of Galeazzo

Ciano who had married the Duce's eldest daughter and, after a brief stint in the ministry of press and propaganda, took over the ministry of foreign affairs on June 6, 1936. Mussolini made several significant changes in his government during the summer and fall of that year. . . . Alessandro Lessona took over the ministry of colonies, Ferruccio Lantini that of corporations, Dino Alfieri that of press and propaganda, and Bottai returned to the government in charge of national education. Finally, party secretary Starace was granted ministerial rank in January 1937. Mussolini thus gave up the colonies and corporations, whose importance was increasing, but retained all the military ministries and the ministry of the interior. . . .

But the most significant innovation was unquestionably the appointment of the young Ciano to the key post of minister of foreign affairs. It pointed first of all to the increasing influence of Mussolini's family entourage on the conduct of public affairs. Until his death in 1931 it had been Arnaldo, Mussolini's younger brother, . . . who had acted as mediator between the Duce, public opinion, and the party; now the young Ciano took over the role of arbitrator between Fascist circles and the *frondeurs,* between Roman society and the head of government, steadily and persistently interfering with questions of internal politics. It is revealing, for instance, that as early as 1934 he should have intervened in favor of Curzio Malaparte who had been interned because of his book *Technique du coup d'etat* (1931) and for having spoken out against Italo Balbo. Meanwhile, the family of Clara Petacci, who was the new mistress and consoling angel of Mussolini, also worked quietly behind the scenes.

To sum up, Mussolini's role in the government began to diminish around the end of 1936 and the beginning of 1937, at least in the area of routine administration. The new foreign minister, with all his vanity, his social connections and family ties, his reputation as the darling of Fascist politics, and in spite of the zeal and intelligence that he brought to his work, was bound to spread confusion within the inner circles of the regime. Mussolini's exalted image as the founder of the empire placed the Duce on a sort of "pedestal" (it was Ciano's word as referred by Cantalupo) where he was removed from most of his collaborators in the government, the party, from the increasingly more infatuated and servile press, and the everyday life of the country. The party was declining as a result of Starace's flamboyant leadership and the loss of meaningful duties as intended and carried out at Mussolini's request. The system simply lacked alternate avenues for development. The dominant mood was one of tired realism and opportunism that stopped short of being revisionist, while marginal, extremist, democratizing, moralizing, and pretentious aspirations smoldered beneath the ashes. The increasing centralization of power stifled the economy and the administration as fascism reached out to every corner of society. Opportunities for reform dwindled even at the legislative level (the only exception was Bottai's reform of the school system in 1938), and the government's efficiency, its capacity to function, and its chain of command were seriously impaired.

Although the regime survived, it began to show signs of internal exhaustion in both its central and peripheral agencies. As it reached out to embrace more, it lost part of its vigor, unity, and political vitality. The dictatorship began to crack and deteriorate. All subsequent "progress" was more nominal than real, quantitative rather than qualitative. The *Gioventù Italiana del Littorio* was established in 1937 by bringing together and coordinating the activities of the various youth organizations, which had a total membership of 6,122,535. In that same year, the ministry of press and propaganda became the ministry of popular culture, which was expected to coordinate all propaganda activities. But it was already apparent, even in government circles, that party leaders were no longer effectively in command. The dictator was losing his grasp, wavering more and more in his decisions, while all around him there was a clash of factions and rival groups that spread moral and political uneasiness throughout the land. Although the presence of Ciano and the new ministers injected new blood in the political leadership, the cream of the younger generation, regardless of whether they were Fascist or anti-Fascist, was beginning to question the basic premises and orientation of the system. The most sensitive people in the government and the party, particularly Ciano and Bottai, felt compelled to take into consideration, or at least to flirt with, the internal critics who were now appearing everywhere within the regime. Even Mussolini's image was somewhat tarnished, although the cult of Mussolini continued.[8]

The entire Fascist movement was affected slowly and gradually as the deadening impact of increased bureaucratization touched all its political and economic structures. The party, which was the backbone of the state and the regime, had to face once again the insoluble problem of defining its role in the nation and its relationship to particular vested interests. Additional confusion resulted from the appearance of competing Fascist groups elsewhere in Europe, particularly in Germany. The revolutionary pretensions of Italian fascism were being put to the test. It now became increasingly urgent to reconcile its promises of social reform with its imperialist practices. The earlier goals of restoring domestic tranquillity and putting the economy in order gave way to a dominant interest in foreign policy and to a rigid but unconvincing military posture that in turn created new problems.

A number of problems came to light soon after the Ethiopian war. Dissension over such issues as the makeup and function of the ruling class, the organization and function of the party, regime, and state, in other words, over the ultimate goals of fascism, became so divisive that it could no longer be contained by the conformist outlook of the party leadership and the government's well-coordinated propaganda. For instance, in May 1936 a young correspondent who had joined the expedition to Ethiopia put his finger on the fundamental and insoluble predicament of fascism, without however really understanding its full seriousness. His analysis was particularly significant because it originated within the regime and the movement. With the war over and the "euphoria" generated by the African conquest dispelled, there was a growing "pensiveness about the problems of the future." The "efficiency of the empire builders" had to be tested. They were not simply faced by the technical problem of forming a class of colonial administrators, or the ideological one of instilling in the people "a feeling of *virtù* in the Roman sense of the word." According to Indro Montanelli, "The Italian people have plunged into this enterprise with magnificent zest. No other people could have made better soldiers. They have not lost their cool when faced by the reality of war. On the contrary, they have embellished it with the poetic spirit of the action squads and have accepted it as a thrilling adventure. They have accepted it like young, wholesome people who can turn even their lack of experience to good advantage as long as they are led by a disciplined ruling class." The most crucial problem of all, that of the ruling class, thus emerged in spite of the ambiguous rhetoric. Behind the immediate issue of the country's relationship with its colony there was also the awareness that the problem was not "simply colonial." [9] In other words, the shortcomings and difficulties of the regime were partly noticeable even in the wake of its greatest triumph. The gap between the leaders of the regime and the people was already growing and would certainly not be narrowed by subsequent developments. The Ethiopian war created problems and aspirations that the regime expressed almost unconsciously by placing the leader on a pedestal, expanding the party membership, extending the role of the bureaucracy throughout the country, subverting every intellectual endeavor, erecting an enormous propaganda machinery piece by piece, and pursuing its nebulous dreams of empire and universality.

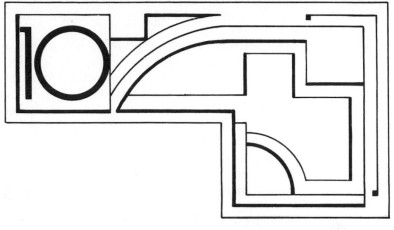

FASCIST
IMPERIALISM
AND RACISM *

Fascism and aggression have become almost synonymous in the minds of those who remember the international events of the 1930's. What is not always remembered is that Fascist expansionism transformed the domestic as well as the international image of fascism. The glorification of war had always been an important element of Fascist ideology, but in the 1930's it became the dominant theme of Fascist propaganda as illustrated by the currency given to such slogans as "war is to man what motherhood is to woman."

War and imperialism were also justified in the 1930's by ref-

* From Luigi Preti, *Impero fascista, africani ed ebrei* (Milan: Mursia, 1968), pp. 87–113. By permission of the publisher.

erence to concepts that had previously played a very marginal role in Italian fascism. Racism is the obvious example. The fact that Italian fascism became racist in the late 1930's is often attributed to the rising influence of German nazism in Italy. That explanation is probably valid insofar as the desire to strengthen the political alliance between the two countries by completing the ideological alignment of fascism and nazism was certainly present. At the same time, Fascist racism was not without domestic roots that were present more in the logic of Fascist imperialism than in the mentality of the Italian people who were not particularly receptive to racist arguments. Once the regime had committed itself to large-scale colonialism in Africa, racism was perceived as a means of promoting nationalist pride and consolidating Italian rule in the colonies.

The following selection discusses the domestic roots of racism with particular reference to the official attitude toward natives in the colonies and Jews at home. The author of the selection is Luigi Preti, who was born in 1914 and is well known in Italy for his contributions as a scholar, novelist, and political figure. His writings include a major study of agrarian struggles in the Po Valley and a documentary novel on the Fascist period, which has been translated into English under the title *Through the Fire of Fascism* (1968). As a prominent Social Democrat and a member of parliament since 1946, Preti has acted at various times as minister of finance, budget, international trade, and bureaucratic reform.

■

RELATIONS BETWEEN ITALIANS AND AFRICANS IN THE COLONIES AFTER THE FOUNDING OF THE EMPIRE

The official publication *Partito e Impero,* issued by the Fascist party in November 1938, clearly illustrates the effect of the conquest of Ethiopia on the imperialist policy of the regime. The pamphlet raised the following question: "What is the role of the party now that, having contributed greatly to the founding of the empire, the empire is in fact a reality?" It gave the answer that "as a political force par excellence, as the custodian of the ideals of the revolution, the party has a permanent duty to create and foster in the generation of today and in those of the future not simply a static acceptance of the empire but, rather, a dynamic imperialist and expansionist mentality."

The official publication went on to say that "Italy cannot yet consider itself successful. . . . We must have the willpower to always strive for new goals, to resist weariness. . . . Whoever gives up will lose. This is the injunction of the party: never to allow the Italian people to rest, to urge them on, to foster among them the urge to expand indefinitely in order to survive, to instill in them a sense of the superiority of our race over the blacks. . . . In short, we must try to give the Italian people an imperialist and racist mentality."

The first official statements on racism were issued in connection with the question of cohabitation between Italians and natives in the colonies. The specific context was Mussolini's policy of differentiating Italian imperialism from that of other countries by promoting massive settlements of Italians in Africa. The regime's colonial designs were in fact spelled out by the party's official publication when it went on to specify that tens of thousands of families would be transferred overseas to the new empire in order "to create in the heart of the African continent a powerful and homogeneous nucleus of whites strong enough to draw those populations within our economic orbit and our Roman and Fascist civilization."

Madamismo was a widespread phenomenon among officers and civil servants in the colonial administrations before the conquest of Ethiopia. The term *madamismo* refers to the cohabitation as man and wife between Italian males and native women who were called *madame*. These relationships often produced offspring who, for the most part, were considered illegitimate. Such cases had never previously preoccupied the government because the small number of Italian residents in itself limited the practice. But when the conquest of Ethiopia opened up to Italy a more densely populated territory and brought to Africa hundreds of thousands of fellow countrymen, *madamismo* became much more prevalent.

Mussolini became so concerned over the prevalence of the phenomenon that he pushed through the decree-law No. 880 of April 19, 1937, which set a penalty of from one to five years imprisonment for those Italian citizens who, either at home or in the colonies, should establish relations of a conjugal nature with the colonial subjects of Italian East Africa—Ethiopia, Eritrea, Somaliland—or with any foreigners whose cultural traditions, customs, and legal concepts were similar to those of the subjects of Italian East Africa. It should be noted that the law penalized only Italians of either sex and not their colored partners. Fascism argued that only the former were responsible because their actions injured the prestige of their race—because, as members of a higher form of civilization, they showed by contracting an illicit relationship that they had forgotten their own duties as citizens.

No ruling was issued against marriages because they were hardly ever contracted. Marriages between Italian citizens of Aryan stock and members of a different race were prohibited only later, in November 1938, when a new decree-law to protect the race was promulgated.

On the other hand, the Fascist regime attributed no importance whatsoever to purely sexual relations between members of different races. Relations of a purely mercenary nature continued to be allowed as demonstrated by the fact that, whenever logistics made it possible, colored troops had at their disposal the same mobile houses of prostitution that were normally reserved for Italian officers. These brothels were supplied regularly with native prostitutes, called *sciarmute,* who were recruited from nearby towns by senior aides with the help of residing colonial officials.

The principle of racial separation was rigidly applied in the case of the offspring. The aim was to prevent the birth of racially mixed children who might pollute the Italian race. It was not simply a question of color, but also of intelligence. Fascism denied that people with brown or black skin could ever acquire the moral qualities or intellectual capacities of whites even if reared in the European tradition for many generations. Racial inferiority was a permanent and unavoidable fact.

Starting on the assumption that blacks were inferior human beings, the Fascist regime obviously denied them the right to have nationalist feelings. Consequently, the brave guerrillas who continued their fight against the Italians in the mountains and forests of Ethiopia and who continued to resist the occupying forces as long as they remained on Ethiopian soil were considered no better than bandits and marauders. Mussolini authorized the unrestricted use of poison gas against them whenever they came together in large military formations. Drastic orders from Rome made it clear that they were to be immediately put to death when captured, but the orders were not always followed.

In short, the native populations of the empire could expect economic benefits and protection under the law, protected perhaps by the innate humanitarianism of the Italian people, as long as they accepted a permanently subordinate status within the empire. But if they tried to assert themselves in any way, then Fascist Italy would strike them down with the greatest severity. A classic illustration of this attitude was the reaction that followed the attempted assassination of the viceroy of Ethiopia, Marshal Rodolfo Graziani, in February 1937. Italian soldiers were ordered to mete out summary justice. Addis Abeba, the Ethiopian capital, was plundered, hundreds of Abyssinians killed, and their huts burned to the ground remorselessly.

In accordance with the Fascist principle of racial separation, the white and black communities of the empire were expected to develop along separate lines in a pattern of racial apartheid similar to the one prevailing today in the Republic of South Africa.

Mussolini and his collaborators even formulated the absurd theory that acts of rebellion on the part of the Ethiopians were due to the failure of Italian residents to firmly abide by the principle of racial separation. They argued that the only reason rebellion was rampant in Ethiopia was that Italians fraternized too

191

much with the Africans and allowed themselves to be treated as the Africans' equals.

It may seem incredible that the leaders of a civilized country could formulate such a theory, but Mussolini's secret speech of October 25, 1938, before the national council of the Fascist party leaves no room for doubt. Referring to the revolt that had broken out among the Amharic populations in the northwestern corner of Ethiopia, Mussolini made the following assertion:

> The lack of racial dignity has had very serious repercussions in the Amhara where it has caused the Amharic people to revolt. The Amharans had no desire to revolt against Italian rule and nothing to gain by doing so. Proof of this is in the fact that during the Ethiopian campaign five thousand well-armed Amharans greeted Comrade Starace . . . with expressions of obedience and enthusiasm. But when they saw that the Italians went about dressed in rags, that they lived in huts, took away their women, etc., they said to themselves "This is not a civilizing race." And the Amharans rebelled because they are the most aristocratic race in Ethiopia. We know these things which the Catholics seem to ignore. (*A reference to the Vatican's condemnation of racism—Ed.*) This is the reason that the racial laws of the empire will be rigorously enforced and anyone who breaks them will be ousted, punished, and jailed. The empire will be preserved only if we impress the natives with the fact that we are clearly and overwhelmingly superior.

Mussolini would not admit . . . that the revolt was motivated by a sense of national dignity and independence. As a latecomer to colonialism, he deluded himself into believing that such feelings did not exist in the underdeveloped countries.

Fascism was so strongly committed to the separation of the white and black races in the colonies that it simply could not understand that it was aiming at an absurd and almost unprecedented goal. The powers that had previously established colonies outside of Europe had adopted different policies. Where they had found favorable climatic conditions and sparse native populations, as in North America, Australia, New Zealand, Argentina, Siberia, etc., they had established permanent white communities.

192

Where the colonial powers had found instead densely populated territories, as in India and other Asian countries and in most parts of Africa, they had limited themselves to establishing colonies for exploitation, moving into the occupied territories only small elites of officials, soldiers, and business representatives.

It is true that in many parts of Latin America, and later in Algeria, the colonial powers had resettled large numbers of Europeans in spite of the fact that the large native populations made it unlikely that these territories could ever become white nations. But in these areas the colonizers had also understood that racial separation was impractical and that racial fusion, or at least the assimilation of the natives, was necessary (the colonization of Algeria constitutes nevertheless one of the most deplorable episodes of French history). Fascism proposed instead a colonial policy that the European states had always judged impractical. Such a policy was also diametrically opposed to that of ancient Rome, which the Fascists wanted to emulate but which had actually practiced a policy of assimilation rather than discrimination. . . .

Having become imperial, Fascist Italy also had to develop an appropriate policy for its Arab-speaking African colony of Libya. This large desert land, populated by slightly more than one million natives, did not lend itself to large-scale settlement. Mussolini and other Fascist leaders believed nevertheless that by settling there a large Italian population they would bind the so-called *quarta sponda* more securely to the motherland, making it a more secure base for Italian expansion in the Mediterranean.

Plans were therefore prepared to settle thousands of families in selected areas of Tripolitania and Cyrenaica on land wrested from the desert with great effort and tremendous cost. Villages and farmhouses were built, roads opened, wells dug, farm boundaries drawn, and tools and livestock readied to welcome Italian workers.

At its meeting of October 26, 1938, the Fascist Grand Council sent its solemn greetings to twenty thousand colonists who in three days were to sail for Libya where they would carry "the

193

will to work of the Fascist nation to the new provinces of the *quarta sponda*." This army of workers consisted of almost two thousand families recruited from thirty-six provinces by the office for internal migration and selected with fairly rigorous criteria. In view of the expected difficulties of settlement, preference was given to small landowners and sharecroppers. This first spectacular migration was followed by other "expeditions" of Italian settlers.

While he was preparing this program for colonization, which certainly could not please the Arabs in Libya, Mussolini also conceived the idea of posing as the protector and defender of the Moslem nations bordering on the Mediterranean. This project was behind his theatrical voyage to Libya in 1937. He went to Libya in March of that year to inaugurate one of the most gigantic and costly projects of the regime: the shoreline road that ran for almost two thousand kilometers from the Tunisian to the Egyptian border and was named Balbia after the dynamic governor Italo Balbo. During his stay the Duce struck poses worthy of a Roman emperor in a setting of false splendor and make-believe. The imperial ceremonies reached a climax on March 18 when, in the presence of two thousand native cavalrymen, some Arab dignitaries presented him with a "Sword of Islam" that had been made in Florence.

The exaggerated theatricality of the ceremony was documented in the official account, which relates how the Duce, followed by a huge retinue, crossed the whole oasis on horseback until he reached the clearing in front of the castle of Tripoli where he harangued the crowd. After having thanked the Libyans for the sword, which he promised to preserve in Rome "among the dearest souvenirs of his life," and after having praised them for their deep loyalty to Italy during the Ethiopian war, the equestrian orator (did Roman emperors also speak on horseback?) declared emphatically: "After these demonstrations, Fascist Italy wants to assure the Moslem populations of Libya and Ethiopia that it will provide peace, justice, prosperity, respect for the laws of the Prophet, and also wishes to demonstrate with its legislation its solicitude for your better future."

Evidently the dictator did not understand that it was impossible to carry out two contradictory policies at the same time. He could not be a paternal guardian to Moslems living in Italian territories and the friend and protector of the "Moslems of the entire world" (almost implying thereby that the Moslems had neither dignity nor national consciousness) and at the same time assert that the Italian race was superior and prohibit "mixing" with subjects in the colonies. Only a European who promised them independence and equal rights had any possibility of becoming popular in the Moslem world, but that was far from the intentions of Mussolini and the Fascists.

In practice, the mountain gave birth to the mouse. The laws that had been announced with so much fanfare in the speech of March 1937 came late and reflected a petty discriminatory mentality that was perfectly in tune with the exasperated nationalism and puffed-up imperialism of the Fascist regime. On October 26, 1938, the Grand Council solemnly proclaimed that Libya would become an integral part of the national territory. A decree-law was promulgated on January 9, 1939, to implement this decision. It stated that the northern provinces of Libya were an integral part of the kingdom and granted "special Italian citizenship" to their inhabitants. The very title of the law revealed that what was being granted was not full-fledged citizenship but, rather, a form of second-class citizenship that, being based on the principle of discrimination, left the Libyans in their former subject status.

Some civil and political rights had already been granted to the Libyans by a law of December 1934, which guaranteed them individual freedom, the inviolability of home and property, the right to compete for civil and military appointments, and the right to pursue a profession of their own choice within the colony.

In addition to granting special Italian citizenship to the Libyans, the law of January 1939 also upheld their traditional per-

195

sonal and inheritance codes, extended to them syndical and corporative institutions, and made them eligible for membership in the *Associazione Musulmana del Littorio* (Fascist Association for Moslems). The law also opened up military careers in Libyan units, made it possible to be appointed *podestà* in towns inhabited by Libyans and consultant in those of mixed population, opened up executive posts in Libyan trade unions, admitted them to the corporative committee for Libya and to the provincial councils of the corporative economy (*all these agencies had vaguely defined advisory functions in economic matters—Ed.*) and, finally, gave them the right to bear arms. Citizenship was not granted to everyone: it was given by gubernatorial decree only to those who requested it and met specific requirements. Furthermore, Libyans were denied access to posts or roles that might give them authority over Italian citizens in the homeland.

For all intents and purposes, the status of the special Italian citizen was a veritable hoax when compared with the way other countries dealt with their colonial subjects. France, for example, recognized that all its colonial subjects might become full-fledged citizens with all the rights of native Frenchmen and it was not difficult to meet the criteria for eligibility. In an Arab and Moslem country like Algeria, the prerequisites for French citizenship were a minimum age of twenty-five years, the monogamous or celibate state, a clean criminal record, and two years of residence in the same community. Only one additional prerequisite had to be met from the following: service in the French armed forces, literacy in French, ownership of rural or urban property, a post in the public administration, election to public office, or possession of a French decoration.

Although only a few thousand French subjects applied for citizenship in order to avoid a break with the traditions of their people and run the risk of being considered renegades, it was certainly not the fault of French policy. In any case, regardless of whether or not one chose to become a French citizen or to remain a subject, his rights were much broader than those of the so-called Italian citizens of Libya. Algerians could marry Europeans, frequent all the schools of the mother country, including the universities, exercise any profession, and for all practical purposes become fully integrated without renouncing the legal status of their choice.

Even Portugal, which was ruled by a quasi-Fascist regime, set an example of generosity in the treatment of its colonies when compared to Fascist Italy. In fact, the so-called special citizenship of the Libyans guaranteed much less than Portuguese legislation provided for the inhabitants of the colonies of Angola and Mozambique (who were black, not Arab). The inhabitants of those regions were divided into two categories: those who lived in tribal communities and were not eligible for Portuguese citizenship, and those who because of their culture and education could be assimilated. Full Portuguese citizenship was granted to the latter by administrative procedure as long as they knew Portuguese and could show that they were self-supporting. Those who obtained citizenship could pursue regular careers in the civil and military administrations on a footing of equality. Three or four percent of the native population enjoyed these prerogatives at the time. Even those subjects who were deprived of citizenship because they lived in tribal communities were permitted to marry Portuguese citizens and had free access to Portuguese schools, including the universities. It would be pointless to cite the legislation of other European countries to draw the conclusion that the colonial legislation of Fascist Italy was the most backward.

■

MUSSOLINI ENGINEERS THE ALLIANCE OF ANTI-SEMITIC POLITICIANS AND RACIST THEORETICIANS

Roberto Farinacci, a veteran of the war in Africa, where he had "heroically" lost a hand while fishing with hand grenades, and recently decorated for his valor, wrote as follows in his newspaper *Il Regime Fascista* on September 12, 1936:

> We must admit that in Italy the Jews, who are a very small minority, while they have intrigued in a thousand ways to capture positions in finance, business, and in the schools, have not opposed our revolution. We must admit that they have always paid their dues and done their duty even in war. But, unfortunately, theirs is a passive attitude which arouses some suspicion because they have never said a convincing word to persuade the Italian people that they do their duty out of conviction rather than fear or cowardice. There is no tangible evidence that they intend to separate themselves from all the Jews of the world whose only aim is to assure the triumph of international Jewry. They have not yet denounced their coreligionists who are guilty of massacres, who destroy churches (perhaps he was alluding to Spain), sow hate, who are bold and evil exterminators of Christians. There is a widespread feeling that soon all of Europe will be engulfed in a religious war. Then they will all shout that they are Fascists, but it won't be enough. They will have to prove conclusively that they are Fascists first and Jews second.

Farinacci's reference to the Spanish civil war, which had recently begun (July 18, 1936), was clear. Nor were his arguments without foundation. Leaving aside the foolish slogan about the triumph of international Jewry, it was true that Jewish elements, who were often influential in the free countries, were opposed because of their democratic convictions to the aggressive policies of the totalitarian states.

Just as they had previously deplored the aggression against Ethiopia, Jews now sympathized with republican Spain. And it was to be expected that if the religious war envisaged by Farinacci broke out, international Jewry (or rather, the Jews living in the free nations) would side with the democratic states. This first attack by Farinacci, based on purely political arguments (the Fascist *ras* from Cremona never did become a "biological" racist), did not condemn Italian Jews as a group because he allowed that individuals might demonstrate that they were Fascists first and Jews second. Farinacci was able, however, to draw the attention of Mussolini and of fascism to the rather important fact that, in those countries where they could express themselves freely, Jews took a stand against totalitarianism. Could the Duce fail to take this into account?

There is no doubt that Farinacci's arguments impressed Mussolini. Two important considerations contributed later on to turning the Duce against the Jews: (1) the growing closeness with anti-Semitic Nazi Germany strengthened by their joint support of General Franco and sanctioned by Galeazzo Ciano's much publicized visit to Hitler in October 1936 and (2) the irritation toward France whose leftist government under Leon Blum was decidedly hostile to fascism and was strongly supported by many Jewish personalities.

It was on such grounds that Mussolini launched his first written attack against the Jews. On December 31, 1936, *Il Popolo d'Italia* featured a short unsigned article entitled "Too Much Is Too Much," which justified anti-Semitism as a reaction to the aggressiveness and exclusiveness of the Jews. The Duce spoke out in these terms:

> Absent-minded people, or those who pretend to be so, ask themselves how anti-Semitism is born, how and why we become anti-Semitic without any prompting from nature. The answer is very simple: anti-Semitism is inevitable wherever Semitism becomes too obtrusive, too aggressive, and therefore too powerful. Too much Jewishness generates anti-Jewishness. Is an explanation for the revival of anti-Semitism in France needed? Let's read the article by Beraud in the latest issue of *Gringoire*, which shows, mentioning names, that under the government headed by the Jew Blum a Jewish cell has grown in every ministry of the republic from where they rule France undisturbed. . . .
>
> This list of names speaks for itself. Do you wish to know what proportion of the French people is Jewish? Two percent. No one can deny that there is a striking disproportion between the number of Jews and the positions which they occupy. Now invert the percentages. Imagine a France in which 2 percent of the people were Christian and 98 percent Jews. Clearly, given the ferocious exclusivism of the tribe, Christians would be totally banished from public life. At the very most, they would be allowed to work like slaves in order to let the Jews rest on the Sabbath.

> The forerunner and justifier of anti-Semitism is always and everywhere the same: the Jew who exaggerates, as he so often does.

Only a few people in Italy learned that the article had been written by the Duce personally, but everyone knew that *Il Popolo d'Italia* was his newspaper and did not broach delicate subjects without his permission. The anonymous piece by Mussolini consequently gave freedom of action in 1937 to anyone willing to bend with the wind and who had something to say against the Jews. It would no longer be isolated voices, though influential ones like Farinacci's, who would speak out against the Jews.

The most authoritative attack on the Jews came from the well-known inventor of catchphrases Paolo Orano who, like Farinacci, confined himself to political arguments. Orana's book *Gli ebrei in Italia,* published in April 1937 and jokingly described as "Orano's bomb" because of its noisy impact, drew for the first time the attention of the entire country to the Jewish question.

Paolo Orano began with a criticism of the Zionist movement, asserting that it was a tool of English foreign policy. The eventual creation of a Jewish state in Palestine could only arouse the most serious concern among Christians over the fate of the Holy Places and provoke a legitimate reaction among the Arabs whose friendship Italy had to cultivate. From this anti-Zionist premise based on considerations of international politics (which Mussolini had also hinted at earlier), Orano went on to criticize Italian Jews. Italian Jews, he said, "should concern themselves with nothing more than their religion." They should not think of making themselves unassailable by always boasting of their patriotism. The only way they can prove that they are good Italians is to sever their ties with Zionism and with international Jewry. They must also give up the idea of using their synagogues as centers for sports, social welfare, and cultural activities.

One reason why Orano's book caused great alarm among Italian Jews is that it was reviewed favorably by *Il Popolo d'Italia* on May 25, 1937. The newspaper asked the Jews to make up their minds whether they considered themselves Jewish guests in Italy or Italians of Jewish religion. After that, how could Italian Jews still think that Orano had not been prompted by Mussolini himself?

Orano's book did not please the extremists, who had suddenly come out into the open. Their aim was to impose on Italy the theory of the Aryan race, and they argued that race was what differentiated the Jews from other people rather than religion or traditions. These doctrines were essentially similar to Hitler's and were the same ones that Mussolini had fought and condemned in his writings and speeches of 1934 and which had been officially rejected by the *Enciclopedia Italiana* in 1935 when it had replaced the concept of race for that of a people. But many things had changed in three years. Now, whoever subscribed to the ideas of the "German comrades" no longer had to worry about falling in disfavor.

There was also the fact that a policy of discrimination against the natives based on the concept of race had been implemented in East Africa where white had been pitted versus black. The concept of race could therefore no longer be ignored. Whoever chose to apply it to the Jews could argue with some justification that he was following those who had legislated for Ethiopia. . . . It could be argued that the kind of racism which took only the color of the skin into account was narrow and primitive because it was based on the sole element of skin pigmentation and not on the full range of racial traits.

After many years of waiting on the sidelines, Giovanni Preziosi finally saw anti-Semitism rising in Italy. In June 1937 he wrote a harsh review of Orano's book in his own periodical, *La Vita Italiana,* charging that the author had stopped at an anti-Semitism that was based on ethical and cultural arguments and had lost himself in intellectual and cultural lucubrations when the problem could instead be resolved in summary fashion by openly persecuting everything that smacked of Jewishness, be it religion or Zionist politics. According to the extremists, Paolo Orano was wasting time by asking Italian Jews to break definitely and unequivocally with international Jewry because his proposal implied that the Jews would cease to be a problem once they had severed their international ties with their coreligionists. The extremists believed instead that Zionism was a secondary issue. The truth was that Jews would always be Jews because of their race and because the Talmud left them no choice.

Other authors published books in 1937 which, unlike Orano's, did go beyond the Jewish question to examine more generally the problem of race. Guido Cogni, an Italian living in Hamburg, in a very muddled book entitled *Razzismo,* endorsed the Germanic concepts of biological racism, asserting from the start that the concept of nation derived from nineteenth-century romanticism and idealism was politically and spiritually obsolete. "At first sight it seems," specified Cogni, "that, regardless of origin, everyone is free to choose his national loyalties if for no other reason than that he is a thinking being." He explains, however, that this is an illusion because reality manifests itself only through the theory of race: "To go back to the blood, in this profoundly cultural sense, means going back to the deep spring, to the origin of the real community which is always, let us admit it frankly, more or less in the soil and in the flesh. He who understands the face of a Nordic woman understands the depth of the Nordic spirit." In spite of Cogni's best efforts to insert some spiritual considerations into his concept of race, his work had little success because it was an obvious rehash of Nazi ideas. As such, it was incompatible with the self-esteem of the Fascists who did not wish to look like servile carriers of ideas that they had just recently rejected because of their extremism. In the Vatican, the Congregation of the Holy Office hastened to condemn Cogni's work, a condemnation that was widely publicized by *L'Osservatore Romano.*

Among those who vied for attention as theoreticians of racism, considerable success was attained by Julius Evola, who tried to strike out on his own in order to avoid both the biological racism of German theoreticians and the moderate, purely political racism of Paolo Orano. Since neither Paolo Orano nor Roberto Farinacci thought of themselves as theoreticians of racism, and since the "precursor" Giovanni Preziosi was not in everyone's good graces, Evola hoped to become the theoretician of an original Italian version of racism that would constitute an independent ideological platform and spare the regime the humiliating charge of plagiarism should it decide to pursue a racist course.

According to Evola, race reveals itself in basic behavior that is rooted in a community's desire to be unique. The concept of race is important, above all, because it disposes once and for all of the abhorrent idea of "abstract and leveling universalism." As such, it is opposed to the principle of internationalism. Race is a product of the spirit and of the traditions and customs emanating from the spirit. Evola defined his own work as an attempt to spiritualize the concept of race. He did not reject the biological racism of the Germans, instead, he claimed that he had transcended it.

One commentator clarified Evola's concept in these terms: "The notion of bodily race must be complemented by the notion of the race of *soul* and spirit." Physical race may be corrupted by the environment, may be distorted and miscegenated, but in the superior races the spirit remains pure, recognizable, and unchanged. Race is therefore an attribute of the spirit and not of the body. In short, race as conceived by biologists, anthropologists, and materialistic racists is not the whole racial reality but only the substance, which is subject to the higher reality of the spirit. Tradition is in every people the product of this fusion between the basic, mixed corporal element and the force of the spirit. The superior races are not those who preserve their physiognomic or somatic features, but rather those who are conscious of the uniqueness of their traditions. Evola then went on to develop a theory of racial hierarchy based on the concept of the superiority of the Aryan race, which he presented as a regular super-race. The Nordic-Germanic line of the Aryan race was indeed a large and important branch but was not its elite as the Nazis claimed.

The proliferation of such publications could only cause concern among Italian Jews who began to fear that these dissertations on race might lead to a new government policy toward the Italian Jewish community. When they tried to remedy the situation, they were confronted with the realization that in the inner circles of the regime the mood had turned against them.

Worried by Orano's book, many Jews declared in Mussolini's *Il Popolo d'Italia* that they "profess to be exclusively Italian and Fascist, clearly and publicly rejecting every international bond, every Zionist commitment." The newspaper, after having published on June 10 the names of these Jews, went on to state the following: "Alongside the Jews who in these circumstances publicly declare themselves anti-Zionists and good Italians, there are still many Jews who will not commit themselves and do not forswear their closed racial circle and their very dangerous mentality, who know how to adjust but remain basically the same and . . . deserve careful watching." Commenting on the declaration of other Jews, the same newspaper pointed out on June 1 that "Nobody thought of subjecting . . . Jews to an investigation. Only a warning has been issued to all those, particularly the leaders, who have not understood that Zionism is incompatible with fascism."

Other major newspapers that took up the problem, including the *Corriere della Sera* and *La Gazzetta del Popolo*, expressed the same attitude: open criticism of Zionism, mistrust of Jews for their suspected lack of loyalty to the Fascist homeland, resentment of international Judaism for its hostility toward the totalitarian nations, etc. However, there were never words of hatred for the Jews as such, nor explicit demands for racial discrimination, nor other gross, Nazi-type condemnations of the "Jewish race."

It is sad to have to say that the Fascist University Groups (GUF) were at the forefront of the anti-Jewish campaign at that time. The most hard-hitting articles appeared in university newspapers and the most blatant anti-Jewish demonstrations occurred in student circles.

Mussolini, on his part, indirectly encouraged the anti-Semitic and racist campaign without taking an official position. He had by now decided to take some steps, perhaps because he would no longer tolerate Zionism among Italian Jews, or because he was extremely irritated by the political attitude of the so-called "international Jewish circles," but he did not yet have a clear idea of what to do. Meanwhile, he tried to create the impression that the upsurge in anti-Semitic and racist feelings was spontaneous, so as to be able to justify government action at the right moment.

The government's official policy was to reassure those leaders and political groups abroad who showed their preoccupation with this beginning of an anti-Semitic campaign. Everyone was told that the articles which had appeared in newspapers and magazines simply expressed the personal views of the journalists and writers who signed them, as if in a totalitarian country an organized press campaign were possible without the tacit consent of the government. To the well-known Italian-American leader Generoso Pope, who during his visit to Rome had expressed his personal concern, the Duce himself gave ample assurances: "I authorize you to declare," Mussolini said to him on June 11, 1937, "and to inform the Jews of America . . . that their concern for their brothers living in Italy is without foundation, being the result of hostile reports. . . . I do not contemplate racial discrimination of any kind."

On February 6, 1938, Galeazzo Ciano wrote in his diary: "We have also spoken with the Duce about the Jewish problem. I expressed myself in favor of a solution that will not create a problem that fortunately does not exist among us. The Duce is of the same opinion. He will pour water on the fire but he will be careful not to smother it."

The ambiguous stand taken by the head of the government, who intended to put the Jews in their place without resorting to outright discrimination and persecution, was reflected in the same month in note number 14 of *Informazione Diplomatica*, which may be considered the first official statement on the Jewish question and may have been prepared by Mussolini. The note began as follows: "The recent newspaper polemics may have created the impression in certain foreign circles that the Fascist government is ready to launch an anti-Semitic campaign. Responsible Roman circles point out that the impression is completely mistaken." It went on to declare that the same "responsible Roman circles believe that the Jewish problem can be solved in only one way: by creating a Jewish state in some part of the world other than Palestine."

After having specified that Italian Jews scarcely numbered fifty to sixty thousand out of a total population of forty-four million, the note declared that the Fascist government did not intend "to take political, economic, or moral measures against the Jews as such." * The government, however, reserved the right to "keep watch over those Jews who have recently entered our country and to make sure that the role of the Jews in national affairs is not out of proportion to their intrinsic and individual merits and to the numerical size of their community."

After this, it seemed as if Mussolini would only take some precautionary steps against those foreigners who had taken refuge in Italy and introduce a quota system for Italian Jews.

For the latter, however, the blow was serious enough. Even admitting that Mussolini would only impose on them the mentioned quota system, they were still coming to the end of an era

---

* Preziosi calculated that in 1934 there were no more than 56,000 Jews in Italy. More precise figures released in 1941 by official sources give an even better idea of the small size of the Jewish community and confirm the absurdity of the persistent persecution of Jews under fascism. The official estimate of 1941 . . . reveals that as of January 1, 1932, there were 45,410 Jews who held Italian citizenship. Of these, 5,966 expatriated between 1932 and October 15, 1941. According to the same figures, there were also 5,012 Jews of foreign nationality residing in the country as of June 1, 1940. Of these, 1,338 had left the country by October 15, 1941. In conclusion, as of October 15, 1941, there were in Italy 39,444 Jews who were Italian citizens, and 3,474 of foreign nationality. Anticipating the adverse consequences that the publication of these figures would have on Italian and foreign public opinion, Preziosi complained against their publication in *La Vita Italiana* in an effort to minimize their importance.

in which they had enjoyed the same rights as other citizens, regardless of their religious beliefs.

Given the semi-official character of the note in *Informazione Diplomatica,* all the Jews who held public office or who were in charge of public organizations immediately resigned from their posts. Clearly, if the quota system was to go into effect, a Jew could not stay on as mayor of a town where the Jews might be no more than 1 or 2 percent of the population, or be in charge of an organization of merchants or industrialists where the Jews might also be a meager minority.

The government remained silent for a few more months, while the press continued to speak out with increasing frequency on the racial question and on the role of the Jews. The newspapers evidently had to whip up public opinion while Mussolini, who had not yet decided what to do, continued to study the reactions of the Catholic Church and of groups abroad.

The Duce now had to decide whether to stop after having adopted a quota system or to go beyond that. He may have been encouraged to adopt a policy of full-fledged racial discrimination by the atmosphere created by Hitler's trip to Rome in May 1938 when he returned an earlier visit to Berlin. The visit developed into a veritable apotheosis of totalitarianism and certainly strengthened the bonds between the Fascist and Nazi regimes.

Changeable and easily enthused as he was, Mussolini must have believed at that moment that a racist policy would enhance the image of his totalitarian regime, particularly because anti-Semitic tendencies were present in the Fascist regimes and movements rising everywhere in Europe.

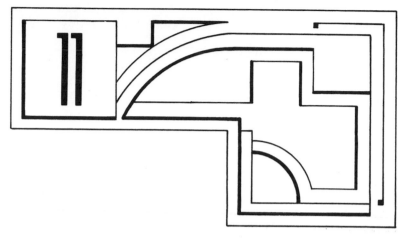

PUBLIC OPINION
IN ITALY BEFORE
THE OUTBREAK OF
WORLD WAR II *

W hen World War II broke out in September 1939, the Fascist regime in Italy was already showing signs of exhaustion and deterioration. These signs could not simply be ascribed to the fact that Italy had been on a constant war footing since 1935, although the long war effort certainly contributed to the general feeling of malaise and dissatisfaction. More fundamentally, there was the dawning realization that fascism had reached the stage of almost complete political and ideological bankruptcy. Domestically, it had already played all its major

* Alberto Aquarone, "Lo spirito pubblico in Italia alla vigilia della seconda guerra mondiale," *Nord e Sud*, XI (January 1964), pp. 117–125. By permission of the publisher.

cards with disappointing results. The syndicates had been established, the machinery of the corporative state was functioning, the economic crisis had been endured, the Fascist leadership was securely entrenched in the government and the administration, special vested interests had been won over to the regime if not to Fascist ideology, and youth had been organized more or less systematically under the control of the party.

Each of these achievements had had the unexpected result of dispelling an important Fascist myth. The appearance of the syndicates had not ushered in an era of greater social justice, the emergence of corporative institutions had not resolved the problems of bureaucracy and decision-making, the economic crisis had revealed that the Fascist economy was not immune from the cyclical disturbances that plagued capitalist systems, the "fascistization" of the government and the public administration had simply created a new privileged caste of middle-aged careerists, the regard shown for the interests of powerful groups had exposed the promises of revolutionary change as being mostly empty rhetoric, and the regimentation of youth contradicted the earlier claims that fascism would always express the aspirations and dynamism of the young.

Only Mussolini's personal prestige was still strong enough to hold the regime together. The politician in him could still come up with new tricks and play off one faction against another. By the late 1930's he enjoyed the additional prestige of being the dean of Fascist dictators, and he could boast of having launched a successful colonial war, stopped communism in Spain, and thrust Italy into the center of international diplomacy. The whole world had seen Mussolini's "compromise" proposals accepted by the representatives of the great powers at the Munich conference in September 1938, the fact that these proposals were actually Hitler's not being generally known at the time.

Not even the myth of Mussolini's infallibility, however, could convince the Italian people that Italy ought to join Germany in war in September 1939. As Alberto Aquarone points out in the following article, public opinion seized hopefully upon

210

every sign that Mussolini intended to keep the country permanently out of World War II. Public reactions thus indicate that, in spite of the most persistent propaganda, fascism failed to convince the people that war is preferable to peace. The rejection of the warlike ethic of fascism by the vast majority of the Italian people points to the limitations of Fascist totalitarianism. The Fascists could control individual behavior by setting up a pervasive police state, but they could not create the *homo fascistus*.

Aquarone's documentation makes it perfectly clear that the Fascist leadership was fully aware of the popular desire to avoid new military ventures. Although Mussolini found these peaceful inclinations most annoying and preferred the term "non-belligerence" to "neutrality" as a description of Italy's policy after September 1939, he nevertheless kept the country out of the war until June 10, 1940. His mood during this period of military inactivity alternated between calm acceptance of the policy of non-intervention and unconcealed resentment that Italy's military unpreparedness forced him to play the role of idle spectator while Germany was scoring impressive military victories.

The explanation for Mussolini's eventual decision to go to war probably lies partly in the psychology of the man and partly in his erroneous but reasoned evaluation of military developments. Did he fear that unless the regime faced up to the ultimate and decisive test of success in a major war fascism might be completely discredited and the very survival of the regime endangered? Or was his decision to go to war based on the cold political calculus that unless Italy entered the war before Germany had defeated the western powers Italy would be shut out of the peace settlement and formally reduced to the rank of a second-rate power? Was Fascist foreign policy based on ideological considerations or on power politics? Much work remains to be done before any of these questions can be answered convincingly. From what Aquarone tells us, however, it is clear that by the time World War II broke out the Fascist regime could no longer count on public support for large-scale military adventures. The military reverses suffered by Italy in World War II widened that fissure between the Fascist leaders and the people to the point that the regime, which had prided itself on its mass basis, fell victim to a handful of conspirators.

■

It is generally agreed today, even by those who held positions of responsibility under the regime and who do not hide their nostalgia for fascism and its enterprises, that in 1938–1939 Italian public opinion was generally perplexed, if not downright hostile, with regard first to the policy of friendship and subsequently of full-fledged alliance with Nazi Germany. Most of all, it seems clear that public opinion was strongly opposed to the idea of waging a war at the side of Nazi Germany against England and France. A serious difference of opinion over the desirability of precisely such a policy emerged at that time even in the inner circles of the Fascist leadership. Such a rift reflected the far broader and deeper feelings of resentment and distrust prevalent among the better informed citizenry toward Mussolini's increasingly more warlike and pro-German foreign policy.

One of the most interesting documentary sources that convey the mood of the country during the critical year preceding Germany's attack on Poland and the outbreak of World War II consists of reports that were sent regularly by party informers to the office of the party secretary in Rome. These reports are now kept in the *Archivio Centrale dello Stato* in Rome. The most striking feature of these reports (which were regularly examined by Starace and often passed on to local secretaries) is the insistence and virtual unanimity with which they convey feelings of hostility, tinged with fear, toward the German alliance and of loathing as it became progressively clearer that Italy might have to go to war. To be sure, when the local secretaries received copies of these reports from the party secretary, in which such feelings were amply described and commented upon, they did occasionally protest that they were only malevolent rumors and downright lies, boasting instead of the popular enthusiasm for Fascist foreign policy in all its aspects. It was a predictable reaction. But the continuous attention with which these reports were followed at headquarters indicates that the officials in Rome considered them a reliable indicator of public feelings toward the alliance with Germany and the prospect of going to war. At the same time, even if we recognize that the informers were likely to emphasize the feelings of pessimism among the people in order to stress the importance of their own work, the uniformity of the reactions from the most diverse provinces and from different informers indicates that the information is highly reliable.

Feelings of uneasiness toward Hitler's expansionist policies and resentment of the German people became evident soon after Germany's annexation of Austria in March 1938. This is what an informant from Turin reported on May 23, 1938:

> Public opinion is once again worried about the threat of war. The fear this time results from the complications that have developed between Czechoslovakia and the Germans. The prospect of having to fight for the interests of a nation that is already considered too powerful and enjoys no popular support arouses no one's enthusiasm. Currently they are saying that the Germans are beginning to exaggerate.[1]

Even the students, particularly those in the universities, on whom the regime could normally rely to arouse public opinion against France and England and stir up popular enthusiasm for war, were responding in an unexpected, apathetic manner. Here, for example, is what one informer wrote on December 21, 1938:

> I have attended student demonstrations in Vicenza, Padua, and Venice that were held in protest against the recent French provocations. I must say frankly that, to put it kindly, these demonstrations were animated more by the usual spirit of student rowdiness than by an awareness of the seriousness of our grievances against France. I regret having to point out that I have observed such lack of understanding in everyone and everywhere. The demonstrations in Rome attracted very little support in the various segments of the population. As usual, the middle classes are absolutely opposed. The general impression is that the people are tired and afraid of wars and of economic crises. It is strange to see how our old frictions with the so-called "Latin sister" have been forgotten.[2]

Feelings of apprehension increased steadily throughout 1939, especially after Hitler's attack on Czechoslovakia in March 1939 and the evident failure of the Munich settlement. Revulsion at the prospect of war and hostility toward Nazi Germany increased apace. Such was the case in Rome:

> Germany's behavior and the excessive power which she has acquired and will acquire continue to be the objects of bitter and violent criticism. There is considerable apprehension about what all this will mean for Italy. There are those who grumble that Italy is already on her way to becoming one of Hitler's client states because she is no longer in a position to break the Axis alliance even if she wanted to. The public, meanwhile, believes that Germany's attitude will be the indirect cause of war and loses no opportunity to express its hostility.[3]

Shortly thereafter, another report from Rome stated the following:

> The people follow the current political situation with the greatest interest because they are aware of its delicacy and do not hide its dangers. The possibility of war is generally deprecated. The people, particularly the less wealthy classes, consider it with evident reluctance because they are afraid of having to endure the greatest sacrifices.[4]

But the middle and upper middle classes were equally firm in their feelings of disapproval and dissatisfaction. This, for instance, is what an informer wrote from Milan on May 4, 1939:

> In professional circles the opposition to Germany is dominant and there is no hesitation in saying that in case of war Germany will be solely responsible because, not being satisfied with what she has attained in the last few years, she wants to take unreasonable advantage of the military unpreparedness of France and England. This last theme reveals the tendentious character of the criticism and echoes almost identical expressions in the foreign press. It is also necessary to remember that, because of the nature of their activities, both professional and industrial circles can more easily be in contact with elements

interested in spreading alarm, thereby confusing public opinion. People in these circles are fond of recalling Germany's role in World War I and to conclude that Italy today in being called upon to support those same German ambitions against which the people fought when they were led to believe in ideals that today are being denied and in atrocities, which it is now claimed were never committed. It would not be accurate to say that these criticisms are voiced by the common people. They are worried only by military call-ups, the rising cost of living, and the scarcity of some basic food items. For the moment, therefore, the mood of apprehension stems mainly from materialistic concerns, but that does not mean that skillful propaganda could not transform it into moral uneasiness, which would pose a far more serious threat to the nation's power of resistance.[5]

Business groups, particularly commercial ones, were exasperated by the general stagnation of business caused by the ever greater uncertainty of the international situation. Their exasperation was so keen that, although basically opposed to the war, they ended up hoping that a conflict would break out as soon as possible if that was the only way to end the economic impasse and the state of psychological tension. For example, this is what an informer reported on May 12, 1939:

> Milan is full of German spies and people go around whispering that they are the new masters. They also say: let it happen fast! May this cursed war break out. The dreadful is better than the anxiety or the tension of waiting. Better a wartime economy, which gets things moving, than this stillness that ruins everything and creates misery upon misery.[6]

The reaction that may be described as "may the war come and let's get it over with once and for all" was also reported from other provinces, particularly from Genoa, Rome, and the region of Venetia. It did not, however, indicate a shift in public opinion in favor of war. On the contrary, it was an indication of the deep-seated anxiety with which people from one end of the country to the other regarded the possibility of having to go to war:

from Sicily (where one informer reported that "both in Trapani and Palermo most people are opposed to the idea of the Axis"),[7] to the capital, to the large industrial centers of the north, to small provincial cities throughout the peninsula. The picture was the same everywhere.

> Certainly—wrote an informer on June 10, 1939—the idea of a war with France is not very popular, even admitting the legitimacy of the Italian claims. It could actually be said that, almost instinctively, our people seem to deny the possibility of a conflict between the two countries. This opinion prevails everywhere in the countryside and in the cities of Venetia and Tuscany. The inhabitants there are not mentally prepared for every eventuality. The emergence of currents that look upon a war with France as an act of madness on the part of fascism could undermine the country's will to resist if Italy should be dragged into a war in spite of its desire for peace.[8]

From Genoa it was reported that "the warlike sentiments of the people of Liguria are at a very low level." [9] Additional comments came a few weeks later:

> The entire population has very little feeling for the war; they don't want it and they disapprove of it. The uneducated element, which includes the man in the street, does not perceive the necessity of the Italian claims, while the part that reads and discusses, if nowhere else than in the cafés, is convinced that Germany will drag us into a war and will reap the greatest benefits from a victorious conflict, while Italy will suffer great damage of incalculable proportions because it is infinitely more exposed to air and sea attacks. In short, they are convinced that Italy's particular geographical position makes it extremely vulnerable and that it will have to sustain incalculable sacrifices mostly for the benefit of its ally. They also assert that Germany is an ally in name only because Italy will be the first to suffer from the future consolidation of German hegemony.

The informer then went on to report the extremely low morale and inadequate fighting spirit of most of the draftees:

Conscripted officers have expressed some serious reservations about the draftees, many of whom have already fought in one or two wars and are fed up. If the rumor is true, there are draftees who say that it is possible to shoot either to the front or to the rear. To those who have objected that machine guns are often placed in the rear to avoid precisely such surprises, they have reportedly replied that even machine guns can be turned around and that, if worse comes to worse, one can always shoot the machine gunners.[10]

Italy's obvious vulnerability in case of war with France or England was a cause for serious alarm among all classes everywhere. It was particularly common in the large centers of the Tyrrhenian coast where England's traditional supremacy was not easily forgotten. These fears were particularly widespread in Naples and Genoa. This is what one informer reported in August 1939:

> The democracies are getting better armed with every day that passes. With the resources that they have at their disposal, they may well be the stronger in spite of the fact that they are not eager for war. People conclude from this that our situation will get progressively worse because, with the development of our coastal regions, with coastal roads, communications, and cities, we are extremely vulnerable. Even if we should win, we are destined in the near future to become the southern outpost of Hitler's Reich. This is the unanimous feeling, and even greater dangers are foreseen.[11]

Hatred of Hitler's Germany took on more precise overtones as the war appeared more and more inevitable. In Padua, a chorus of voices "was raised against Hitler who is never satisfied, who never has enough, and who is responsible for everything." [12] An informer reported the following from Milan a few months later:

> . . . disgust and hostility for all things Germanic grow fuller and deeper in Italy. The alliance is considered a grave danger

for us because of the ill will of the Germans who want us tied
to their cart. In Milan there is a desperate and widespread desire to break with them because, with their habit of interfering
and the excessive power which they have gained everywhere in
Italy, they are considered extremely dangerous.[13]

The disgust and hostility sprang logically from the spreading and deepening belief that Italy was increasingly losing its
freedom of action and that it "had chained itself by submitting
to Germany." [14] Even before the Pact of Steel was signed on May
22, 1939, Italian public opinion overwhelmingly displayed a
highly pessimistic but accurate capacity for predicting the inevitable consequences should Italy and Germany find themselves
fighting side by side.

There were not many people who believed that the two
countries were being pushed into war by the need to protect vital
interests and that it was almost a question of life and death.
Rather the contrary was true. A few days before the beginning of
the conflict, on August 27, 1939, an informer writing from Turin
described the state of mind that prevailed everywhere in the
country:

> Many people are grumbling that it is absurd to fight a
> war over Danzig or any of the other issues relating to an orderly
> and practical settlement in Europe, particularly if we consider
> how successful both Germany and Italy have been in acquiring
> new territories. One hears insinuations that national interests
> are no longer at stake, only rivalries and the desire to get even
> on the part of the few people who lead the nations and that the
> common people will have to pay for them with endless sacrifices
> and suffering.[15]

In this connection, it is revealing to read the comments
made by the party secretary in Turin in a letter dated September 1 to Starace in which he acknowledged receipt of the above
information: "This time the informer is an honest man who
sums up fairly and accurately the situation in Turin, as I myself
have already described it to you."

Considering that this was the state of public opinion throughout the spring and summer of 1939, it is not surprising that once Germany's attack on Poland had unleashed the conflict, the vast majority of the Italian people welcomed the declaration of non-belligerence with a sigh of relief, hoping that the country would stay out of the war permanently. That attitude was particularly evident in the large cities of the north and surrounding regions. This is what . . . a police superintendent wrote in a telegram to national police headquarters on September 1 with regard to Lombardy:

> The population of Milan and surrounding provinces has until now maintained utmost calm and unlimited faith in the enlightened leadership of the Duce. Today's announcement from the council of ministers has reinforced this faith because, regardless of what else may be said, everyone thinks that our intervention would enable the democratic powers to exert upon Italy and her colonies all that pressure which they could not easily apply to Germany because of her more favorable geographic position.[16]

The same police superintendent was even more explicit on the following day when he stressed the people's general desire for peace:

> Public opinion remains unchanged. Favorable comments are still being made on the decisions of the council of ministers. There is still blind faith in the Duce's ability to keep us out of the war. On the other hand, lack of warmth for Germany is evident everywhere. Among other things, the Germans are now accused of having concluded the pact with Russia behind Italy's back, thus compromising our Mediterranean policy and friendship with Japan.[17]

Attitudes toward the war, of course, did not remain unchanged in all quarters during the following months, particularly when the German armies began to score rapid and blazing victories in the spring of 1940. The impression made by these developments and by the impact of incessant Fascist propaganda undoubtedly convinced an increasing number of people, particularly among the young, that it was in Italy's interest to intervene in the war in order to share the fruits of victory, particularly in view of the fact that the collapse of France and England seemed certain. It also seems certain, however, that the desire for peace and hostility toward Germany remained dominant by far. But the problem does become more complicated for the final part of the period of non-belligerence. It ought to be examined in detail as part of a larger study of the entire crucial period of non-belligerence . . . which has not yet found its historian.

At the beginning of World War II in September 1939, before the transitory myth of the invincibility of the German armed forces had seized people's minds and distorted their judgment, Italian public opinion was overwhelmingly and unequivocally opposed to the war. Even if we recognize that this consensus might subsequently have weakened, the general attitude was still the one expressed by those *Alpini* recruits (mountain troops) who (as the worried prefect hurriedly reported) went through the streets of Verona one morning near the end of August singing loudly "a defeatist song, based on a popular tune, which ended with the refrain *vogliamo la pace e non vogliamo la guerra* (we want peace, we don't want war)." [18]

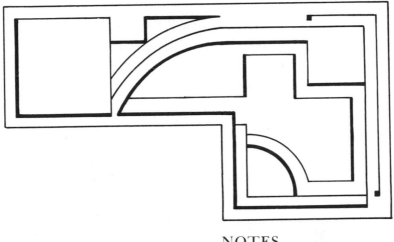

NOTES

INTRODUCTION

[1] See A. James Gregor, *The Ideology of Fascism. The Rationale of Totalitarianism* (New York, 1969). There is no similarly thorough study of the mixed social basis of fascism, but some interesting leads may be found in Renzo De Felice, *Mussolini il fascista. I. La conquista del potere, 1921–1925* (Turin, 1966), pp. 6–11.

[2] See, for instance, Giuseppe A. Borgese, *Goliath: The March of Fascism* (New York, 1938).

[3] Renzo De Felice, *Le interpretazioni del fascismo* (Bari, 1969), p. 210.

[4] The reactions of political parties to fascism may be followed in Renzo De Felice, ed., *Il fascismo e i partiti politici italiani. Testimonianze del 1921–1923* (Bologna, 1966). The most comprehensive discussion of the political context in which fascism developed is Roberto Vivarelli's *Il dopoguerra in Italia e l'avvento del fascismo (1918–1922). I. Dalla fine della guerra all'impresa di Fiume* (Naples, 1967). Only the first volume has appeared so far.

[5] Quoted in Ottavio Dinale, *Quarant'anni di colloqui con lui* (Milan,

1953), p. 321. See also Harry Fornari, *Mussolini's Gadfly: Roberto Farinacci* (Nashville, Tenn., 1971).

[6] Bottai's career is best followed from his own writings, a representative cross-section of which appears in his *Scritti* (Bologna, 1965), edited by Roberto Bartolozzi and Riccardo Del Giudice. There is still no good study of Starace.

[7] The admiring view comes across strongly in one of Mussolini's earliest biographies, Antonio Beltramelli's *L'uomo nuovo (Benito Mussolini)* (Milan, 1923). Socialist writers, always mindful of Mussolini's "betrayal" of socialism, insisted on his lack of principles and accused him of having "sold out." On Mussolini's break with the Socialist party in the fall of 1914, see Brunello Vigezzi, *L'Italia di fronte alla prima guerra mondiale. I. L'Italia neutrale* (Milan, 1966), pp. 936–973.

[8] For a survey of some recent writings on Mussolini, see Charles Delzell, "Benito Mussolini: A Guide to the Historical Literature," *The Journal of Modern History*, Vol. XXXV (December 1963), pp. 339–353.

[9] The third and latest volume of this biography covers Mussolini's career up to the plebiscite of March 1929. The rest will be covered in two forthcoming volumes. The three published so far are: *Mussolini il rivoluzionario, 1883–1920* (Turin, 1965); *Mussolini il fascista. I. La conquista del potere, 1921–1925* (Turin, 1966); *Mussolini il fascista. II. L'organizzazione dello Stato Fascista, 1925–1929* (Turin, 1968).

[10] See Vivarelli, *Il dopoguerra in Italia*, p. 220.

[11] Early writers were aware of the diversity of fascism. See, for instance, Giovanni Zibordi's "Critica socialista del fascismo," originally published in 1922 and reprinted in De Felice, ed., *Il fascismo e i partiti politici italiani*, pp. 359–420. An awareness of the mixed social bases of fascism also appears in Guido Dorso, *Benito Mussolini alla conquista del potere* (Turin, 1949), p. 230, and Gaetano Salvemini, *Lezioni di Harvard* (1943), in *Scritti sul fascismo* (Milan, 1963), edited by Roberto Vivarelli, Vol. I, pp. 572–575.

[12] The following provide good coverage of the major interpretations of fascism: Costanzo Casucci, ed., *Il fascismo. Antologia di scritti critici* (Bologna, 1961); Renzo De Felice, ed., *Il fascismo. Le interpretazioni dei contemporanei e degli storici* (Bari, 1970); A. William Salomone, ed., *Italy from the Risorgimento to Fascism. An Inquiry into the Origins of the Totalitarian State* (Garden City, N.Y., 1970).

[13] On Rocco's ideology, see Paolo Ungari, *Alfredo Rocco e l'ideologia giuridica del fascismo* (Brescia, 1963).

[14] Alberto Aquarone, *L'organizzazione dello Stato totalitario* (Turin, 1965), p. 47.

[15] Antonio Gambino, *Storia del PNF* (Milan, 1962), p. 149. Dante L.

Germino's *The Italian Fascist Party in Power. A Study in Totalitarian Rule* (Minneapolis, Minn., 1959) is thorough on the organizational structure and chain of command of the party but fails to pay sufficient attention to the larger political context in which the party functioned.

[16] On Fascist aspirations for Italian expansion before the march on Rome, see Giorgio Rumi, *Alle origini della politica estera fascista (1918–1923)* (Bari, 1968). The expansionist aims of Fascist diplomacy in the 1920's are discussed in Alan Cassels, *Mussolini's Early Diplomacy* (Princeton, 1970). The domestic background of that expansionist policy is covered in Giampiero Carocci, *La politica estera dell'Italia fascista (1925–1928)* (Bari, 1969).

CHAPTER 1

[1] ACS (*Archivio Centrale dello Stato* in Rome), *Ministero dell'Interno, Direzione Generale di P[ubblica] S[icurezza], Divisione Affari Generali Riservati*, 1923, folder 47, circular dated January 31, 1923, signed by De Bono.

[2] *Ibid.*, telegram no. 15,364, dated July 2, 1923.

[3] *Ibid.*, cablegram from the Ministry of the Interior to the Ministry of War, no. 3838, dated February 1, 1923.

[4] *Ibid.* See Mussolini's telegram of January 30, 1923, no. 2247, where he urged the prefects "to end, once and for all" this state of affairs. Also, Mussolini's other telegram to the prefects, dated July 11, 1923, no. 16,238, instructing them to "eventually adopt every conceivable precautionary or repressive measure in order to restrain current sporadic outbreaks of individual violence."

[5] *Ibid.* See Mussolini's circular to the prefects, no. 1222, dated January 16, and De Bono's circular to the prefects, also dated January 16.

[6] *Ibid.* Different instructions had apparently been given by De Bono to the prefects in telegram no. 5,193, dated March 4, 1923: "There is never any news about Fascists being disarmed. Whoever commits violence in the name of fascism is not to be considered a Fascist. Everyone must be disarmed who illegally retains and uses weapons. Send your reassurances." See also circular no. 2968, dated February 7, also on the question of armed Fascists: "These instances of illegality must end; refer in such cases to my circular 1223, dated January 16 u. s. I still notice some reluctance on the part of officials, mostly the *Carabinieri*. Signed De Bono." De Bono's instructions may have been misleading because he referred precisely to the circular allowing the Blackshirts to retain "shoulder firearms."

[7] *Ibid.* (*The author quotes from a letter dated May 27, 1923, in which Mussolini informed De Bono that he had received protests from Catholic leaders to the effect that groups belonging to the religious organization Catholic Action had been harassed by Fascists in several towns. A long letter from the president of Catholic Action, Luigi Colombo, and a reply from a police official explaining the incidents are also quoted at length.—Ed.*)

[8] *Ibid.* De Bono requested information on the infiltration of Mafia elements (telegram no. 2,036, dated January 27) from the prefect of Palermo Giovanni Gasti who replied on March 23: "Mafia elements tried initially to infiltrate Fascist sections in order to influence the movement's policies, particularly in rural areas, and to obtain rapid advance information concerning the attitude of the party and the government toward the Mafia."

[9] *Ibid.* See Mussolini's telegram of December 8, 1923, no. 27,721, to the prefect of Reggio Emilia in reference to "Corgini's ambiguous movement." Also, in ACS, *Ibid.,* folder 48, there is a telegram dated August 19 in which Mussolini told the prefect of Alessandria that "The condition of fascism in Alessandria can only arouse the most severe censure. Please convey that Signore Sala's attitude is unacceptable. Should he be expelled from the party, I urge you to cooperate with local authorities and to use all means, I repeat all means, from arrests to the use of gunfire, to maintain order. Inform local Fascist leaders that what is happening in Alessandria revolts me." (*Corgini and Sala spoke for Fascist dissidents who objected to the influx of political opportunists into the ranks of fascism and deplored Mussolini's slowness in curbing local bosses.—Ed.*)

[10] *Ibid.,* folder 47, telegram no. 13,652, dated June 13, 1923.

[11] Cesare Rossi, "La critica alla critica del fascismo," *Gerarchìa,* April 25, 1922.

[12] Roberto Farinacci, "Oggi sono tutti fascisti," *Cremona Nuova,* November 9, 1922. Farinacci was the *ras* of Cremona and an intransigent Fascist who opposed all efforts at reconciliation.

[13] "Genealogie fasciste," *Il Popolo d'Italia,* November 9, 1922.

[14] Farinacci, "È ora che l'Italia conosca qual è il pensiero di D'Annunzio poeta: parlate chiaro," *Cremona Nuova,* December 16, 1922.

[15] ACS, *Ministero dell'Interno, Gabinetto Sottosegretario Finzi (1922–1924),* folder 7, telegram no. 34,321, dated December 17, 1922. (*The author also quotes additional corroborating material from the same source.—Ed.*)

[16] A. Tamaro, *Venti anni di storia, 1922–1943* (3 vols.; Rome, 1953–1954), Vol. I, p. 305. See also G. Lumbroso, *La crisi del fascismo* (Florence, 1924), pp. 76ff., and M. Rocca, *Come il fascismo divenne una dittatura* (Milan, 1952), pp. 122ff.

[17] Rocca, *op. cit.,* p. 120. Rocca also recalls (p. 121) that "as early as the beginning of 1923 Cesare Rossi asked in vain that the prefect of Turin be

transferred because he was an excessively partisan protector of Fascist extremists against other Fascists and the rest of the population."

[18] See A. Aquarone, *L'organizzazione dello stato totalitario* (Turin, 1965), pp. 15ff., and P[artito] N[azionale] F[ascista], *Il Gran Consiglio nei primi dieci anni dell'era fascista* (Rome, 1933).

[19] Rocca, *op. cit.*, p. 122.

[20] See G. Perticone, *L'Italia contemporanea* (Milan, 1926), p. 1023, particularly his comments on the historiography of fascism; also by Perticone, *Politica italiana nell'ultimo trentennio* (Rome-Florence, 1945).

[21] The report is not dated, but Mussolini's reply to the report carries the date April 20, 1923. ACS, *Segreteria particolare del Duce*, Bastianini, 242/R.

[22] On this point, see the preface by Renzo De Felice to the anthology *Il fascismo e i partiti politici italiani (1921–1923)* (Bologna, 1966). It is also worth remembering the words of Camillo Berneri in *Giustizia e Libertà*, December 27, 1935: "The leftist pronouncements of the Fascist program of 1919 have misled many but they were not meant to deceive. . . . Political movements respond to political pressures and the rational empiricism of programs is almost always destined to yield to the irrational, that is to say, to history in the making." De Felice stresses the subversive and revolutionary nature of early fascism which was slow to die. See also Rocca's "Un neo-liberalismo?" in *Risorgimento*, September 1921: "The left wing is not likely to . . . impose its program on fascism. It will nevertheless leave its imprint. . . . The pro-labor left is morally justified by the presence of an extreme right . . . made up of certain members of the bourgeoisie, particularly landowners and impoverished aristocrats, who have always looked upon fascism as a means of self-defense and offense to be exploited as cheaply as possible in times of fear."

[23] *(In two successive footnotes the author cites articles from several Fascist periodicals emphasizing the internal diversity of fascism and the government's desire to restrain those Fascists who broke the law. The most explicit statement to this effect appeared in* Il Popolo d'Italia *on November 16, 1922: "Fascists who do not respect the law do not respect their Chief; whoever breaks the law of the land implies that Mussolini is inept and shows lack of faith in him."—Ed.)*

[24] O. Dinale, *Quarant'anni di colloqui con lui* (Milan, 1953), p 181.

[25] Lumbroso, *op. cit.*, pp. 72–73.

[26] See the article "Orientamenti nuovi e pericoli vecchi nella Milizia fascista," *Camicia Nera* (Fascist daily of Treviso), which stated: "Let us speak clearly: many Fascists are disillusioned by this first phase of 'military' activity which supersedes the squads. Many have seen it as marking the end of fascism as we know it, of that fascism which was always synonymous with sin-

cerity, courage, and individual heroism carried to the point of sacrificing one's life."

[27] (*The author lists many minor Fascist groups that were competing for power. The source for this list is a study by a Communist writer, Giulio Aquila (pseud. Sas), which may be consulted in De Felice's anthology,* Il fascismo e i partiti politici italiani.*—Ed.*)

[28] Bottai, "Note e appunti sul movimento fascista," *Corriere Italiano,* December 1, 1923.

[29] Rocca, "Fascismo e paese," *Critica Fascista,* September 15, 1923.

[30] See the following articles in *Corriere Italiano,* "Governo e fascismo nella realtà politica," September 16, 1923; F. Lantini, "Fascismo e Partito Fascista," September 18, 1923; "Un problema di assestamento. Una intervista con il Comm. Giovanni Marinelli," September 19, 1923.

[31] See also the comments by Giacomo Cipriani-Avolio in *Polemica Fascista,* May 24, 1923, to the effect that the party should choose a new type of leadership because it was not to the party's advantage to perpetuate a dictatorship. Cipriani-Avolio argued that the party was wedded to an obsolete mode of leadership.

[32] On the proposal to dissolve the party, see the debate of September in *Corriere Italiano,* "Governo e fascismo nella realtà politica," September 16; "Fascismo e Partito Fascista," September 20, and all pertinent statements in the issues up to September 25.

[33] (*The author cites several hostile replies to Rocca's appeal, the most well known coming from Farinacci in* Corriere Italiano, *September 25, 1923.—Ed.*)

[34] De Marsanich, "Revisionismo," *Critica Fascista,* August 1, 1923.

[35] (*The author summarizes information from several issues of* Corriere Italiano *to indicate that the temporary victory of the revisionists strengthened the authority of the state. The following quotation, from the October 20, 1923, issue, is typical: "The authority of the state as represented by the prefects and high public officials must in no way be nullified or obstructed by members of a party that was born and fought strenuously to restore the authority of the state in all sectors of public life."—Ed.*)

[36] (*The author describes the events that led to the assaults against Forni and Sala on Giunta's orders and to Giunta's subsequent resignation when he came under fire during the Matteotti crisis.—Ed.*)

[37] ACS, *Ministero dell'Interno, Direzione Generale di P[ubblica] S[icurezza], Divisione Affari Generali Riservati, 1903–1945,* folder 501. The note goes on to examine in detail the state of fascism in Lombardy, with particular reference to the autonomous Fascist groups of Como under former deputy Filippo Ostinelli, to the situation in Pavia, Cremona, Seregno, Rho, Legnano, the Brianza district, and certain areas of Venetia.

CHAPTER 2

[1] De Felice, *Mussolini il rivoluzionario,* p. xxii. The reference is to the views expressed by Gramsci in the deliberations of the political committee of the Third Congress of the Communist Party of Italy held on January 20, 1926. See the *Bollettino: Documenti del III Congresso Nazionale del PCI* (no place or date of publication), p. 41.

[2] *La Civiltà Cattolica,* February 15, 1919. Also, A. Gemelli and F. Olgiati, *Il programma del PPI come non è e come dovrebbe essere* (Milan, 1919), pp. 59–60, and ACS, *Carte Nitti,* file II, box 1. Letter from Nitti to Cardinal Gasparri, dated August 26, 1929. Consult the speeches by Farinacci and Michele Bianchi arguing that the Popular party was no longer needed since Mussolini had become the defender of the Church, *L'Osservatore Romano,* March 14, 17, and 28, 1923. For an analysis of the ecclesiastical policies of Liberals, Nationalists, and Fascists, see the editorial "Nazionalismo, fascismo, valori spirituali," *L'Osservatore Romano,* February 28, 1923.

[3] *(Mussolini's attempts to move toward negotiations with the Holy See are discussed on pp. 124–130 of Margiotta Broglio's book.—Ed.)*

[4] De Felice, *Mussolini il rivoluzionario,* p. xxv.

[5] On the views of Mussolini and the Fascists on Church policy through the end of 1919, see pp. 71–81 of Margiotta Broglio's book.

[6] See the letters of Carlo Enrico Barduzzi, a negotiator for Cardinal Gasparri, and Senator Salvatore Contarini, secretary general in the Italian ministry of foreign affairs, written in May–June 1923 *(see Margiotta Broglio's book, pp. 111–112n.—Ed.)* On the turning point of January 3, 1925 . . . , see the succinct and lucid comments in the entry on "Fascism" written by De Felice for the encyclopedia being currently published by Herder of Freiburg. . . . It stresses that fascism survived the crisis of 1924–1925 largely because of the support it received from the most conservative quarters and from the Church, which feared revolution and domestic disorder. The crisis "accelerated and definitely sanctioned the conservative stabilization" of fascism and turned Mussolini into the "prisoner of a state that was still the old conservative state, which, in spite of the corporative reforms that were imposed from above and the attempts to expand public enterprise and government control, was not only unable to change the structure of society but accepted traditional social relationships and continued to move in the same direction in spite of some minor resistance." The steps that led to the Lateran pacts are part of the same political process that led to the Fascist regime of the 1930's. That regime is described by De Felice as "an equilibrium of conservative interests, bolstered in turn by welfare policies, and where they did not suffice, by the police state and a popular consensus based on the myth and the habitual acceptance of the Leader as the one . . . best

qualified to pursue the goal of national greatness." See also the perceptive comments in the entry under "Fascism" written by L. Paladin for Volume XVI (currently being published) of the *Enciclopedia del Diritto*. Paladin categorically denies that fascism represented a new principle of social order. . . . He also points out the difficulty of ascertaining "at which precise point after the rise of the regime the alleged break with tradition might have occurred" because of the "extremely gradual pace at which the Fascist regime constructed its juridical system," because the speech of January 3, 1925 . . . "was still a political rather than a juridical break," and because "it is only with the laws of December 24, 1925, no. 2263, and January 31, 1926, no. 100, that the Fascist regime begins to develop a juridical personality of its own."

[7] A. Rocco, "Chiesa e Stato," *Il Resto del Carlino*, April 4, 1922 and the editorial "Nazionalismo, fascismo, valori spirituali," *L'Osservatore Romano*, February 28, 1923. . . . The editorial concluded as follows: "We who have never misunderstood or misrepresented the spiritual essence of Nationalist and Fascist thought have never disparaged their work or their leader . . . by comparing them with the work and the leaders of the Catholic social movement. We have dutifully noted, as they themselves have, all the good things they were doing for the country by suppressing harmful rivalries, propagating useful values, guiding citizens' minds toward the long-invoked and proper pacification of Italian society."

[8] (*Rocco established the committee on February 12, 1925, when he commented that the Fascist government had created a new political climate in which relations between church and state could be "reexamined in a profoundly new spirit and perhaps resolved.*" *ACS*, Ministero dell'Interno, Direzione generale affari di culto, Commissione per la riforma delle leggi ecclesiastiche, *folder 175, file 459, 1925, minutes of the meeting of February 13, 1925.—Ed.*)

[9] De Felice, *Mussolini il rivoluzionario*, p. 460ff.

[10] *Ibid.*, pp. xxiii.

[11] ACS, *Segreterìa particolare del Duce, Autografi del Duce*, 1927, box 5, file VI, subfile F, no. 6, *Autobiografia del Duce*.

[12] It is worth noting that Mussolini erased a passage in the first draft of the *Autobiography*. . . . The passage, which does not appear in the French and English editions, referred proudly to the religious expressions in his speech of 1921 before the chamber, to the reintroduction of the crucifix in the classroom, the restoration of religious instruction, and went on to state the following: "But I had to see deeply into the simple soul of our humble people who want the comfort of the faith, want to believe that a divine law stands above the common law of man, want to venerate their dead in the knowledge that the soul is immortal. It is for these reasons that, in the schools and in all public actions, my politics are the politics of faith that draw inspiration from the fruitful principles of religious and civil ethics."

ACS, *Segreterìa particolare del Duce, Autografia del Duce*, 1927, *Autobiografia del Duce*. These phrases were probably erased because he apparently sensed that they were too patently false and absurd.
[13] *Ibid*.

CHAPTER 3

[1] Volt, "L'esercito fascista resterà," *Il Popolo d'Italia*, October 24, 1922.

[2] "Dopo il Gran consiglio fascista. Gli scopi ed il significato della milizia per la sicurezza nazionale," *Il Popolo d'Italia*, December 17, 1922. The Militia was officially established at the beginning of February and was sworn in in April.

[3] C. Zoli, "L'esercito e la milizia," *L'Idea Nazionale*, October 28, 1923. The article reappeared, with additional details on the vicissitudes of the "spirit of victory," as C. Zoli, "La sistemazione della milizia," *Il Secolo*, August 5, 1924.

[4] "Le direttive e le finalità della milizia nazionale," *Il Popolo d'Italia*, September 30, 1923. Notice the reinterpretation of the myth of the "armed nation," a reference to the notion that the entire nation must be mobilized to attain victory. (*The concept of the "armed nation" had first been formulated by Liberal patriots in the nineteenth century as a means of achieving national unification.—Ed.*)

[5] P. Gramantieri, *Esercito e fascismo* (Turin, 1924), pp. 15, 17. This pamphlet was originally written in December 1922 and published fifteen months later in the series "Biblioteca fascista di cultura politica diretta da Pietro Gorgolini." It expressed the desire to establish an armed nation like Switzerland, based on a friendly understanding between fascism and the army. General Gramantieri's professions of democratic faith were not new. In 1919 he had intervened at La Scala to defend Leonida Bissolati against the catcalls of the Futurists and Mussolini's *arditi* (*Mussolini's followers noisily interrupted a political conference held by the Social Democrat Bissolati at the La Scala Opera House in Milan on January 11, 1919.—Ed.*). However, the general reconciled himself to the regime in 1925 and became a collaborator for *Il Popolo d'Italia*.

[6] As an example, see F. Zugaro, "Esercito regolare e milizia di partito," *Il Mondo*, November 25, 1922, which envisaged the possibility that the presence of the Militia might facilitate a reduction in the term of service and numerical strength of the army as well as greater economies. The editors of the newspaper disagreed with their military expert.

[7] "Per il riordinamento della milizia su nuove basi prevalentemente militari," *Il Popolo d'Italia*, July 25, 1923, and "I nuovi concetti informatori della milizia nazionale," *Cremona Nuova*, July 25, 1923. It could be inferred

from these articles that approval of the plan was certain. That, at least, was the understanding in F. Zugaro, "La trasformazione della milizia nazionale," *Il Mondo*, July 26, 1923 (the newspaper expressed its approval in a feature article), and in "Mussolini e De Bono riorganizzano su nuove basi la milizia delle camice nere," *Il Giornale d'Italia*, July 25, 1923. Agreement was also evident in "Le attribuzioni e i compiti della milizia nazionale," *Esercito e Marina*, July 31, 1923.

[8] "Il Gran consiglio fascista. Dichiarazioni del presidente sulla milizia nazionale," *Il Popolo d'Italia*, July 26, 1923. Point 3 provided that the Militia was to consist of 300,000 men for the first levy, with 200,000 in reserve for the second. Point 5 specified that the Militia was not to engage in ordinary police duties.

[9] R. Farinacci, "Dissipare gli equivoci," under a full-page banner headline which read, "Questioni nostre. La milizia nazionale è e deve rimanere una forza politica," *Cremona Nuova*, August 16, 1923.

[10] This is Point 6 of the Grand Council's resolution of July 25 on the duties of the Militia, from the already cited article in *Il Popolo d'Italia*, July 26, 1923.

[11] Colonel Fulvio Zugaro was so enthusiastic over this proposal that for its sake he was willing to accept less attractive aspects of the Militia, such as the reassertion of its partisan character. See. F. Zugaro, "L'evoluzione della milizia nazionale," *Il Mondo*, July 29, 1923. The newspaper, however, did not agree with its expert and replaced him in the following months with General Roberto Bencivenga, who was politically close to Representative Giovanni Amendola, a Liberal opponent of fascism and the editor of *Il Mondo*.

[12] E. Sailer, "L'istruzione premilitare," which appeared in *Il Popolo d'Italia* on July 4, 1923, and *Esercito e Marina*, July 7, 1923. This is the source for the number of recruits, who were enrolled in two separate courses and belonged to 550 associations. There were from 25,000 to 35,000 men ready to take their qualifying exams. Notice the uncertain figures, which were also widely exaggerated. Government sources state precisely that the number of recruits who were certified as having received premilitary training was 4,365 for the class of 1902, 8,266 for 1903, and 14,273 for 1904 (who were called up in 1922, 1923, and 1924 respectively). These are the only available official figures on premilitary trainees for the postwar period. See "Relazione della sottocommissione Guerra e Marina sullo stato di previsione del ministero della Guerra per l'esercizio 1924–25," in *Atti del Parlamento Italiano, Camera dei Deputati*, XXVII Legislature, Document 12-A. The report was presented on October 31, 1924. . . .

[13] "Mobilitazione industriale," *Esercito e Marina*, May 29, 1923. The article proposed that the Militia be put in charge of premilitary training (which elicited the editorial comment quoted above). It also proposed that the Militia be entrusted with organizing industrial mobilization and was im-

mediately rebutted by an expert on the army's general staff. See F. Foschini, "Milizia nazionale e mobilitazione industriale," *Esercito e Marina*, June 22, 1923. Similar views were also expressed in the following articles from *Esercito e Marina*: A. V. L., "L'istruzione premilitare," July 13, 1923; Nestore, "La premilitare," July 21, 1923; Ersa, "L'istruzione premilitare," September 25, 1923.

[14] From the already cited article in *Il Popolo d'Italia*, September 30, 1923. The bulletin even foresaw a reduction in the army's term of service as a result of the pre- and post-military training within the Militia. It was also published under Timone, "Note del giorno," *Esercito e Marina*, October 2, 1923, with a hesitant but not hostile editorial comment.

[15] From the already cited article in *Il Popolo d'Italia*, July 26, 1923.

[16] *Opera Omnia di Benito Mussolini* (Florence, 1951–1963), Vol. XIX, p. 402n.

[17] We must not forget that relations between the army and the Militia were only one aspect of a crisis that also involved liberal-democratic opponents and rival groups among the Fascists.

[18] For the military plan, see C. R., "Esercito e milizia. Dopo il progetto Ferrari," *L'Idea Nazionale*, January 9, 1924, and R. Guerra, "Per l'istruzione premilitare," *Il Giornale d'Italia*, January 4, 1924. Mussolini's reply came in a speech before the commanding officers of the Militia, who gathered in Rome on February 1 to commemorate the first anniversary of the founding of the Militia: "The heads of the army have approached us. We are now examining ways of integrating the Militia with the other military forces so that they may maintain order at home and protect the country's interests abroad. I cannot foresee how the fusion will take place. It is a delicate problem because I do not intend to diminish the Militia's ties to fascism until conditions totally change." From "Parla il duce del fascismo," *Il Popolo d'Italia*, February 2, 1924. It was at this meeting that Balbo claimed 300,000 trained men and 180 legions for the Militia.

[19] L. Segato, "Fin dove e come l'ingranamento della milizia nazionale?" *Esercito e Marina*, April 8, 1924. This was the policy favored by the military biweekly, as indicated by the following articles: the already cited article of February 12, 1924; "L'ingranamento della milizia nazionale," March 25, 1924, L. Segato, "Fusione ma non sostituzione," June 10, 1924; L. Segato, "L'inquadramento della MVSN nell'esercito," July 15, 1924 (followed by an even more unyielding editorial comment). Their very explicit reservations are always accompanied by declarations of profound esteem for fascism and for the political and moral functions of the Militia.

[20] In a letter to *Impero*, reprinted by *L'Idea Nazionale* on December 17, 1924, the Militia General Vittorio Verné gave the following figures: nearly 750 officers on permanent duty (high ranking or assigned to clerical duties), 550 cohort commanders, 1,670 centuries commanders, 5,000 maniples

commanders (corresponding to majors, captains, and lieutenants respectively). [21] Some changes did occur in 1923–1924. As of December 1924, for instance, all sixteen zone commanders were army generals on leave. See "Chi sono i comandanti della milizia nelle 16 zone," *Cremona Nuova,* December 21, 1924. Judging from the protests, however, the changes were minor.

[22] Use of Militia units in wartime implied parity of rank between Militia and regular army officers. Furthermore, since the Militia consisted of infantry units only, the army would have had to provide them with artillery, logistical support, and matériel at its own expense.

[23] See, for instance, General Pier Luigi Sagramoso, "Esercito e milizia nazionale," *Il Giornale d'Italia,* January 25, 1924, and most of all in *Il Mondo,* R. Bencivenga, "L'organizzazione dell'esercito," January 5, 1924; "Esercito nazionale e milizie volontarie," January 8, 1924; "Polemiche militari," January 11, 1924; "Esercito e milizie volontarie," January 13, 1924. All these articles took a strong line against the Militia and fascism, accusing them of wanting to destroy the army because it was the last obstacle to their excessive demands for power.

[24] IOTO, "L'ingranamento della milizia nazionale nell'esercito," *L'Idea Nazionale,* June 10, 1924, reprinted intact in *Cremona Nuova,* June 20, 1924. The article stated that there was no desire to merge the two officer corps but, rather, to agree on a common hierarchial order that would establish norms for saluting and, in some cases, determine who was subordinate to whom.

[25] Cited article in *L'Idea Nazionale,* June 10, 1924.

[26] General Luigi Segato's defense of the Militia as a political body . . . was more representative of army feelings than the previously cited criticisms. See the already cited article in *Esercito e Marina,* July 15, 1924.

[27] See General Antonino Di Giorgio's speech in *Atti del Parlamento Italiano. Camera dei Deputati,* December 13, 1924, p. 1494, and M. C., "Il riordinamento dell'esercito negli intendimenti del ministro Di Giorgio," *La Stampa,* January 25, 1925. It seems that there were 50,000 rifles at the militia's disposal as of June 1924. Right after the assassination of Matteotti, however, it withdrew an additional 100,000 from the army's deposits that had been placed at its disposal by Diaz. The withdrawal was authorized by the government, but not without the consent of the army.

CHAPTER 4

[1] Mussolini, *Opera Omnia,* ed. G. Pini and E. Susmel (Florence 1951–), Vol. 21, pp. 238–239. Subsequent references to Mussolini's speeches or writings are, unless otherwise stated, taken from this source.

[2] *Ibid.*, Vol. 20, pp. 61–62. See also his speech to the Assembly of the Fascist party January 28, 1924: "The Fascist revolution is not bedecked with human sacrifices; it has not created special tribunals; the rattle of the firing squads has not been heard; terror has not been exercised; emergency laws have not been promulgated." *Ibid.*, p. 164.

[3] *Popolo d'Italia*, August 5, 1924, speech of V. Pellizzari.

[4] C. Pellizzi, *Problemi e realita del Fascismo* (Florence: 1924), pp. 103, 164.

[5] ACS (Archivio Centrale dello Stato), Carte Michele Bianchi, fasc. 43, May 1, 1923.

[6] *Pagine di critica fascista* (Florence, 1941), p. 221.

[7] See G. Lumbroso, *La crisi del fascismo* (Florence, 1925), *passim*.

[8] Head of Mussolini's press office and a member of the Direttorio of the PNF. Arrested for complicity in the murder of Matteotti.

[9] ACS, *Min. Interno, Gabinetto, Uff. Cifra*, tel. in partenza, May 30, 1924, n. 12000.

[10] G. Salvemini, *Scritti sul fascismo*, Vol. I, ed. R. Vivarelli (Milan, 1963), p. 219.

[11] *St. Antony's documents*, June 14, 1924 (correspondence relating to cabinet changes). *Ibid.*, reference of Acerbo, September 18, 1924, to the "conspirators . . . of the 14th of June."

[12] *Giornale d'Italia*, December 30, 1924. This count included the Liberals Casati and Sarrocchi, the two moderate Fascists De Stefani and Oviglio, the ex-Nationalist Federzoni, the Catholic Nara, and the two military ministers.

[13] M. Rocca, *Come il fascismo divenne una dittatura* (Milan: 1952), p. 124.

[14] G. Sarrocchi, *Ricordi di un esule da Palazzo Madama* (Florence: 1950), p. 27 n. On January 1, 1925, *Popolo d'Italia* wrote: "The government is Fascist and Mussolinian, because no one can govern against fascism and against Mussolini."

[15] *Opera Omnia*, Vol. 21, p. 240. *Popolo d'Italia*, January 3, 1925: "to restrain the Fascists it is necessary to restrain the press which provokes them. . . . The Government's order prohibiting rallies and meetings and promoting an enquiry into the Florence incidents is a new proof of the intentions of the right honorable Mussolini and his collaborators. . . . The Government desires a legalitarian settlement."

[16] *La Nazione*, November 25, 1924: "If the creature did not obey its creator it might even happen that the latter would leave it to its destiny."

[17] *Popolo d'Italia*, November 29, 1924.

[18] ACS, Carte Michele Bianchi, fasc. 2, Arnaldo Mussolini to Bianchi, November 27, 1924.

[19] Balbo's successor was General Gandolfo; he was an ardent Fascist who had previously been prefect of Cagliari. Balbo had been appointed "temporary" C in C of the Militia on the resignation of De Bono.

[20] *Atti Parlamentari, Senato, Discussioni, 27 legisl. sessione 1*, pp. 379–385 (December 4), (Giardino), pp. 485–488 (December 9), (Zupelli), pp. 415–416 (December 5), (Caviglia). For Mussolini's reply see *Opera Omnia*, Vol. 21, pp. 197–199.

[21] See *ACS, Min. Interio Gabinetto Uff. cifra*, December 8, 1924, n. 26, 409: General Gandolfo asks the zone commanders to report the impression made on the consuls "by the new directives of the Militia."

[22] ACS, Carte Farinacci, fasc. 3, 1924, s/fC., December 26, 1924.

[23] E. Galbiati, *Il 25 Iuglio e la MVSN* (Milan: 1950), pp. 37–39; R. Montagna, *Mussolini e il processo di Verona* (Milan: 1949), pp. 22–29; A. Tamaro, *Venti anni di storia*, Vol. 2 (Rome: 1952–1954), pp. 60–62; E. M. Gray, "La genesi del 3 gennaio," *Il meridiano d'Italia*, January 23, 1949. The Militia consul commanded a legion, at full strength about 1,500 men.

[24] L. Salvatorelli and G. Mira, *Storia d'Italia nel periodo fascista* (Turin: 1956), p. 330.

[25] Gray, *loc. cit.*; G. Pini and D. Susmel, *Mussolini, l'uomo e l'opera* (Florence: 1953), Vol. 2, p. 403.

[26] *St. Antony's documents;* ACS, *Min. Interno, Dir. Gen. P.S. AGR* (Affari Generali e Riservati), 1924, b. 91 fasc. *Ferrara*, November 29, 1924, b. 95, fasc. *Ravenna*, November 30, 1924.

[27] *Corriere della Sera*, November 30, 1924.

[28] ACS, *Min. Interno Dir. Gen. P.S. AGR*, 1924, b. 89 fasc. *Bologna*, December 1. Prefect of Bologna to Mussolini.

[29] ACS, *Min. Interno, Dir. Gen., P.S. AGR*, 1924, b. 87, fasc. MVSN, s/f, Sistemazione dei gradi nella Milizia, prefect of Bologna to Mussolini, December 11, 1924.

[30] ACS, *Min. Interno Gabinetto Uff. cifra*, Tel. in arrivo, December 10 n. 39997, prefect of Perugia to Minister of Interior; *ibid. Dir. Gen. P.S. AGR*, b. 95, fasc. *Perugia*, December 15, *ibid*.

[31] ACS, *Min. Interno Gabinetto Uff. cifra*. Tel. in arrivo, December 17 n. 40680.

[32] R. Montagna, *op. cit.*, p. 23. According to Gray six consuls obtained an audience with Mussolini on the 23rd: but this is probably a confusion, as the other versions do not mention the fact. Or the meeting may have taken place, but have had no significance.

[33] ACS, *Min. Interno Gabinetto Uff. cifra*. Tel. in partenza. December 23.

[34] *Ibid*. tel. arrivo, December 23 prefect of Perugia to Mussolini: "For the reasons I explained to you personally permit me to insist on the most rapid possible settlement for Gen. Agostini."

[35] *Ibid.* December 29 Agostini's enemy, the *federale* of Perugia, Felicioni, was the source of the information: this suggests it was thought to be compromising.

[36] See also, in *St. Antony's documents*, report of March 28, 1925, from prefect of Milan to Mussolini describing Tarabella and Galbiati as the leaders of that part of the Militia which resented the appointment of generals to the zone commands and feared that the system might be extended to the legions. They wanted instead to give the Militia "a squadrist character with its own leaders." Their associates were Moschini (Mantova), Testa (Mirandola), and Candelori (Rome). This corroborates the later accounts, which mention Testa and Candelori as among the leaders, with Tamburini, Tarabella, and Galbiati.

[37] *Popolo d'Italia*, November 30, 1924. "Fascism–Government should be like a general staff, which should never be put into the difficult position of thinking that its will is not respected by the soldiers, or even discussed."

[38] *Ibid.* December 1, 1924.

[39] ACS, *Min. Interno Gabinetto Uff. cifra.* Tel. in arrivo, 1924, n. 39048, November 30. Prefect of Florence to Mussolini.

[40] Salvemini, *op. cit.*, pp. 134–136; C. Ronchi Bettarini, "Note sui rapporti tra fascismo 'cittadino' e fascismo 'agrario' in Toscana," in *La Toscana nell Italia unita* (Florence: 1962), p. 372.

[41] *Giornale d'Italia*, November 27, 1924.

[42] ACS, *Min. Interno dir. Gen. P.S. AGR*, 1924, b. 93 fasc. *Milano*, November 30. Prefect of Milan to Mussolini.

[43] G. Bottai, *Pagine di critica fascista*, p. 325.

[44] December 6, A. Luchini: the delimitation between party and government was necessary as the government "shows itself . . . extremely ill-adapted, we do not say to realize the postulates of the Fascist revolution, but even . . . to direct the movement."

[45] Interview with *La Stampa*, December 23, 1924.

[46] *St. Antony's documents*, de Stefani to Mussolini, January 5, 1925.

[47] R. Paolucci, *Il mio piccolo mondo perduto* (Bologna: 1947), p. 256.

[48] *Giornale d'Italia*, December 19, quotes their circular: "some deputies who are old Fascists have felt the necessity for an exchange of ideas among those who are best able to understand the absolute necessity of the defense of the ideals, and the political and moral program of fascism."

[49] Paolucci, *op. cit.*, pp. 257–258.

[50] *Resto del Carlino*, December 20, 1924.

[51] Salandra resigned before the publication of the Rossi memorial. For its motivation, see G. B. Gifuni, *Il Risorgimento*, February 1962, "Dalla crisi Matteotti alla proposta liberale delle dimissioni di Mussolini nella seduta del Consiglio dei ministri del 30 Decembre 1924."

[52] The actual measures taken were: (1) an instruction by Federzoni to

the prefects to apply the press censorship decree with rigor; (2) the arrest and search of the organizers of *Italia Libera*. (ACS, *Min. Interno, Gabinetto, Uff. cifra*, tel. in partenza, December 30).

[53] See G. B. Gifuni, *Il Risorgimento*, October 1962, "Verso la dittatura. Il Diario Salandra del gennaio 1925," pp. 52–53; 196–197. The Milanese Liberal associations, led by De Capitani, voted a motion of "absolute collaboration" with the government on December 28; ACS, *Min. Interno Gabinetto Uff. cifra*, tel. in arrivo n. 41560, prefect of Milan to Mussolini.

[54] *Giornale d'Italia*, December 25, reports that the extremist deputies were to hold a meeting on December 28 and the moderates on January 2.

[55] *La Conquista dello Stato*, December 21, 1924.

[56] Suckert commented that "Devotion cannot be carried to the point of suicide." *La Stampa*, December 26, 1924.

[57] *Giornale d'Italia*, December 30, 1924.

[58] The journal of the Florentine Fascists, *Battaglie Fasciste*, published Suckert's next attack: "All, even Mussolini, must obey the warning of integral fascism." *La Conquista dello Stato*, December 28, 1924.

[59] Salvemini, *op. cit.*, pp. 111–112; ACS, *Min. Interno Gabinetto Uff. cifra*, tel. in arrivo December 31, 1924 n. 41835, *ibid.* n. 41867, *ibid.* January 1, 1925 n. 23. *Battaglie Fasciste*, January 4, 1925; *Nuovo Giornale*, December 31, 1924.

[60] *Battaglie Fasciste*, January 4, 1925.

[61] *Cremona Nuova*, January 2, 1925; *Popolo d'Italia*, January 1, 1925: "The Fascist assemblies, summoned by local initiative and not that of the *Direzione* of the party, have been provoked by the perfidy of the opposition."

[62] G. B. Gifuni, *op. cit.*, p. 199; Sarrocchi, when he saw Salandra on January 5, "did not dissent from my opinion concerning the responsibility of the government for, or rather their direct instigation of, the Florence disorders." *Ibid.*, p. 200.

[63] *La Conquista dello Stato*, January 18, 1925.

[64] Montagna, *op. cit.*, p. 24.

[65] *St. Antony's documents.*

[66] ACS, Carte Michele Bianchi, fasc. 6, September 17, 1924.

[67] Even at Florence, the "second wave" was preceded by a number of arrests carried out by the police (Salvemini, *op. cit.*).

[68] *Cremona Nuova*, December 23, 1924.

[69] *Ibid.* December 24, 1924.

[70] Montagna, *op. cit.*, pp. 28–29. Besides Torre, Acerbo and Balbo had been members of the Piazza Gesu freemasonry. (A. Tasca, *Nascita e avvento del Fascismo* (Florence: 1965), p. 504. Tamburini and Suckert are also listed, but the source is dubious.

[71] Galbiati, *op. cit.*, pp. 47–62; *St. Antony's documents.*

⁷² My italics. ACS, *Segreteria Particolare del Duce, Carteggio riservato*, 242 R, *Roberto Farinacci*, Chiavolini to Prefect of Cremona, February 20, 1925.

⁷³ *St. Antony's documents*, January 4, 1925, Sarrocchi to Mussolini. A concern with legality is apparent in Federzoni's instructions to search the houses of *Italia Libera* leaders, "deputies excluded." (ACS, *Min. Interno, Gabinetto, Uff. cifra*, tel. in partenza, December 30. Federzoni to prefect of Genoa.)

⁷⁴ *La Conquista dello Stato*, January 4, 1925. *Ibid.*, January 18, claimed that Mussolini's measures were essentially directed against the Fascist movement, and to frustrate an integralist *coup*.

⁷⁵ *Giornale d'Italia*, January 13, 1925.

CHAPTER 5

¹ See "Le forza del combattentismo è miseramente finita," *Cremona Nuova*, March 3, 1925, which was followed by similar articles. Also, Farinacci's *Un periodo aureo del Partito Nazionale Fascista* (Foligno, 1927), p. 28.

² See Farinacci's "Tagliamo i viveri" (requesting the termination of the parliamentary mandate for members of the Aventine) and "Siamo sempre più convinti" (demanding the death penalty, political confinement, and loss of citizenship for the "renegades"), in *Cremona Nuova*, respectively February 18 and April 16, 1925, reprinted in Farinacci's *Andante mosso, 1924–25* (Milan, 1929), p. 200ff and p. 208ff. Also, his speech at Robecco d'Oglio (April 12), in which Farinacci demanded, in addition to the already mentioned measures, the banning of Albertini, Turati, Donati, De Gasperi, and the immediate arrest of the leaders of the Aventine on the ground of "criminal conspiracy against the power of the state." Farinacci, *Un periodo aureo*, p. 76ff. (*The author points out that these requests were not accepted by the government but Mussolini did order all members of the government to avoid contacts with members of the opposition. On October 30, for instance, he sent the following telegram to his ministers: "I renew the recommendation to rigorously ignore opposition deputies without any exception. Letters from the secessionists are to remain unanswered." ACS, Presidenza del Consiglio dei ministri, Gabinetto (1919–36), folder 382, dossier 1/5-1, no. 9336; also in ACS, Mussolini, Autografi-Telegrammi, folder 1.—Ed.*)

³ See "Sire, siate meno generoso," *Cremona Nuova*, June 13, 1925, reprinted in Farinacci, *Andante mosso*, p. 220ff.

⁴ See *Cremona Nuova*, August 7, 15, 18, 25, 26, 28, 1925 (the article of August 7, entitled "Ora basta!" is reprinted in Farinacci's *Andante mosso*, p. 227ff). Also, Farinacci, *Un periodo aureo*, p. 219ff and p. 247ff. (*The author*

refers to several Fascist newspapers which also polemicized against the Holy See.—Ed.)

[5] See *Corriere della Sera*, April 8, 1925. For the concession of other honorary membership cards to leading social and cultural personalities, see the issue of March 24, 1925.

[6] See Farinacci's *Un periodo aureo*, pp. 32, 95ff. Farinacci's attitude toward labor at that time was extremely unyielding and in some ways more extreme than that of the government and even of the party. As he said in Cremona on April 21, Fascist syndicalism "must be under the control and direction of the party which must assume responsibility for the labor movement, the two being one and the same." From this premise, he went on to argue that all producers must join syndical associations, that these associations be officially recognized by the government, that labor contracts negotiated by them be legally binding, that compulsory arbitration be introduced, labor courts be set up to adjudicate labor disputes, and representatives of the syndicates be admitted to legislative bodies. These proposals were rejected by the syndicalists at that time because they realized that they would have remained dead letter, particularly if Farinacci had succeeded in putting the syndicates under the control of the party.

[7] See *Cremona Nuova*, March 3 and July 9, 1925. The second article, entitled "L'uomo del dovere," is reprinted in Farinacci's *Andante mosso*, p. 223ff.

[8] Efforts to regain the loyalty of dissidents were most successful in Emilia. For the general picture, see Ministero dell'Interno, *Direzione Generale di Pubblica Sicurezza, Divisione Affari Generali e Riservati (1925)*, Folders 86 (dossier *Milizia Adriatica*), 87, 91 (dossier *Napoli*), and above all, 95 (dossier *Fascisti dissidenti-Affari generali*). Farinacci would not give in with Edorado Torre, a dissident who warned Mussolini that the Nationalists might be planning to take over the government and liquidate fascism, in spite of the fact that Torre had written to him soon after his nomination as party secretary (which he thought of as a move against the Nationalists) with the suggestion that he and his followers might rejoin the party. See ACS, *R. Farinacci*, dossier 5, insert T. He was equally unrelenting toward Aldo Oviglio, a former minister of justice, whom he had expelled from the party. See *Corriere della Sera*, August 27 and 28, 1925. Also, ACS, *R. Farinacci*, dossier 5, insert O. *(The author goes on to mention that in October 1925 sixteen deputies were also expelled from the party and gives a list of newspapers which were either Fascist or friendly to fascism.—Ed.)*

[9] After June 1925, Farinacci could rely on a party directorate appointed by himself whose members included Roberto Forges-Davanzati, Giorgio Masi, Pier Arrigo Barnaba, Maurizio Maraviglia, Serafino Mazzolini, Alessandro Melchiorri, Augusto Turati, and Renato Ricci.

[10] According to what Farinacci reported at the national congress of the

party on June 21, 1925, as of that date two youth organizations, the Avanguardia and the Balilla, had increased memberships, with the Avanguardia
having 84,280 members (from 53,829 at the end of 1924) and the Balilla,
34,085 members (from 7,120). See Farinacci, *Un periodo aureo*, p. 156.

[11] (*The author discusses Farinacci's decisive fight against the leaders of
the Fascist Militia (Galbiati, Tarabella, Tamburini, Testa, and Candelori),
who in December 1924 had given Mussolini the ultimatum to eliminate the
political opposition. These "pentarchs" tried to force regular army officers
out of the Militia and reestablish the old independent squads. Farinacci had
the two leaders, Galbiati and Tarabella, expelled from the party on charges
of being in collusion with the Masons. Galbiati and Tarabella retaliated by
revealing that Farinacci had joined a Masonic lodge back in 1915. They were
both readmitted to the party after the controversy subsided. The author lists
the following sources: ACS,* Segreterìa particolare del Duce, Carteggio riservato [1922–43], *dossier 186/R, "Consoli Galbiati e Tarabella," and R. Farinacci, dossier 5, "Precedenti massonici." Also, Enzo Galbiati,* Il 25 luglio e la
MVSN [*Milan, 1950*], *p. 52ff, "Aldo Tarabella,"* Corriere della Sera, *February 25, 1967 [letter].—Ed.*)

[12] See Gentile's "Commento a Farinacci," *La Montagna*, March 1, 1925.
There is no good study of Gentile's reform. By Gentile, see *Educazione e
scuola laica* (Florence, 1921) and, most of all, *Il fascismo al governo della
scuola (nov. 1922–aprile 1924). Discorsi e interviste* (Palermo, 1924), edited by
F. E. Boffi.

[13] See Bottai's "Farinacci e noi," *Critica Fascista*, October 1, 1925. On
the general position of *Critica Fascista*, described as following "a discreet but
evident orthodoxy in relation to the intransigent directives of fascism," see
L. Freddi, "Rivista delle Riviste," *L'Ordine Fascista*, September 30, 1925, p. 96ff.

[14] We should not conclude, however, that Forges Davanzati, and Rocco
in particular, openly supported Farinacci's policies, as claimed by Federzoni
in *Italia di ieri per la storia di domani* (Milan, 1967), p. 105. For a correct
understanding of Rocco's position, see P. Ungari, *Alfredo Rocco e l'ideologìa
giuridica del fascismo* (Brescia, 1963).

[15] ACS, *Segreterìa particolare del Duce, Carteggio Riservato (1922–43)*,
dossier 242/R. Also, ACS, *R. Farinacci*, subdossier 25, insert G.

[16] It is significant that in September 1925, after the death of General
Asclepio Gandolfo, Mussolini chose General Maurizio Gonzaga as the new
commanding general of the Militia. General Gonzaga, who was a career officer, asked for the king's permission before accepting the post. He had nothing to do with the turbulent world of Militia commanders and former
squadristi. A year later, when the party and the Militia were reorganized,
Mussolini took over the post. See ACS, *Segreterìa particolare del Duce, Carteggio Riservato (1922–43)*, dossier 186/R, "Gonzaga Maurizio comandante
generale MVSN."

[17] See Federzoni, "Fascismo di governo e fascismo di pártito," *Gerarchìa*, June 1925, p. 344.

[18] See Forges-Davanzati, "Premesse fasciste per il Congresso," *Gerarchìa*, June 1925, p. 344.

[19] It is significant that the nomination of A. Teruzzi (he took the place of D. Grandi who was considered a moderate too close to Federzoni and was transferred to the ministry of foreign affairs) was welcomed enthusiastically by *Cremona Nuova*. On the nomination, see Federzoni's comments in *Italia di ieri per la storia di domani*, p. 100, and F. Turati and A. Kuliscioff, *Carteggio*. VI. *Il delitto Matteotti e l'Aventino (1923–25)* (Turin, 1959), edited by A. Schiavi, p. 402ff. Above all, see the mimeographed bulletin *Note di informazioni per i comitati dell'Aventino*, dated May 18, 1925, which is particularly rich in information on the events surrounding the nomination and on the conflict between Farinacci and Federzoni. The bulletin indicates, among other things, that Federzoni tried to have the Honorable Italo Lunelli, who was considered more politically neutral, nominated in Teruzzi's place.

[20] According to Federzoni's imprecise recollections in *Italia di ieri per la storia di domani*, p. 103ff, at the most critical point of Mussolini's illness with gastric ulcers in 1925, Farinacci allegedly began to think of preparing his own candidacy for the succession. Although it is not improbable that he did so, the information is not confirmed by other sources.

[21] See Farinacci, *Un periodo aureo*, p. 194ff.

[22] See "Si riparla di elezioni," *Cremona Nuova*, March 26, 1925.

[23] See, in addition to the article cited in the preceding note, his speeches of June 26 in Milan and July 13, 1925, in Palermo, in Farinacci, *Un periodo aureo*, pp. 176, 181.

[24] According to the testimony of a man who was very close to him, Emilio Canevari in "Roberto Farinacci, II," *Il Meridiano*, July 25, 1958, Farinacci envisaged a parliament elected solely by party members who would number no more than 300,000 and would be drawn mostly from the lower bourgeoisie loyal to fascism.

[25] On the incident, in addition to the press, particularly *Cremona Nuova*, June 18, *L'Impero*, July 5–8, and *La Tribuna*, July 7, see also G. Rossini, *Il delitto Matteotti tra il Viminale a l'Aventino* (Bologna, 1966), p. 166ff.

[26] ACS, *Segreterìa particolare del Duce, Carteggio Riservato (1922–43)*, dossier 242/R, and *R. Farinacci*, subdossier 8, inserts A, B; from Mussolini to the prefect of Cremona. Farinacci protested strongly against the order, reasserting his freedom of action as secretary of the party and hinting that Mussolini had been unduly swayed by others.

[27] ACS, *Mussolini, Autografi-Telegrammi*, folder 1.

[28] All pertinent quotations are from ACS, *Ministero dell'Interno, Dire-*

zione Generale di Pubblica Sicurezza, Divisione Affari Generali e Riservati (1925), folder 85, dossier "Fasci-Affari Generali."

[29] ACS, *Segreterìa particolare del Duce, Carteggio Riservato (1922–43)*, dossier 242/R. Also, *R. Farinacci*, subdossier 25, insert C.

[30] According to the censuses of 1911 and 1921, the number of landowners rose during this period from 2,257,266 to 4,177,800, increasing from 21 percent to 36 percent of the entire agricultural sector. For an evaluation of these statistics, see M. Bandini, *Cento anni di storia agraria italiana* (Rome, 1963), p. 116ff.

[31] *(The author cites the results of a survey carried out in March 1932 indicating that of 191 participants at the first meeting of the Milan* fascio *on March 23, 1919, only 103 were still members of the party, 19 were dead, 2 had turned against fascism, 6 were no longer members, and 61 could not be located.* ACS, Segreterìa particolare del Duce, Carteggio Riservato [1922–43], *dossier "Il Popolo d'Italia," subdossier "Elenco e fogli informativi dei Sansepolcristi."—Ed.)*

[32] *(The author refers to a report written on October 23, 1928, by the chief of the political police who pointed out that dissidents were still sufficiently influential in the provinces to confuse public opinion but that they were not strong enough to change anything.* ACS, Ministero dell'Interno, Direzione Generale di Pubblica Sicurezza, Divisone Affari Generali e Riservati [1928], *folder 158, "Movimento Sovversivo," dossier "Organizzazione squadrista."—Ed.)*

[33] At times these arguments were so violent that they sparked rumors of possible pronunciamentos. A typical case occurred in July 1926 when Mussolini heard that some southern Fascists (particularly in the Puglie region) and Fascists in Rome, Cremona, and other places were ready to make a decisive move against Federzoni and "his friends" to prevent the "contamination" of fascism. ACS, *Segreterìa particolare del Duce, Carteggio Riservato (1922–43)*, dossier W/R, "Caradonna on. Giuseppe."

CHAPTER 6

[1] Fascism was becoming "ministerialized." Dissatisfied leaders in large numbers were looking for jobs in the public administration. Scores of men wanted to become police chiefs, prefects, plenipotentiary ministers, or simple consuls. Mussolini acceded to the requests of the petitioners and selected those revolutionary followers whom he wished to get rid of to fill, for the common good, particularly sensitive positions in the public administration. The so-called *ventottismo* was thus born in all its forms as a Fascist onslaught on domestic governmental careers . . . and on the diplomatic service.

But the onslaught on the latter turned out to be more sizable than on the former. See Yvon De Begnac, *Palazzo Venezia. Storia di un regime* (Rome, 1950), p. 415.

² *Loc. cit.* This is what another Fascist historian had to say about the massive influx of Fascists in the foreign service: "The introduction of the *ventottisti* did not yield the desired results because of the carelessness demonstrated by the party in selecting candidates and because of the candidates' almost complete lack of experience and training, nor was a true fusion between the *ventottisti* and the *carrieristi* [career men] ever achieved." See Attilio Tamaro, *Venti anni di storia, 1922–1943* (Rome, 1953), Vol. II, p. 322.

³ *Atti del Parlamento Italiano, Camera dei Deputati,* XXVIII Legislature, Session 1929, *Discussioni,* Vol. I, p. 728. Meeting of June 6, 1929.

⁴ Ministero delle Corporazioni, *Ruoli di anzianità del personale al 1° aprile 1937–anno XV* (Rome, 1937), pp. 7–8. There were seven director generals, two of whom were temporary. There were two general inspectors and twenty division heads. Very scanty information appears in Taylor Cole, "Italy's Fascist Bureaucracy," *American Political Review,* Vol. XXXII (December 1938), pp. 1143–1157. It does contain a few useful hints.

⁵ Alfredo Rocco, *La formazione dello Stato fascista (1925–1934)* (Milan, 1938), p. 924.

⁶ *Ibid.,* p. 923.

⁷ See, for instance, Nicola Coco, "La legge sul Primo Ministro nei lavori preparatori," *Rivista di Diritto Pubblico e della Pubblica Amministrazione in Italia,* 1926, Part I, pp. 105–108. The author emphasized the fact that the report to the Chamber, drawn up by Balbino Giuliano . . . seemed to hint at some kind of chancellorship. From its affirmation that "in perfect accordance with the constitution, the law reaffirms the responsibility of the government toward the king and only toward the king," it was possible to deduce, in contrast with Rocco's statements, the complete elimination of the parliamentary system. Interesting retrospective comments on the character of the law and the way it was applied were made by Giuriati in a letter to Mussolini dated July 17, 1943 *(see pp. 610–612 of Aquarone's book—Ed.).* See also, Silvio Trentin, *Les transformations récentes du droit public italien. De la Charte de Charles-Albert à la création de l'Etat fasciste* (Paris, 1929), pp. 258ff.

⁸ *Atti del Parlamento Italiano, Camera dei Senatori,* XXVII Legislature, First Session 1924–1926, *Discussioni,* Vol. IV, pp. 4373–4374. Meeting of December 19, 1925. On Mosca's attitude toward fascism, see Mario Delle Piane, *Gaetano Mosca: classe politica e liberalismo* (Naples, 1952), pp. 368ff.

⁹ The text of the law appears on pp. 395–396 of Aquarone's book.

¹⁰ For a copy of the report attached to the bill in question as presented to the council of ministers, see ACS, *Presidenza del Consiglio, Gabinetto A, 1937–1939,* folder 1/1-26, no. 996, subfile 2-3. In subfile 3-7 there is a copy of a

letter, dated September 1, 1940, sent by the presidency of the council to all the ministers. The letter clarified the reach of the bill in question, which had already been approved by the Senate and by the Chamber of Fasces and Corporations, the official name of the Chamber of Deputies after January 1939.

[11] Partito Nazionale Fascista, *Il Gran Consiglio nei primi dieci anni dell'era fascista* (Rome, 1933), pp. 48–49, and Luigi Ferraris, "Sull'ordinamento amministrativo di Roma città-capitale dello Stato italiano," *La Vita Italiana*, Vol. XI (June 15, 1923), pp. 468ff. According to the plan presented by the technical council, the executive municipal power was to be exercized by an official appointed by the government, whereas legislative power was to be exercised by two councils, partly elected and partly government appointed, one having jurisdiction over the urban zone of the municipality, the other over the rural zone. On the subject, see also Alberto Aquarone's article, "Aspirazioni tecnocratiche del primo fascismo," *Nord e Sud*, Vol. XI (April 1964), pp. 115–116.

[12] The governorship crisis is amply documented in ACS, *Ministero dell' Interno, Direzione Generale di Pubblica Sicurezza, Divisione Affari Generali Riservati*, 1926, folder 75, file *Governatorato di Roma*. This is how a police informer described the popular mood as of December 1, 1926: "The law establishing the governorship is misconceived because it is based on the premise that the government is incorruptible. Instead, Senator Cremonesi has yielded to the demands of Fascists who have made millions off the administration's budget. Even the public works in Rome aroused a gold fever and Senator Cremonesi had to fight against two competing groups." According to the defenders of the governor, he had become the victim of the intrigues of former Nationalists who were led by a well-known public works contractor. Other information on the motives which might have led Cremonesi to resign were mentioned in a report dated December 6, which referred information gathered at the Hunting Club.

[13] See the report of December 1, 1926, cited in the preceding note.

[14] See pp. 412–413 of Aquarone's book.

[15] *Ibid.*, pp. 414–415.

[16] *Atti del Parlamento Italiano, Camera dei Deputati*, XXVII Legislature, Session 1924–1929, *Disegni di legge e relazioni*, Vol. XX, No. 1118A.

[17] For the text of this letter, see pp. 416–417 of Aquarone's book.

[18] After having reaffirmed the principle of parity of representation between employers and white- and blue-collar workers combined, and the assignment of one-third of the workers' representatives to the white-collar element, Article 7 of the measure went on to state the following: "Within the above-mentioned guidelines, the number of representatives assigned to each productive activity is established by the prefect on the basis of impartial but discretional criteria, according to the importance of each of these ac-

tivities, to their territorial extension, their specific nature, and their relative function in the national economy."

[19] The administration of the various provinces was entrusted to a director and to a provincial directory consisting of the director and of rectors whose number could vary from four to eight depending on the population of the province. They were all appointed by the government. The director took over all the duties which, according to the law on the provinces, belonged to the president of the provincial delegates and to the delegates themselves. The directory took over the duties . . . reserved for the provincial council. The measure, which could be renewed, was to remain in force for four years.

[20] The new provincial executive committee, the *giunta provinciale amministrativa,* consisted of the prefect (or his substitute), the vice-prefect, a prefectural adviser chosen each year by the prefect, the superintendent of finance, the director of accountancy or chief accountant of the superintendency of finance, and of one permanent and one temporary member who were chosen by the secretary of the Fascist party and appointed by royal decree to a four-year term at the recommendation of the minister of the interior. Four additional temporary members were chosen by the prefect and the superintendent of finance. When in executive session, the committee was composed of the prefect, two prefectural advisers, the superintendent of finance, and the member chosen by the Fascist party.

[21] On this point, see ACS, *Presidenza del Consiglio, Gabinetto A,* 1925, folder 1/6-1, no. 3553.

[22] The following officials could expect to be summoned by the prefect under normal circumstances: the superintendent of finance, the local director of education in those provinces where one resided, or, for the other localities, an official or school principal chosen by the director, the administrators of estates in abeyance, the chief engineer of public works, the provincial director of postal services, the forestry inspector, the directors of itinerant agricultural aid agencies, the chief engineer of the division of mines, the labor inspector, the harbor masters in the main maritime ports in the province.

[23] Luigi Federzoni, "Le memorie di un condannato a morte," *La Nuova Stampa,* installment of June 6, 1946.

[24] The text of the oath read as follows: "I swear to carry out my professional duties with loyalty, honor, and diligence, and with concern for the highest goals of justice and the best interests of the nation."

[25] The text of the circular appeared in the *Bollettino Ufficiale del Ministero della Giustizia e degli Affari del Culto,* Vol. XLVII (November 4, 1926), p. 841. On this point, Rocco referred to the provisions of Article 93 of the regulatory measures issued on August 26, 1926, No. 1683, on how to implement the law on the reorganization of the legal profession. Concerning the obligation to take the oath as provided by Article 2 of the royal decree

of May 6, 1926, the regulations established the following: "For those who are currently registered in the professional rolls, the regulations of the preceding clauses 3 and 4 are to be applied within three months after the present law goes into effect." It should also be remembered that between May and December 1926, following the reorganization of the legal profession, the government proceeded to dissolve the various local associations of lawyers and prosecutors and, while waiting for new associations to be set up, appointed special commissions to exercise the functions of the old ones. A royal decree of May 24 dissolved the associations of Ancona, Aquila, Bari, Palermo, Rome, and Perugia. A decree of June 3 dissolved those of Catanzaro, Florence, Genoa, Bologna, Cagliari, Catania, Messina, Milan, Brescia, Naples, Potenza, Turin, and Venice. Finally, a decree of December 13 dissolved those of Trent and Trieste.

[26] Camera dei Deputati, XXVII Legislature, *La legislazione fascista, 1922–1928 (I–VII)* (Rome, no date), Vol. I, p. 391.

[27] On May 28, 1925, Federzoni sent a telegram to the prefects calling their attention to the new outbreaks of Fascist violence against the newsstands and exhorting them to intervene and repress such acts. On the whole question, see ACS, *Ministero dell'Interno, Direzione Generale di Pubblica Sicurezza, Divisione Affari Generali Riservati,* 1925, envelope 57, subfile *Boicottaggio giornali dell'opposizone.* In a letter to the high command of the police, the prefect of Ravenna replied, with perhaps unintended irony: "It is not true that in Faenza, as has been reported to Your Excellency, we continue to prevent the sale of opposition papers with the threat of serious reprisals. It is rather the newspaper vendors themselves who have explicitly stated that they no longer wish to be bothered with the sale of some opposition papers." *Ibid.,* folder 85, subfile *Boicottaggio di giornali d'opposizione.*

[28] For the chronology of the confiscations of *Rivoluzione Liberale,* see Piero Gobetti, *La Rivoluzione liberale. Saggio sulla lotta politica in Italia* (Turin, 1964), pp. xxxiii–xxxvi, with an introductory essay by Gaspare de Caro.

[29] In connection with the latter, see the article "I casi del *Mondo* e del *Risorgimento,*" *Il Mondo,* December 18, 1925. The article stated: "Since November 5, these newspapers have been subjected to repressive measures which we believe are without precedent. Every evening, shortly after being distributed, the issues of *Mondo* . . . are systematically confiscated. For nearly a month and a half, *Mondo* has been almost completely cut off from its readers, in spite of the fact that, to avoid giving the prefect any pretext for intervening . . . the newspaper has reduced itself to a shadow of its former self. It has limited itself to printing only the items carried by Stefani and the events of the day, abstaining from any political comments that might justify in any way . . . the order to confiscate." The motivation to confiscate, as

normally mentioned in the prefectural decrees, was the following: "It is compiled in such a way as to overexcite people, with the danger that it may disrupt public order."

CHAPTER 7

[1] Renzo De Felice, *Mussolini il fascista*. I. *La conquista del potere, 1921–1925* (Turin: Einaudi, 1966), pp. 666–670. Also, *Opera Omnia di Benito Mussolini* (Florence: La Fenice, 1951–1963), Vol. XXI, pp. 56–59; 102–105; 124–125.

[2] *Ibid.*, Vol. XXI, pp. 250–251.

[3] Giovanni Balella, "Sul riconoscimento giuridico dei sindacati," *Rivista di Politica Economica*, Vol. XV (January 1925), pp. 4–8, and Umberto Ricci, "Il sindacalismo giudicato da un economista," *Rivista di Politica Economica*, Vol. XV (February 1925), pp. 97–115. Also, De Felice, *Mussolini il fascista*, Vol. I, 691n.

[4] CGII, *Annuario 1925* (Rome: Cooperative Tipografica Castaldi, 1925), p. 166. The strike is discussed in Franco Catalano, "Le corporazioni fasciste e la classe lavoratrice dal 1925 al 1929," *Nuova Rivista Storica*, Vol. XLIII (January 1959), pp. 34–41. See also, *L'Organizzazione Industriale*, April 1, 1925, p. 53.

[5] CGII, *Annuario 1925*, pp. 172–174.

[6] *Atti del Parlamento Italiano. Camera dei Deputati*, 1929–1931, Vol. IV, p. 4532.

[7] *L'Organizzazione Industriale*, October 15, 1925, p. 145; September 1, 1929, p. 311. On the CGII's opposition to the introduction of factory trustees, see its *Circolare 442*, dated September 29, 1925, from Volume III of a collection of circulars preserved in the library of the General Confederation of Italian Industry in Rome.

[8] CGII, *Circolare 444*, Vol. III, dated October 10, 1925.

[9] *La Finanza Italiana*, Vol. XVII (October 10, 1925), p. 386. Curiously, these same words were used by Mussolini to justify the Vidoni agreement. See *Opera Omnia*, Vol. XXII, p. 43. Olivetti's apprehension about the possible consequences of Fascist totalitarianism for organized industry are evident in a letter of September 1924 to the industrialist Giuseppe Mazzini, who was then president of the Industrial League of Turin. Olivetti advised Mazzini that, should Mussolini decide to destroy the CGII, the industrialists should disband and abandon all political activity. The industrialists, although Olivetti does not mention it, actually concentrated all power in the hands of the CGII the better to resist Fascist totalitarianism. The letter is quoted in Mario Abrate, *La lotta sindacale nella industrializzazione in Italia, 1906–1926* (Turin: Franco Angeli, 1967), p. 426.

[10] *Rivista di Politica Economica*, Vol. XV (May 1925), pp. 487–488.

[11] *Atti. Camera*, 1924–1926, Vol. V, pp. 4888–4889.

[12] *Ibid.*, p. 4960.

[13] *Ibid.*, pp. 4964–4965.

[14] Alberto Aquarone, *L'organizzazione dello Stato totalitario* (Turin: Einaudi, 1965), pp. 133–136.

[15] *Atti. Camera*, 1924–1926, Vol. V, pp. 4931–4936.

[16] Renzo De Felice, *Mussolini il fascista*. II. *L'organizzazione dello Stato totalitario, 1925–1929* (Turin: Einaudi, 1968), pp. 270–278.

[17] Giuseppe Bottai, *Esperienza corporativa (1929–1935)* (Florence: Vallecchi, 1935), p. 27, and *Opera Omnia*, Vol. XXIV, p. 216.

[18] *Atti. Camera*, 1924–1926, Vol. V, pp. 4931–4934.

[19] See Benni's interview in *Il Popolo d'Italia*, March 19, 1927, p. 2. For a discussion of the charter's background, see De Felice, *Mussolini il fascista*, Vol. II, pp. 286–296.

[20] Aquarone, *L'organizzazione dello Stato Totalitario*, pp. 198–201.

[21] The steps whereby the industrialists obtained satisfaction on most demands may be followed in *Atti. Camera*, 1929–1930, Vol. II, pp. 1627–1628, 1652–1653; 1929–1931, Vol. IV, pp. 4533–4534. Also, *L'Organizzazione Industriale*, January 31, 1931, pp. 41–42; September 15, 1933, p. 500; December 15, 1933, p. 722. For a description of the structure and functions of the corporations, see William G. Welk, *Fascist Economic Policy* (Cambridge: Harvard University Press, 1938), pp. 121–133.

[22] From Benni's speech to the annual convention of industrialists sponsored by the CGII, in *Rivista di Politica Economica*, Vol. XVIII (June 1928), p. 559.

[23] There was considerable debate over the structure of the corporations. The final compromise was apparently worked out under Mussolini's personal supervision. In addition to the cycle corporations mentioned, there were other single-trade corporations. See *L'Organizzazione Industriale*, September 15, 1933, p. 499; September 30, 1933, pp. 529, 533; October 31, 1933, pp. 607–608; November 15, 1933, pp. 643–650; January 13, 1934, p. 1.

[24] *L'Informazione Industriale*, November 27, 1931, p. 2, and *Rivista di Politica Economica*, Vol. XXII (February 1932), pp. 195–200.

[25] The industrialists' commitment to a deflationary policy and monetary revaluation is discussed in Roland Sarti, "Mussolini and the Industrial Leadership in the Battle of the Lira, 1925–1927," *Past and Present*, No. 47 (May 1970), pp. 97–112. The industrialists' opposition to stabilizing the currency at *quota 90* is emphasized in De Felice, *Mussolini il fascista*, Vol. II, pp. 246–258.

[26] On the controversy between Benni and Arnaldo Mussolini, see *Il Popolo d'Italia*, April 8, 1930, p. 1, and April 15, 1930, p. 1.

[27] In the absence of adequate economic analysis, it is difficult to gener-

alize about the cartels' impact on the structure of production. Most observers agree that they did not promote rationalization or improve productivity to any significant degree. For general comments along these lines, see Rosario Romeo, *Breve Storia della grande industria in Italia* (Rocca San Casciano: Cappelli, 1963), pp. 158–160. For an interesting case study, see Tullio Ortu Carboni, "La concorrenza nell'industria meccanica," *Rivista di Politica Economica*, Vol. XXIII (February 1933), pp. 164–171.

[28] *Atti. Camera*, 1929–1932, Vol. VI, pp. 6765–6766.

[29] The brief history of the steel cartels is discussed in ASIA [Associazione fra le Società Italiane per Azioni] and CGII, *Relazione sull'attività degli Uffici economici (28 novembre 1932–XI)* (Rome: Cooperativa Tipografica Castaldi, 1932), pp. 75–77, and CGII, *Annuario 1933–XI* (Rome: Tipografia del Senato, 1933), pp. 464–468.

[30] *Opera Omnia*, Vol. XXVI, pp. 150, 356. Also, Pirelli's speech of October 15, 1934, to the general assembly of the CGII in *Rivista di Politica Economica*, Vol. XXIV (September–October 1934), pp. 954–963.

[31] CGII, *Annuario 1937–XV* (Rome: Tipografia del Senato, 1937), pp. 661–666. The figures given by the CGII probably fall far short of the actual number of cartels in operation. According to the law on cartels, a voluntary cartel could be based on an unregistered verbal agreement among the participating firms. For a description of the major industrial-commerical cartels, see Confederazione Nazionale Fascista del Commercio, *Commercio 1922 (I)–1932 (X)* (Rome: Confederazione Nazionale Fascista del Commercio, 1933), pp. 403–405. References to other important cartels appear in *L'Organizzazione Industriale*, April 31, 1931, pp. 242–248; June 30, 1932, p. 380; July 15, 1932, p. 402; July 31, 1932, pp. 439–441; September 15, 1932, p. 359; March 10, 1934, p. 1; August 11, 1935, p. 1; January 16, 1936, pp. 1, 5.

[32] *L'Organizzazione Industriale*, June 28, 1938, p. 1. Labor leaders were often critical of the lack of public controls on the cartels. See Pietro Capoferri, "La posizione dei consorzi nell'economia corporativa," *L'Economia Nazionale*, Vol. XXX (September 1938), pp. 4–5. For penetrating comments on the function of the cartels, see Giulio Scagnetti, *Gli enti di privilegio nell'economia corporativa italiana* (Padua: CEDAM, 1942), pp. 226–231.

CHAPTER 9

[1] E. Caviglia, *Diario, aprile 1925–marzo 1945* (Rome, 1952), pp. 126–137.

[2] One of the first expressions of Fascist interest in colonialism was the speech by the representative Carlo Baragiola, *Aspetti attuali del problema africano* (Rome, 1931). See also Enrico Mandillo, *Colonie e imperi* (Genoa, 1930), presented by the Ligurian section of the *Istituto Fascista di Cultura*, which favored the establishment of an Italian colonial empire. On the Flor-

ence symposium, see Regio Istituto Cesare Alfieri, *Atti del Primo Congresso di studi coloniali* (Florence, 1931), 7 volumes. Among the many other publications . . . , see Mario Napoletano, *Colonie e fascismo* (Naples, 1932); Dante Maria Tuninetti, *Emilio De Bono agricoltore* (Rome, 1932); Sandro Sandri, *Il generale Graziani* (Rome, n.d.), edited by *L'azione coloniale;* Tommaso Sillani, *Luigi di Savoia* (Rome, 1930). Also of interest is the study by Colonel O. Morrica, *Trattato di arte militare coloniale* (Rome, 1930), with a preface by Rodolfo Graziani.

[3] See, for example, Lidio Cipriani, *Considerazioni sopra il passato e l'avvenire delle popolazioni africane* (Florence, 1932), with a preface by Corrado Gini, sponsored by the Italian Society of Genetics and Eugenics. The author uses typically racist arguments to defend the necessity for Italian emigration to Africa.

[4] On the moves and countermoves made by rival imperialist economic groups, see Antonio Zischka, *Abissinia. L'ultimo problema insoluto dell'Africa* (Florence, 1935), in its Italian translation. On the Italian interest groups, which in addition to being backed by the government were also separately represented by Raimondo Franchetti, who had organized a holding company to finance the economic penetration of Ethiopia, see Alessandro Lessona, *Verso l'Impero. Memorie per la storia politica del conflitto italo-etiopico* (Florence, 1939), pp. 13–15. In 1932, when it became evident that Franchetti had failed in his effort to set up a joint Italo-Ethiopian company, he asked the government to adopt the "strong manner." The Ethiopian Senate had in fact decided that all roads should fan out from the capital to the provinces of the empire rather than vice versa and should be built by outfits already established in Ethiopia. Franchetti's expectations were frustrated by the opposition of Ethiopian nationalist groups and by the competition of American, German, and Belgian financial enterprises. The emperor's suspicions, however, had also been aroused by Italian military works under construction in Eritrea and by rumors of war.

[5] Emilio De Bono, *La preparazione e le prime operazioni* (Rome, 1937), p. 81.

[6] Italy's political penetration, which had previously been peaceful, limited to the border regions, implemented by special propaganda agencies attached to the various consulates, and directed mostly at the chieftains who opposed the emperor and at the Coptic clergy, was beginning to take on an offensive character. See Lessona, *op. cit.,* chapter entitled "La penetrazione offensiva italiana." The ministry of colonies prepared a plan along these lines for both the northern and southern regions of Ethiopia. In the regions of Gojjam and Aussa these efforts were supported by Senator Iacopo Gasparini, a former governor of Eritrea and a concessionaire in the irrigated lands near Tessenei, and by Baron Franchetti.

[7] According to the census of April 21, 1937, out of 124,000 hectares of

land assigned to Italian owners (79,801 of which were developed), a full 103,000 belonged to 131 large firms. Italo Balbo, who was governor after 1934, even referred to the situation as a form of "capitalist" colonization and of "latifundian" concessions, and aimed at reversing the policies that had been adopted by former governor Giuseppe Volpi in 1923–1925 but subsequently modified during the governorships of De Bono and Badoglio. As of that date (April 21, 1937), only 1,299 families had been settled over this vast area (colonial agencies and government holdings accounted for an additional 68,884 hectares). During 1936–1937, however, a more crowded type of settlement was adopted, based largely on personal holdings and on peasant villages scattered throughout the countryside. But the preceding system of concessions and the provisions for paying off the land slowed down and complicated the change in settlement policy, particularly in the western provinces. It was anticipated that as of the end of 1938 there would be only 123 new peasant holdings. The land seized from the natives and taken over by the government increased by approximately 500,000 hectares from 1934 to 1938, reaching a total of 246,455 in Tripolitania and 491,861 in Cyrenaica. The local populations were left to take care of stock-raising, with special reserves being set aside for them outside the "Green Belt" of the Gebel. A vast "labor fleet" composed of seventeen ships carrying about 20,000 settlers reached Libya on October 28, 1938, whose arrival had been timed to coincide with the anniversary of the march on Rome. See Italo Balbo, "Coloni in Libia," *Nuova Antologia,* November 1, 1938.

[8] The situation deteriorated when the Duce began to suffer once again from his old ulcer ailment that would then continue to afflict him until the end of his life. The German physician who looked after him in 1943–1945 argued that the illness took a turn for the worse in 1940, but other sources suggest that the disturbance reappeared somewhat earlier. See Georg Zachariae, *Mussolini si confessa* (Milan, 1966). Mussolini was on a strict diet as early as the beginning of 1937, but at that time he could still boast of being in perfect health. See the interview entitled "Ho fatto del mio organismo un motore costantemente sorvegliato e controllato cha marcia con assoluta regolarità," given to Webb Miller of United Press and published in *Il Popolo d'Italia,* March 9, 1937.

[9] Indro Montanelli, "Dopo la guerra," *Civiltà Fascista,* May 1936.

CHAPTER 11

[1] ACS, *Partito Nazionale Fascista, Situazione politica delle provincie,* folder *Torino.*

[2] *Ibid.,* folder *Padova.*

[3] *Ibid.,* folder *Roma.*

[4] *Ibid.,* folder *Roma.* The report is dated March 30, 1939.

[5] *Ibid.,* folder *Milano.*

[6] *Ibid.,* folder *Milano.*

[7] *Ibid.,* folder *Palermo.* The report is dated April 12, 1939, from Trapani.

[8] *Ibid.,* folder *Pisa.*

[9] *Ibid.,* folder *Genova.* The report is dated July 1, 1939. The party secretary in Genoa, Giuseppe Massa, had been protesting since the spring that the informers' reports were one-sided and misleading. This is what he wrote in one of his letters, dated April 8, to the secretary of the party: "All the information contained in reports No. 48652/B, 48656/B, and 48672/B absolutely does not correspond to the truth. The people of Liguria, not just those from the city of Genoa but also those from the eastern and western parts of the Riviera, have no fear of war nor do they bear any resentment against Germany. I have sent trusted agents on the eastern and western train lines and they have reported that all the comments they heard indicate approval of the government's decisive course of action. Public opinion in general is increasingly anti-French and absolutely opposed to the actions of the French and British governments." Considering that the Fascist secretaries were directly responsible for propaganda work and for the state of public opinion in their respective districts, it is not surprising that their comments to the central authorities of the party were considerably more optimistic than those of the informers. Still from Genoa, this is what an informer wrote on April 25, 1939: "Genoese public opinion, which was already deeply worried because it feared an imminent war with France, has been taken by surprise by the sudden occupation of Albania, reacting to it without excessive alarm in the hope that this "detour in the Adriatic," as our undertaking in Albania is called, will put off the danger of war between France and Italy."

[10] *Ibid.,* folder *Genova.* The report is dated July 25, 1939.

[11] *Ibid.,* folder *Napoli.* The report is dated August 24, 1939.

[12] *Ibid.,* folder *Padova.* The report is dated April 3, 1939. The informer went on to comment that "The women are particularly worried because, remembering the unfortunate incidents that occurred in Padua during the last war, they are afraid of aerial bombardments."

[13] *Ibid.,* folder *Milano.* The report is dated July 28, 1939. The party secretary in Milan, Rino Parenti, also complained about what he considered to be misleading statements by party informers on the state of public opinion. This is what he wrote in his letter of August 17 to the secretary of the party: "In reply to your last comments, the themes that recur in the "carnival songs" of these professional liars are exceedingly monotonous. Economic restlessness and hostility toward the alliance between Italy and Germany have already become the traditional refrains of their tragic tales."

[14] *Ibid.,* folder *Milano.* The report is dated May 12, 1939.

[15] *Ibid.*, folder *Torino*.

[16] ACS, *Ministero dell'Interno, Gabinetto, Ufficio cifra, Telegrammi in arrivo*. Telegram no. 38,860, dated September 1, 1939, sent to police headquarters from Milan.

[17] *Ibid.*, telegram no. 38,958, dated September 2, 1939, also to police headquarters from Milan.

[18] *Ibid.*, telegram no. 88,505, dated August 30, 1939, from the prefect of Verona to police headquarters. The incident ended with the arrest of three of the approximately ten participants.

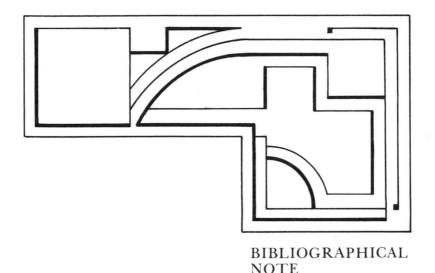

BIBLIOGRAPHICAL NOTE

A short bibliographical note cannot possibly do justice to the vast literature on Italian fascism. The titles mentioned here represent only the tip of the iceberg. More detailed discussions appear in several bibliographical articles which should be used in conjunction with the often excellent bibliographies appearing in a number of general works. A good bibliographical starting point is Geneviève Bibes, "Le fascisme italien. État des travaux depuis 1945," *Revue Française de Science Politiques*, Vol. XVIII (December 1968), pp. 1191–1244. This extensive article lists and discusses the relevance of nearly three hundred works. Also useful, but considerably less informative, is Piero Melograni, "Bibliografia orientativa sul fascismo," *Il Nuovo Osservatore*, Vol. VII (May 1966), pp. 421–438, and in the same journal, Vol. VII (November–December 1966), pp. 962–982. Definitely outdated, but still worth reading for its many perceptive comments, is Paolo Alatri, "Recenti studi sul fascismo," *Studi Storici*, Vol. III (October–December 1962), pp. 757–836. American writings on fascism are discussed in

257

Philip V. Cannistraro, "Il fascismo italiano visto dagli Stati Uniti: cin-quant'anni di studi e di interpretazioni," *Storia Contemporanea*, Vol. II (September 1971), pp. 599–622. A good general discussion of the his-toriography of fascism is Renzo De Felice, *Le interpretazioni del fas-cismo* (Bari: Laterza, 1969). Unfortunately, this very useful book lacks a bibliography.

Bibliographical articles in English tend to be either narrower in focus or to treat the literature on fascism in the larger context of Ital-ian scholarly production. The first article in order of time, and also the most comprehensive, is Emiliana P. Noether, "Italy Reviews Its Fascist Past," *American Historical Review*, Vol. LXI (July 1956), pp. 877–899. Charles F. Delzell's "Italian Historical Scholarship: A Decade of Recovery and Development, 1945–1955," *Journal of Modern His-tory*, Vol. XXVIII (December 1956), pp. 374–388, devotes a few pages to the literature on fascism. Two other articles by Delzell help to up-date the coverage: "Benito Mussolini: A Guide to the Bibliographical Literature," *Journal of Modern History*, Vol. XXXV (December 1963), pp. 339–353, and "Mussolini's Italy Twenty Years After," *Journal of Modern History*, Vol. XXXVIII (March 1966), pp. 53–58, which dis-cusses a few major works. Marxist interpretations of fascism are sum-marized in John M. Cammett, "Communist Theories of Fascism, 1920–1935," *Science and Society*, Vol. XXXI (Spring 1967), pp. 149–163. Claudio Pavone's "Italy: Trends and Problems," *Journal of Contemporary History*, Vol. II (January 1967), pp. 49–77, is definitely of marginal interest as far as the literature on fascism is concerned.

GENERAL HISTORIES

No existing general history of the Fascist period is likely to satisfy the demanding scholar, but a number of them are informative if not altogether well balanced. The standard work is Luigi Salvatorelli and Giovanni Mira, *Storia d'Italia nel periodo fascista* (Turin: Einaudi, 1964), revised edition. Attilio Tamaro's *Venti anni di storia, 1922–1943* (Rome: Tiber, 1953–1954), 3 vols., and *Due anni di storia, 1943–1945* (Rome: Tosi, 1948–1950), 3 vols., covers the entire period in great de-tail and with a generally sympathetic attitude. Enzo Santarelli's *Storia del movimento e del regime fascista* (Rome: Editori Riuniti, 1967), 2 vols., brings a Marxist slant to the topic and steadily probes for the shortcomings of the regime. A recently published work by Edward R. Tannenbaum, *The Fascist Experience. Italian Society and Culture, 1922–1945* (New York: Basic Books, 1972) covers the period in topical fashion. A most noteworthy and original feature of this volume is its concern with popular perceptions of the regime.

Several good short histories are available in English. Federico Chabod's *History of Italian Fascism* (London: Weidenfeld and Nicolson, 1963) reveals the superb touch of that master historian but is at times a bit disjointed and uneven, probably because it is based on a series of lectures that Chabod gave at the Sorbonne in 1950. Extremely concise and to the point is Alan Cassels' *Fascist Italy* (New York: Thomas Y. Crowell, 1968). Elizabeth Wiskemann's *Fascism in Italy: Its Development and Influence* (New York: St. Martin's Press, 1969) covers a lot of ground but is often puzzling in style and organization. S. William Halperin's *Mussolini and Italian Fascism* (Princeton: Nostrand, 1964) interprets fascism as a projection of Mussolini's flawed personality. The volume also features excerpts from many important documents of the Fascist period. Stimulating insights into the nature and operation of the Fascist regime abound in H. Stuart Hughes' *The United States and Italy* (Cambridge: Harvard University Press, 1965), revised edition, and in Denis Mack Smith, *Italy: A Modern History* (Ann Arbor: University of Michigan Press, 1969), revised edition.

BIOGRAPHIES OF MUSSOLINI

Given Mussolini's pervasive role, any comprehensive biography of the dictator is bound to resemble a general history of the Fascist regime. Such is indeed the case with Renzo De Felice's projected five-volume biography of which only three volumes have appeared so far: *Mussolini il rivoluzionario, 1883–1920* (Turin: Finaudi, 1965), *Mussolini il fascista. I. La conquista del potere, 1921–1925* (Turin: Einaudi, 1966), and *Mussolini il fascista. II. L'organizzazione dello stato totalitario* (Turin: Finaudi, 1968). Although often difficult to read, this work is a must for anyone who wishes to probe deeply into the history of the regime. The best way to approach Mussolini, however, is through his own voluminous writings and speeches, which have been collected in the *Opera Omnia di Benito Mussolini* (Florence: La Fenice, 1951–1963), 36 vols., edited by Edoardo and Duilio Susmel.

259

Of the several biographies in English, the most reliable and informative is still Ivone Kirkpatrick's *Mussolini: A Study in Power* (New York: Hawthorn, 1964), which fills in the political background. Mussolini's early years are the topic of Gaudens Megaro's classic work *Mussolini in the Making* (Boston: Houghton Mifflin, 1938), which has now been largely superseded by the first volume of De Felice's biography. Laura Fermi's *Mussolini* (Chicago: University of Chicago Press, 1961) is rich in personal details but weak on the political background. Paolo Monelli's *Mussolini. The Intimate Life of a Demagogue* (New York: Vanguard, 1954) still manages to deliver more than its title suggests. Christopher Hibbert's *Il Duce* (Boston: Little, Brown, 1962) and Roy MacGregor-Hastie's *The Day of the Lion. The Life and Death of Fascist Italy, 1922–1945* (New York: Coward-McCann, 1964) give no indication of either original research or new insights. Mussolini's latest biography in English, Richard Collier's *Duce! The Rise and Fall of Benito Mussolini* (London: Collins, 1971), relies heavily on eyewitness accounts but adds little to our knowledge of Mussolini and is replete with annoying artificial effects ("Solemnly, rhythmically, his fork was enmeshing the long yellow ribbons of tagliatelle"). The bibliography is excellent. Mussolini's final years are covered exhaustively and expertly by F. W. Deakin in *The Brutal Friendship: Mussolini, Hitler and the Fall of Fascism* (New York: Harper and Row, 1962), which is also available in a shorter version, *The Six Hundred Days of Mussolini* (Garden City: Doubleday, 1966).

FASCIST IDEOLOGY

The ideology of Italian fascism is discussed in a number of works that attempt to give an overall view of fascism as a general phenomenon. The interplay between Fascist thought and action is the theme of Ernst Nolte's widely acclaimed book *Three Faces of Fascism: Action Françàise, Italian Fascism, National Socialism* (New York: Holt, Rinehart and Winston, 1966). Unfortunately, this thought-provoking book is marred by unnecessarily dense and cryptic prose. A more easily intelligible but considerably less subtle approach characterizes A. James Gregor's *The Ideology of Fascism. The Rationale of Totalitarianism* (New York: The Free Press, 1969). Gregor argues the debatable point that Fascist politics were guided by ideological considerations. It is nevertheless an important contribution to the debate over the nature of fascism. An admirable little book that also takes Fascist ideology seriously and discusses Fascist movements on a comparative basis is Eugen Weber's *Varieties of Fascism* (Princeton: Van Nostrand, 1964). John Weiss's *The Fascist Tradition: Radical Right-wing Extremism in Modern Europe* (New York: Harper and Row, 1967) stresses the conservative configuration of fascism. The links between the cult of youth, the idea of revolution, and the expansionist thrust of Fascist ideology are explored concisely in Michael A. Ledeen, *Universal Fascism: The Theory and Practice of the Fascist International, 1928–1936* (New York: Howard Fertig, 1972).

There are a number of books that throw light on the ideology of fascism by focusing on specific personalities and problems. Among these, the excellent study by Henry S. Harris, *The Social Philosophy of Giovanni Gentile* (Urbana: University of Illinois Press, 1960), deserves special mention. The ideas of another seminal figure are discussed in Paolo Ungari's *Alfredo Rocco e l'ideologia giuridica del fascismo* (Brescia: Morcelliana, 1963). The rise of political anti-Semitism in Italy is discussed in Renzo De Felice's well documented study *Storia degli ebrei italiani sotto il fascismo* (Turin: Einaudi, 1962) which is about to appear in English.

FASCIST INSTITUTIONS

The influence of Fascist ideology was certainly evident in the formal institutional framework of the Fascist state. The most concise guide to the social institutions of fascism is G. Lowell Field's *The Syndical and Corporative Institutions of Italian Fascism* (New York: Columbia University Press, 1938) The internal struggles and compromises that accompanied the rise of the Fascist state are taken into account in Alberto Aquarone's first-rate study *L'organizzazione dello Stato totalitario* (Turin: Einaudi, 1965). Still very useful is the older book by Herman Finer, *Mussolini's Italy* (London: Gollancz, 1935), which has also been reissued in paperback (New York: Grosset and Dunlap, 1965). Dante L. Germino's *The Italian Fascist Party in Power. A Study in Totalitarian Rule* (Minneapolis: University of Minneapolis

Press, 1959) is good as a description of the formal chain of command within the party but pays insufficient attention to the larger political context.

POLITICS AND PRESSURE GROUPS

The larger political context, which brings into the open the clash of ideologies and factions within and around fascism, is brought out in great detail in De Felice's already mentioned biography of Mussolini. Party politics in the early years of the regime are also covered in Giuseppe Rossini, ed., *Il delitto Matteotti tra il Viminale e l'Aventino* (Bologna: Il Mulino, 1966). Harry Fornari's *Mussolini's Gadfly: Roberto Farinacci* (Nashville: Vanderbilt University Press, 1971) also sheds some light on the intramural disputes of fascism. A fascinating insider's view emerges from Giuseppe Bottai's *Vent'anni e un giorno (24 luglio 1943)* (Milan: Garzanti, 1949).

Powerful outside groups found it easier to accept fascism because they could always identify with specific Fascist currents and figures that they found congenial. The army's response is the topic of Giorgio Rochat's *L'esercito italiano da Vittorio Veneto a Mussolini (1919–1925)* (Bari: Laterza, 1966). The reactions of big business are discussed in Ernesto Rossi's *Padroni del vapore e fascismo* (Bari: Laterza, 1966), revised edition, and in Roland Sarti's *Fascism and the Industrial Leadership in Italy, 1919–1940* (Berkeley: University of California Press, 1971). The dialogue between fascism and the Church is discussed admirably in Daniel A. Binchy's *Church and State in Fascist Italy* (London: Royal Institute of International Affairs, 1941). The negotiations leading to the reconciliation between Church and state are well documented in Francesco Margiotta Broglio's *Italia e Santa Sede. Dalla Grande Guerra alla Conciliazione. Aspetti politici e giuridici* (Bari: Laterza, 1966). There is no good study of relations between fascism and the monarchy, but interesting material appears in Nino D'Aroma's *Vent'anni insieme. Vittorio Emanuele e Mussolini* (Bologna: Capelli, 1957).

The plight of the political opponents of fascism has been the subject of much discussion. The standard and most reliable work is Charles F. Delzell's *Mussolini's Enemies: The Italian Anti-Fascist Resistance* (Princeton: Princeton University Press, 1961). The Catholic response to fascism, partly sympathetic and partly critical, is clearly outlined in Richard A. Webster's *The Cross and the Fasces: Christian Democracy and Fascism in Italy* (Stanford: Stanford University Press, 1960).

ECONOMIC AND SOCIAL POLICIES

Before World War II utterly destroyed the credibility of Italian fascism, debate raged on whether fascism had developed an original and viable system for settling economic and social problems. Echoes of that debate reappear in S. J. Woolf's essay "Did a Fascist Economic System Exist?" in S. J. Woolf, ed., *The Nature of Fascism* (New York: Random House, 1968), pp. 119–151. Some of the older studies have withstood the test of time remarkably well. Carmen Haider's *Capital and Labor Under Fascism* (New York: Columbia University Press, 1930) was a serious pioneering effort. Louis Rosenstock-Franck's *L'économie corporative fasciste en doctrine et en fait* (Paris: Librairic Universitaire J. Gamber, 1934), and *Les étapes de l'économie fasciste italienne* (Paris: Librairie Sociale et Economique, 1939) are still unequaled as descriptions of how Fascist institutions managed and mismanaged the economy. Gaetano Salvemini's *Under the Axe of Fascism* (London: Gollancz, 1936) manages to be both an anti-Fascist tract and a convincing scholarly work. Carl T. Schmidt's *The Plough and the Sword* (New York: Columbia University Press, 1938) is still the best study of how the agricultural sector fared under fascism. A good overall view of how the Fascist economy functioned emerges from William G. Welk's *Fascist Economic Policy* (Cambridge: Harvard University Press, 1938). Shepard B. Clough's *The Economic History of Modern Italy* (New York: Columbia University Press, 1964) has an excellent informative chapter on "Fascism and Its Economic Policies."

FOREIGN POLICY

The latest and most well-balanced discussion of Fascist foreign policy in the 1920's is Alan Cassels' *Mussolini's Early Diplomacy* (Princeton: Princeton University Press, 1970). Ennio Di Nolfo covers some of the same ground in *Mussolini e la politica estera italiana,*

1919–1933 (Padua: CEDAM, 1960) but with considerably skimpier documentation. Giampiero Carocci takes into account the impact of domestic developments on foreign policy in *La politica estera dell'Italia fascista (1925–1928)* (Bari: Laterza, 1969). We do not have an up-to-date account of Fascist diplomacy in the 1930's, although much about the nature of the decision-making process may be inferred from Galeazzo Ciano's *Diary, 1937–1938* (London: Methuen, 1952) and *The Ciano Diaries, 1939–1943* (Garden City: Doubleday, 1946). Maxwell Macartney and Paul Cremona's *Italy's Foreign and Colonial Policy, 1914–1937* (London: Oxford University Press, 1938) still stands up well as a narrative. An excellent monograph on the diplomatic background of the Ethiopian war is George W. Baer's *The Coming of the Italian-Ethiopian War* (Cambridge: Harvard University Press, 1967). The alliance with Germany is discussed in Elizabeth Wiskemann's *The Rome-Berlin Axis: A History of Relations between Hitler and Mussolini* (London: Collins, 1966), revised edition, and in Mario Toscano's detailed *The Diplomatic Origins of the Pact Steel* (Baltimore: Johns Hopkins Press, 1967), revised edition. The Fascist view is restated in unrepentant terms by Luigi Villari in *Italian Foreign Policy under Mussolini* (New York: Devin-Adair, 1956).

PUBLIC OPINION

Popular reactions to the salient features and programs of the Fascist regime are discussed and documented in the already cited work by Edward R. Tannenbaum, *The Fascist Experience*, particularly in the chapters on "Fascist Socialization and Conformity" and "Popular Culture and Propaganda." The reactions of narrower sectors of public opinion to the experience of living under fascism are described in a number of other works. The increasing disillusionment of young, mostly middle-class intellectuals with the social conservatism and authoritarian leadership of the regime in the 1930's is the theme of Ruggero Zangrandi's *Il lungo viaggio attraverso il fascismo* (Milan: Feltrinelli, 1962) and of a documentary novel by Luigi Preti, *Through the Fascist Fire* (London: Secker and Warburg, 1968). On the other hand, Michael A. Ledeen, in his already cited work *Universal Fascism*, shows that the idea of a Fascist mission to arrest the decline and decay of the Western World could still inspire many young Fascists in the 1930's.

BIBLIOGRAPHICAL NOTE

There are many works of fiction that reveal the quality of life under fascism. In a class all by itself is a literary-psychoanalitic essay by the novelist Carlo Emilio Gadda, *Eros e Priapo* (Milan: Garzanti, 1967). With the inimitable stylistic pyrotecnics that characterize his prose, Gadda argues that Italians, particularly the women, were seduced by the exaggerated, domineering masculinity of Mussolini's public image. The plight of human beings stifled and abused under a repressive and lawless regime is portrayed in a number of novels that have been translated into English. The intellectual's search for meaning in the midst of bombast and rhetoric is the implied theme of Elio Vittorini's *Conversation in Sicily* (London: Penguin, 1962). Giorgio Bassani's *The Garden of the Finzi-Continis* (New York: Atheneum, 1965) tells the poignant story of Italian Jews who became the victims of the racial laws. Middle-class reactions, ranging from resigned idealism to unscrupulous zest for money and power, are dissected in Alberto Moravia's *The Time of Indifference* (New York: Farrar, Strauss and Young, 1953). Vasco Pratolini's *A Tale of Poor lovers* (New York: Viking Press, 1949) reflects the mixture of human and political passions governing the life of a Florentine, working-class neighborhood. The plight of the southern peasant is the subject of two novels by Ignazio Silone, *Fontamara* (New York: Atheneum, 1960) and *Bread and Wine* (New York: Atheneum, 1962), while the encounter between the progressive mentality of the north and the backward social realities of the south provides the tension in Carlo Levi's *Christ Stopped at Eboli* (New York: Grosset, 1947).

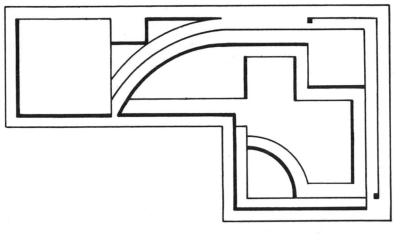

INDEX

276

ABOUT THE AUTHOR

Roland Sarti, Professor of History at the University of Massachusetts, is the author of *Fascism and the Industrial Leadership in Italy, 1919–1940: A Study in the Expansion of Private Power Under Fascism.*